Y0-EIB-949

JUL 1 3 1994

Canada in the Atlantic Economy

50

CANADA IN THE ATLANTIC ECONOMY

Published:

1. David W. Slater, *World Trade and Economic Growth: Trends and Prospects with Applications to Canada*
2. H. Edward English, *Transatlantic Economic Community: Canadian Perspectives*
3. Harry G. Johnson, Paul Wonnacott, Hirofumi Shibata, *Harmonization of National Economic Policies under Free Trade*
4. Gerald I. Trant, David L. MacFarlane and Lewis A. Fischer, *Trade Liberalization and Canadian Agriculture*
5. W. E. Haviland, N. S. Takacsy, E. M. Cape, *Trade Liberalization and the Canadian Pulp and Paper Industry*
6. David E. Bond and Ronald J. Wonnacott, *Trade Liberalization and the Canadian Furniture Industry*
7. Jacques J. Singer, *Trade Liberalization and the Canadian Steel Industry*
8. John M. Munro, *Trade Liberalization and Transportation in International Trade*

Forthcoming:

9. Hirofumi Shibata, *Harmonization of Fiscal Policy under Freer Trade*
10. John F. Earl, *Trade Liberalization and the Atlantic Provinces Economy*
11. G. David Quirin, *Trade Liberalization and the Mineral Industries*
12. R. A. Shearer, G. R. Munro, and J. H. Young, *Trade Liberalization and the British Columbia Economy*
13. Richard E. Caves and Grant L. Reuber, *Canadian Economic Policy and the Impact of International Capital Flows*
14. Jacques J. Singer and Eric C. Sievwright, *Trade Liberalization and the Canadian Primary Textiles Industry*
15. R. A. Matthews, *Easing the Adjustment to Freer Trade: A Program of Transitional Policies for Canada*
16. Eric Hehner, *Non-Tariff Barriers Affecting Canada's Trade*
17. David W. Slater, Bruce W. Wilkinson, and H. Edward English, *Canada in a Wider Economic Community*

Trade Liberalization
and Transportation in International Trade

John M. Munro

Published for the
Private Planning Association of Canada by University of Toronto Press

To William B. Lambert

ERINDALE
COLLEGE
LIBRARY

These studies of "Canada in the Atlantic Economy" are dedicated with respect and gratitude to the late William B. Lambert, Chairman of the Board of the Private Planning Association of Canada from 1965 to 1967, who played a vital role in the development and supervision of the Atlantic Economic Studies Program, on which the publications are based.

His interest went far beyond his formal responsibility; he held a deep conviction concerning the importance of international cooperation among the North Atlantic nations. His untimely death came when the first draft studies had entered the early stages of publication.

HE
215
M8

© University of Toronto Press 1969 / Printed in Canada / SBN 8020 3234 6

Foreword

There have been two outstanding developments in international trade policy during the past twenty years—the multilateral dismantling of trade barriers under the General Agreement on Tariffs and Trade, which has been the agency for several rounds of successful tariff negotiations since its inception in 1947, and the establishment of the European Economic Community and the European Free Trade Association in the late 1950s. In a period of reconstruction and then sustained growth, these policies have helped the participating nations of the Atlantic area to experience the benefits of international specialization and expanding trade. The wealth generated by trade and domestic prosperity has also made possible external aid programs to assist economic growth in the developing countries.

Whatever the trade and economic development problems of the future, it is widely acknowledged that the industrially advanced countries of the North Atlantic region must play an important role. It is also generally conceded that the ability of these countries to maintain their own economic growth and prosperity and to contribute to that of the less advanced nations will be greatly enhanced if they can reduce or remove the remaining trade barriers among themselves. Cooperation among Atlantic countries is now fostered by the GATT and by the Organisation for Economic Co-operation and Development. But the success of these and other approaches depends on the assessment by each country of the importance of international trade liberalization and policy coordination for its domestic economy and other national interests. This is particularly true for countries such as Canada which are heavily dependent upon export markets.

The Atlantic Economic Studies Program of the Private Planning Association of Canada was initiated to study the implications for Canada of trade liberalization and closer economic integration among the nations bordering the North Atlantic. It is planned to issue at least twelve paperbound volumes, incorporating over twenty studies by leading Canadian and foreign economists. Despite the technical nature of much of the subject matter, the studies have been written in language designed to appeal to the non-professional reader.

The directors and staff of the Private Planning Association wish to acknowledge the financial support which made this project possible—a grant from the Ford Foundation and the contributions of members of the Association. They are also appreciative of the help that has been provided by very many individuals in the preparation and review of all the studies— in discussions and correspondence with authors, at the Association's November, 1966, conference on "Canada and the Atlantic Economy," and on other occasions.

H. E. ENGLISH
Director of Research
Atlantic Economic Studies Program

Contents

Preface

This study represents an attempt to analyze the effect of transportation policy on commodity trade between Canada and the United States. Such analysis involves two tasks: the specification and quantification of specific government and industry policies affecting transportation and, second, the identification and measurement of the impact of these policies on trade flows. No one is more aware than the author that his performance in both these tasks falls short of perfection. Yet he hopes that the study as a whole will be of value and that some of its more obvious shortcomings will stimulate further and more specialized research.

There has been little research on the question dealt with in this study. The relationships between transportation and international trade remain in large part unresearched. For trade between Canada and the United States, already the largest two-country trade in the world and destined to grow still larger as trade barriers are lowered, research of this type is almost non-existent.

One reason for the reluctance of researchers to approach these topics may lie in the difficulty of establishing what the operational effects of various transportation policies and practices really are. Another is in the shortcomings of published transportation statistics. In both these "problem areas" this study has benefited greatly from the advice and information of various individuals in government, industry, and universities.

The initial work on this study was undertaken by George W. Wilson of Indiana University, who carried out a survey of its feasibility. Helpful comments on a preliminary outline by the present author were provided by Harry G. Johnson of the London School of Economics and Hans H. Liesner of Cambridge University.

Only a few of those in industry and government who gave generously of their time and effort can be mentioned. D. P. MacKinnon of Canadian National Railways and H. M. Romoff of the Canadian Pacific Railway Company provided the international traffic statistics used in chapter 4. This was much appreciated, as was their assistance in putting the author in touch with other informed individuals in their companies. Helpful discussions were also held with Marius Gendreau of Canadian Trucking Associations and J. O.

Goodman of the Automotive Transport Association of Ontario. The assistance of R. R. Cope, then of the Department of Transport, and of other Department officials was similarly appreciated. Among officials of regulatory agencies, particular acknowledgment should be made of the help of E. J. Shoniker of the Ontario Highway Transport Board and Edward Margolin of the U.S. Interstate Commerce Commission. Two individuals involved as users of transportation likewise deserve special thanks; these are Richard Haupt of the Ford Motor Company and Eric Gracey, then of the Canadian Industrial Traffic League. This list is necessarily short; it includes less than one-fourth of the people who provided substantial help to a grateful author.

The usual disclaimer concerning the sole responsibility of the author for the shortcomings of the study must be accompanied by another. Since conclusions are reached that are diametrically opposed to public positions taken by some of the firms and industries represented by those who assisted the author, it should be emphasized that the analysis and conclusions are those of the author alone. I benefited greatly from the counsel and information of others, but in some cases my evaluation of the facts led me to different conclusions.

J.M.M.

1. Transportation and International Trade

Introduction

This study will examine the role played by transport in trade between Canada and the United States. More specifically, it will attempt to analyze the impact of various government and industry policies and practices on the international flow of goods within North America. Consideration will be given to the degree of influence that transportation has had in determining the patterns of North American trade and to the changes in present transport policy that might be necessary to permit full realization of the potential benefits of freer trade between Canada and the United States. The analysis will cover influences stemming from three broad types of transport policy: regulatory and promotional policies for domestic transportation in each country; regulation and promotion of international transportation between the two countries; and transport industry policies and practices affecting international transportation. Consideration will also be given to the effects that freer trade would be likely to have on transportation industries in Canada. Transport policy harmonization in the interests of freer trade cannot be divorced from the effects that freer trade would itself have on transportation. This is particularly the case in Canada, where government has traditionally used transportation in the pursuit of many non-economic objectives and where the impact of freer North American trade on the transport sector would be greatest.

It is generally agreed that the harmonization of transportation policies among major trading partners enhances the benefits received from international trade. Most of the major free trade groupings in existence today have determined that to some degree the harmonization and rationalization of transport policies are essential to the achievement of their joint economic objectives. This viewpoint is well expressed in the following statement made by the former chairman of the Economic Council of Canada:

In present circumstances the conditions of trade between two countries are not governed solely or in many cases primarily by the height of tariffs or other border restrictions. The conditions of trade are strongly affected by subsidies, direct and indirect; by weight and incidence of taxation; by the scale and level of the social services; by the regulation of monopolies and cartels; by the regulation of credit; by the regulation of transport; and by control over production or prices in industries such as agriculture. Free trade is not established or maintained simply by removing all tariffs and other border restrictions. It is necessary also in the present welfare state to harmonize and co-ordinate government policies over a wide range of economic, fiscal, and social affairs.[1]

Besides the explicit mention of transport regulation in the above quotation, there are also, as we will see, important implications for the transport sector in the provision of direct and indirect subsidies and in the regulation of monopolies and cartels.

An opposing position has been taken by Harry G. Johnson. He contends that, in a free trade area, "the need for harmonization *additional to what is already required* of countries extensively engaged in world trade is relatively slight. . . ."[2] In the particular case of transportation, Professor Johnson bases his conclusion that policy harmonization in the transport sector would not add much to the economic gains of a Canada–U.S. free trade arrangement on these arguments:

1. Canada and the United States have been closely integrated economically for decades, and there is "a long history of adjustment of railway rates and transport arrangements in general."
2. There is intensive intermodal competition in transportation (much more so than in Europe), and this has greatly reduced the opportunities for monopolistic behaviour by any one mode.[3]

In an earlier footnote, Johnson also alludes to the insignificance of transport costs in the market prices of many commodities and suggests that for this reason the over-all effect of transport discrimination between foreign and domestic producers can only be slight.[4]

From what has been said thus far in the present study (and, indeed, from the mere fact that the study has been written), it should be apparent that the author prefers the Deutsch point of view to the Johnson point of view. What remains to be done is to substantiate this preference—to point out how and where prevailing policies in the transport sector have affected trade between Canada and the United States and what changes would be desirable in the interests of more beneficial trade relations between the two countries.

[1]John J. Deutsch, "Selective Free Trade in the North American Bloc as a Defensive Concept," *Third Seminar on Canadian-American Relations*, Windsor, Assumption University of Windsor, 1961, p. 89, quoted in Sperry Lea, *A Canada-U.S. Free Trade Arrangement: Survey of Possible Characteristics*, Montreal and Washington, Canadian-American Committee, 1963, pp. 46–7.
[2]Harry G. Johnson, "The Implications of Free or Freer Trade for the Harmonization of Other Policies," in Johnson, Paul Wonnacott, Hirofumi Shibata, *Harmonization of National Economic Policies under Free Trade*, PPAC series, "Canada in the Atlantic Economy," Toronto, University of Toronto Press, 1968, p. 3 (emphasis as in original).
[3]*Ibid.*, p. 26.
[4]*Ibid.*, p. 14.

Transportation and the location of industry

We will begin by discussing the role of transport costs in location theory and international trade theory. The relationship is close—indeed, it has been argued, at the theoretical level, that "the theory of international trade is only a part of a general localization theory. . . ."[5] This section will consist of a general survey of previous contributions and will be discursive rather than empirical.[6]

The more refined presentations of the theory of location explain the geographic distribution of economic activity in terms of the familiar assumptions of profit-maximizing behaviour. They assume that firms choose their locations for production and distribution activities according to the relative profitability of alternative locations. On the revenue side of the profit equation, firms are said to evaluate the potential market in dollar terms, while on the cost side they compare costs of labour, raw materials, transportation, etc., at the various locations under consideration. The location offering the highest profit is chosen.

A.   PROBLEMS IN LOCATION THEORY

There are several problems that arise when we try to apply location theory to the actual location decisions of actual firms. First, as August Losch, author of what is probably the most authoritative work on location, has pointed out, the location problem is conceptually insoluble.[7] This is because as soon as space is introduced as a variable into a firm's decision process, a virtually infinite number of alternatives present themselves. More simply, a firm cannot hope to evaluate *all* the possible locations for its production and distribution activities; they are essentially infinite in number. Despite this crucial difficulty, location theory still has much to offer. The absence of a formally perfect solution to a location question does not mean that the profitability evaluation of alternative sites should not be the basis for the firm's location decision; it means only that the number of sites considered must necessarily be limited.

Accepting this, we are still faced with two difficulties that arise out of the profit-maximizing assumption. It is clear that firms often do not choose their locations according to any economic criteria. Personal biases and mere

[5]Bertil Ohlin, *Interregional and International Trade*, Cambridge, Mass., Harvard University Press, 1933, p. vii.
[6]A more empirical study of the location of industry under conditions of North American free trade is available in Ronald J. Wonnacott and Paul Wonnacott, *Free Trade between the United States and Canada: The Potential Economic Effects*, Cambridge, Mass., Harvard University Press, 1967.
[7]August Losch, *The Economics of Location*, trans. William H. Woglom, New York, Wiley, 1967, pp. 28–9.

accident may be said to play major roles in the location decisions of many firms. But even when firms do try to follow a profit-maximizing rule in location selection, they are apt to be hampered by special peculiarities of the location decision. Personnel competent to carry out established procedures for other types of decisions are often unsuitable or unavailable for the complex and infrequently required location decisions. This lack gives the location decision a trial-and-error quality. In fact, however, the errors are probably seldom discovered—the firm selects a location and then lives with it. This location is taken as given, and the firm bases its other economic decisions on profit-maximizing criteria operating within the constraint of the already selected location.

This suggests that the gap between normative and positive, between theory and reality, is quite substantial in the realm of location. We should not expect all firms to follow or to have followed the norms of location decision-making.

B. COST-ORIENTED LOCATION THEORY

On the cost side, three categories of cost may be considered important.[8] These are transport costs, labour costs, and fuel and raw material costs. Other locationally variable costs (taxes or interest) are seen as essentially "institutional" in nature and are excluded. The problem is further simplified by viewing fuel and raw material costs in transport-cost terms; more expensive raw materials are treated, for analytical purposes, as though they were located farther away from producing points.

Thus, location involves a trade-off between labour costs and transport costs. The effect of the latter is to disperse industry—to place it in scattered locations. These will be near raw materials when the manufacturing process is weight-losing and nearer markets when the product gains weight during manufacture. Labour costs, on the other hand, tend to encourage the concentration of economic activity. Production is carried on in a few locations so that advantage can be taken of economies of scale and average total costs of production can be lowered.

If transport costs were zero and economies of scale highly significant, then productive activity would be concentrated geographically. If, on the other hand, transport costs were high and economies of scale unimportant, there would be a high degree of dispersion of economic activity. The intermediate case suggests a compromise between the economies of mass production and the economies of reduced transportation requirements.

[8]What follows here is essentially Alfred Weber's cost-oriented version of location theory. Summaries of Weberian location theory are available in Melvin L. Greenhut, *Plant Location in Theory and in Practice*, Chapel Hill, N.C., University of North Carolina Press, 1956, pp. 8–17, and Losch, *The Economics of Location*, pp. 18–26.

C.   MARKET-ORIENTED LOCATION THEORY

The foregoing has assumed that buyers are evenly dispersed—that in fact revenue aspects of the profit equation are of no interest and have no influence on location decisions. Location theorists have not been too successful in improving on this assumption. Two approaches to a market-oriented theory of location deserve mention here. Both carry the assumption, it seems, that the locational influence of differences between transport cost on raw materials and transport cost on finished products has been considered. In other words, a location for production has been tentatively selected. Given this, the size of the market area in dollars of sales revenue is determined.

The first approach, which is the more static of the two, treats each seller as a monopolist selling to buyers distributed evenly around his plant.[9] The size of the market served by the plant depends on the demand schedule of the buyers in relation to the delivered price of the product, i.e., to the f.o.b. plant price plus transport costs. As we move away from the plant, the delivered price rises with transport costs, and the quantity sold declines. Beyond a certain point sales will be zero.

The second approach allows location to vary. It considers the reactions of rival firms to each others' actions—the condition of spatial monopoly is dropped, and both the locations and market areas of firms are seen to vary with changes in the competitive practices of their rivals.[10] The term "competitive practices" is very inclusive and can refer to such strategies as price changes, transport-cost changes, location shifts, marketing changes, and so on. A firm may counter the competitive advantage gained by a rival who obtains lower transport costs by moving nearer the market, by reducing price, by matching the rival's new advantage, or by improving or intensifying its own marketing effort.

D.   TRANSPORTATION'S ROLE IN LOCATION DECISIONS

The location of economic activity can thus be seen to be the result of the working out of many complex and conflicting influences. Moreover, the location decision should be recurring—the location of last year may not be the optimum location for the current year. This is even truer when we measure time in decades. Within the involved evaluation of the cost and revenue characteristics of alternative locations, transport costs are a key consideration.

---

[9]See Losch, *ibid.*, pp. 105–8.
[10]A few sources may be mentioned: Edward H. Chamberlin, *The Theory of Monopolistic Competition*, Cambridge, Mass., Harvard University Press, 1962, pp. 260–5; Greenhut, *Plant Location*, pp. 25–42 and 87–93; and William Alonso, "Location Theory," *Regional Development and Planning*, ed. John Friedmann and William Alonso, Cambridge, Mass., M.I.T. Press, 1964, pp. 79–82 and 94–7.

They influence the delivered cost of raw materials and fuel, and they affect the market attributes of different locations. Relatively high transport costs mean expensive production and restricted markets and, unless offset by some major locational advantage, can act as an absolute barrier to the establishment of economic activity at a certain location or in a certain region. Changes in transportation costs can have similar effects on firms already established at given locations.

Transportation in international trade theory

We move now from examination of the role played by transportation costs in the location of firms to the related question of the effect of transportation costs on the flow of goods between countries.

A. THE EFFECTS OF TRANSPORT-COST CHANGES ON TRADE FLOWS AND LOCATIONS

From the preceding section of this chapter it is clear that transport costs influence location. Any producing location has associated with it certain distribution patterns—certain flows of goods. If transport costs change, then there may be changes in trade flows and/or in location. Whether either or both will occur depends on the circumstances of particular cases. If, after a transport-cost increase, the location can still serve the same markets, there will be no alteration of trade flows. Even if the cost increase does generate a trade-flow change, the existing location may remain sufficiently profitable. Moreover, even when rising freight costs do force changes in location, the event is typically delayed.

But transport-cost changes need not have any effect on trade flows or location. A railroad freight rate increase of 3 percent, to use a recent U.S. example, should not be expected to have any effect on the shipments of U.S. farm-implement manufacturers to Canadian buyers. Even if trade flows do change, there is no guarantee that transport-cost changes will encourage shifts in location. Suppose ocean freight rates charged on newsprint moving from Canada's Atlantic provinces to U.S. Atlantic coast destinations fell by 20 percent. There *might* occur an increase in Canadian newsprint exports, but even then there need be no related shift of the newsprint industry to the Atlantic provinces. Whether a shift from competing locations occurred would depend on, among other things, the relative availability of raw materials and the amount of excess capacity available at various locations producing newsprint.

B. TRANSPORT AND TRADE VOLUME

There has been relatively little work done at either the theoretical or the empirical level on transport costs and international trade. At the theoretical level those specializing in international economics have often found it convenient to assume that transport costs were zero. This is not because, as Beckerman has pointed out,[11] they believed that transport costs actually were zero, but because this abstraction from the influence of transport costs allowed these economists to study other aspects of international trade that were of more interest to them. This analytical device is a recognition of the role that transport costs play in international trade.

What, then, is the effect of transport costs on trade? The existence of transport costs, the fact that space has economic significance, reduces the volume of international trade. If transport costs were zero, if movement of goods between places did not require the use of economic resources, then the volume of international trade would be very large.[12] All goods for which there were any inter-country differences in production cost would be traded internationally, assuming there were no artificial barriers (tariffs, quotas, foreign exchange restrictions, etc.) to international trade. On the other hand, if international transport costs were infinite there would be no international trade at all. Production and consumption would be locally oriented. Between these two unrealistic extremes there is the possibility of a limited international exchange of goods.

However, the limits to the international exchange of goods are not set solely by what has been called the "attenuating influence of distance."[13] International trade patterns are in the first instance determined by the comparative costs of production in different countries. Grapefruit could be grown in Canada, but it is a more efficient use of our resources to devote them to production of other commodities and to import grapefruit from the southern United States. Transport costs play a role in determining this import volume. It cost, in 1964, about $36 to move a ton of oranges and grapefruit by rail from Florida to eastern Canada,[14] and there is probably a smaller quantity of oranges and grapefruit moving between these two areas than if Florida were two hundred miles from this market rather than twelve hundred. But the elasticities of demand and supply are crucial to this role. If Canadian consumers required a fixed quantity of Florida oranges and grapefruit (that

[11]W. Beckerman, "Distance and the Pattern of Intra-European Trade," *Review of Economics and Statistics*, XXXVIII, Feb. 1956, p. 31.
[12]This follows the approach used by Kindleberger. See Charles P. Kindleberger, *Foreign Trade and the National Economy*, New Haven, Yale University Press, 1962, pp. 8–11.
[13]Walter Isard and Merton J. Peck, "Location Theory and International and Interregional Trade Theory," *Quarterly Journal of Economics*, LXVIII, Feb. 1956, p. 114.
[14]See chap. 4 for the source of this and other railroad freight rate statistics.

is, if demand were perfectly inelastic), transport costs would have no effect in determining trade flows. Alternatively, if Florida growers produced a fixed quantity of oranges and grapefruit for the Canadian market each year, regardless of selling price, the influence of transport would again be absent. Perfectly inelastic supply has the same effect as perfectly inelastic demand. Some degree of elasticity in supply and demand is an essential component of the trade-determining power of transportation. This condition, though, is typically fulfilled.

C.   TRANSPORT AND TRADE DIRECTION

We might also mention the impact of national trade policies on international trading patterns. A country can do much to alter its trade flows by direct action involving the imposition of high tariffs or arbitrary quotas on a geographical or commodity basis. The same end can be achieved indirectly by policies related to the country's international balance of payments.

Transport costs can have an influence here, too. They have a limiting effect on the direction of international trade as well as on its volume. Put in simple terms, the influence on direction is that countries tend to trade with their neighbours. While there are obviously other influences at work, it is significant that, in 1964, 60.6 percent of Canada's trade was with the United States and only 1.3 percent with Australia.[15] The economic proximity of the United States must play an important part, along with comparative costs, tradition, and the differing sizes of the U.S. and Australian economies, in explaining this disparity.

D.   THE RELATIVE IMPORTANCE OF TRANSPORT COSTS

The influence of transport costs on the volume and composition of trade flows (between Canada and the United States specifically) is of interest. The most important dimensions of this impact are obvious. For given elasticities of supply and demand, the higher the level of transport costs in relation to delivered price, the greater the influence of transportation in determining trade patterns. In the grapefruit example used earlier in this section, the hypothesis that transport costs are important in determining patterns in U.S.–Canada shipments of this commodity rests on the transport cost/price relationship. According to the best information available, a ton of oranges and grapefruit is worth about $150 in terms of wholesale value at destination.[16]

[15]Dominion Bureau of Statistics, *Canada Year Book*, 1966, Ottawa, Queen's Printer, 1966, pp. 921–2 and 925–6. The percentages refer to the total of domestic exports plus imports.
[16]Interstate Commerce Commission, *Freight Revenue and Wholesale Value at Destination of Commodities Transported by Class I Line-Haul Railroads*, 1959, Washington, ICC, 1961, p. 16. The advantage of this source is that it expresses values in the same

The rail transportation cost of $36 comprises a major part (24 percent) of this value, and its importance in determining trade flows seems obvious.

For commodities where the freight-rate portion of delivered price is much smaller (for example, agricultural machinery),[17] we must be less definite. For many manufactured products transportation charges are less than 5 percent of delivered price, and there must be some question about the effect that these charges have on flows of these commodities. Furthermore, what is the impact of changes in transport cost (which are rarely as substantial as 20 percent) on existing trade flows? The question is really one of buyers' and producers' reactions to changes in price and the real significance of very small price changes. It is clear from other evidence that firms can be very sensitive to slight changes in their costs of production, presumably because they fear the effects of slightly higher product prices on their market positions.

Consider, for example, the number of strikes where only a few cents' difference in wage offers and demands separates employer and union when collective bargaining breaks down. While strikes are rarely caused by a simple disagreement over wages, the willingness of firms to interrupt production over amounts that sometimes represent a very minor proportion of selling price is of some relevance to the present question. We might also refer to the reactions of individual shippers and shippers' organizations when freight-rate increases are proposed. The July, 1967, increase in railroad freight rates in the United States is a case in point. Although the proposed change amounted to only about a 3 percent average increase over existing rates, almost three hundred protests were filed with the Interstate Commerce Commission.[18] Some of these, to be sure, were from industries where freight costs are generally high in relation to selling price, but many were from manufacturing industries with what we would expect to be a rather marginal interest in a freight-rate increase of such slight magnitude.[19] Similar examples of shipper interest in freight-rate changes could be cited from Canadian experience prior to the Freight Rates Reduction Act of 1959.

It is virtually impossible to provide definite guides to state how important transport costs must be before they have a significant impact on international

---

classifications used for railroad freight revenue statistics. It is assumed here that wholesale prices changed little between 1959 and 1964.

[17]Within the United States the 1959 rail freight-rate proportion was only 3.90 percent. *Ibid.*, p. 19.

[18]"Existence of Rails' Financial 'Emergency' Is Disputed in Oral Argument before Entire ICC," *Traffic World*, July 15, 1967, p. 21.

[19]The estimated freight factors (freight-rate proportion of delivered price) for some of the protestants were as follows: Wine Institute (2.99), George A. Hormel, Inc. (4.17), Fibre Box Association (3.29). *Ibid.*, pp. 21 ff.; freight factors from ICC, *Freight Revenue*, pp. 16–21.

trade flows.[20] The trend is obvious, though. A high ratio of transport costs to delivered prices implies greater sensitivity to transport cost and cost changes than does a lower ratio, other things being equal. The calculation of these ratios, or freight factors, is of considerable importance.

E.   PROBLEMS IN THE DETERMINATION OF FREIGHT FACTORS

If all goods involved in foreign trade between two non-contiguous countries were produced and consumed at seacoast locations, if neither country operated a merchant fleet, and if the two countries succeeded in their efforts to keep accurate and consistent balance of payments statistics, the determination of freight factors would be relatively easy. The International Monetary Fund's requirements call for the valuation of internationally traded goods at the frontier of export.[21] With coastal locations for both consumption and production, all freight costs would be recorded for balance of payments purposes and could presumably be made available on a commodity and destination basis.

Inland freight transportation presents a problem, however. If the IMF valuation rule were followed, then non-ocean transport charges would be submerged in merchandise value. When, as is the case with Canada, a different valuation rule is followed, the problem becomes more complex. Canadian exports are valued f.o.b. point of consignment for export,[22] and imports are valued f.o.b. point of shipment in the country of origin. Concerning imports, however, DBS admits that c.i.f. valuation is common, especially in the absence of *ad valorem* tariffs.[23] Moreover, much Canada–U.S. trade is carried by U.S. and Canadian transport firms. Thus, although the f.o.b. frontier rule is not followed, we have the U.S.-carried portion of Canadian imports and the Canadian-carried portion of Canadian exports excluded from Canadian balance of payments estimates. This means that we cannot use the sum of receipts and payments of freight and shipping transactions with the United States ($631 million in 1964)[24] and relate it to the sum of exports to and

---

[20]The problem is somewhat analogous to the determination of the degree of "effective protection" afforded by the Canadian tariff structure. For a discussion of this see Bruce Wilkinson, *Canada's International Trade: An Analysis of Recent Trends and Patterns*, Montreal, Canadian Trade Committee, 1968, pp. 55–63.

[21]Herman F. Karreman, *Methods for Improving World Transportation Accounts*, New York, National Bureau of Economic Research, 1961, p. 16. (Henceforth referred to as *Methods.*)

[22]Some exporters report export values in U.S. dollars. For a discussion of the implications of this practice see Wilkinson, *Canada's International Trade*, pp. 10–11.

[23]DBS, *Trade of Canada* (1967), *Imports by Countries*, January–December 1966, p. 4.

[24]DBS, *The Canadian Balance of International Payments: A Compendium of Statistics from 1946 to 1965* (1967), p. 176. U.S. statistics are also unsuitable. For a general description see Angelos J. Clones and Gary C. McKay, "Transportation Transactions in the U.S. Balance of Payments," *Survey of Current Business*, Aug. 1963, pp. 23–7.

from the United States ($10,600 million in 1964)[25] to obtain a full picture of the transportation content of North American trade.[26] Even less can we use this source of information to provide any insights concerning the transportation costs associated with trade in any particular commodity.

The objective of much of the work that has been done in connection with freight factors has been the refinement of balance of payments statistics. Most researchers have been interested in freight factors on individual commodities so that they might be able to develop freight and shipping accounts for the balance of payments from commodity trade statistics.[27] Our interest does not extend this far; we are concerned with commodity freight factors for their own use in suggesting the impact of transport-cost changes on trade flows.

A standard procedure in balance of payments construction is to estimate the freight portion of imports valued at c.i.f. at 10 percent of the c.i.f. value.[28] A more refined procedure would take account of differences in freight factors for different commodities and origins. Carmellah Moneta's study of German ocean-borne imports in 1951, using actual ocean freight rates and excluding all inland transportation costs, arrives at an average freight factor of 14.3 percent.[29] More important, for our purposes, is the variation in freight factors for different commodities. These showed a wide range, as Table 1 suggests.

Similar information is not available for Canada–U.S. trade. The necessary investigations have not been made and would be extremely involved. The Moneta study was greatly aided by the availability of German statistics relating ocean freight rates to particular commodities imported from particular regions. No such data are available within North America. The best substitute is the U.S. Interstate Commerce Commission report cited above.[30] It

[25]Clones and McKay, *ibid.*, p. 21.
[26]Another difficulty is that U.S. transportation firms do carry some Canadian goods to non-U.S. markets. Few Canadian transport firms, however, carry U.S. goods to non-Canadian markets.
[27]For example, Karreman, *Methods*, and Jacob Viner, *Canada's Balance of International Indebtedness 1900–1913*, Cambridge, Harvard University Press, 1924, pp. 63–79.
[28]Carmellah Moneta, "The Estimation of Transportation Costs in International Trade," *Journal of Political Economy*, LXVII, Feb. 1959, p. 42.
[29]*Ibid.*, Table 2, p. 46.
[30]ICC, *Freight Revenue*. Two alternatives may be mentioned. The "transport-sensitivity" of commodities could be measured in terms of their value per ton. According to this approach, products with a low value per ton are sensitive to transportation-cost influences. However, this approach involves two critical assumptions: that distance from producer to market is roughly the same for all commodities, and that transport costs are solely related to distance. Freight factors could also be developed on the basis of input-output data. The drawbacks to this procedure are mainly statistical. First, the industrial classification used for transportation in input-output studies is at once too inclusive and too incomplete. Second, no satisfactory input-output study is available. The DBS Canadian input-output study of 1949 is dated and, in any event, is unsuitable when applied to external trade. The same criticism may be made of the 1958 U.S. study.

TABLE 1

FREIGHT FACTORS OF SELECTED GERMAN IMPORTS, 1951

Commodity group	Freight factor*
Petroleum, crude	64.3
Iron ore and concentrates	54.9
Fruit and nuts, fresh	17.3
Wheat, unmilled	16.2
Wood shaped or simply worked	15.0
Chemicals, inorganic	9.5
Meat, fresh, chilled, or frozen	8.4
Paper and paperboard	4.0
Iron and steel	2.5
Cotton fabrics	0.9
Machinery, electric	0.5

Source: Carmellah Moneta, "The Estimation of Transportation Costs in International Trade," *Journal of Political Economy*, LXVII, Feb. 1959, Table A2, pp. 57–8.
*Freight factor = (freight charge/c.i.f. value) × 100.

has, however, several shortcomings when used without modification as a source of freight factors for Canada–U.S. trade. Among these are the following:

1. It refers to railroad transportation only.
2. It is limited to the transportation of goods within the United States at U.S. freight rates. There is no reason to suppose similar rates or transportation conditions in rail movements between the two countries.
3. Goods are valued at U.S. prices.
4. 1959 is the latest year for which these data are available. This should introduce a generally upward bias to freight-factor estimates based on this source. Between 1959 and 1965 the U.S. wholesale price index rose by 1.9 points, while the index of freight revenue per ton-mile, using the same base, fell by 12.8 points.[31]

Recognizing these shortcomings, we will set forth information from this publication that is useful in consideration of Canada–U.S. trade.

The only available input-output formulation that integrates the economies of both countries is based on 1949 relationships and includes "trade" with "transportation and storage." See Ronald J. Wonnacott, *Canadian-American Dependence: An Interindustry Analysis of Production and Prices*, Amsterdam, North-Holland, 1961.

[31]Wholesale price index from *Economic Report of the President*, 1966, Washington, U.S. Government Printing Office, 1966, Table C-41, p. 257; freight-revenue index calculated from Association of American Railroads, *Yearbook of Railroad Facts*, Washington, AAR, 1967, p. 36. A more precise evaluation by major commodity groups would reveal differing degrees and directions of bias.

An examination of the estimated railway freight revenues by commodity groups obtained from the freight factors of Table 2 reveals that these ICC statistics cannot be generally applied to international traffic between the two countries. Comparison with railway freight revenue statistics obtained especially for this study shows that the freight factors tend to understate the proportion of freight cost included in delivered price. For example, the freight factor for railway shipments of lumber and plywood to the United States should be of the order of 24, rather than 18 as shown in Table 2. For news-

TABLE 2

FREIGHT FACTORS FOR SELECTED COMMODITIES TRANSPORTED BY RAIL WITHIN THE UNITED STATES, 1959

Commodity group	Freight factor	1964 f.o.b. value of Canada-U.S. trade carried by rail ($ million)	Estimated 1964 freight costs ($ million)
Canadian exports:			
Lumber and plywood	18	306	67
Woodpulp	7	281	21
Newsprint	8	380	33
Fertilizers	19	59	14
Primary and manufactured iron and steel	6	55	4
Aluminum	3	109	3
Nickel and alloys	0.5	63	0.3
Agricultural machinery	5	92	5
Canadian imports:			
Fruit and vegetables	23	70	21
Cotton	3	62	2
Chemicals	10	82	9
Primary and manufactured iron and steel	6	95	6
Industrial machinery	4	—	—
Agricultural machinery	5	—	—
Motor vehicle parts	3	—	—

Sources: Freight factors—weighted averages calculated from ICC, *Freight Revenue* 1959; export values—DBS, *Exports by Mode of Transport, Calendar Year 1964* (1966); import values—author's calculations from various U.S. and Canadian sources (see chap. 2). Note: Unless otherwise stated, quotations from Canadian sources are in Canadian dollars; from U.S. sources in U.S. dollars.

print the freight factor should be approximately 15, instead of 8. Although the freight factors derived from this ICC information should not be used as absolute figures, the relative ranking of different commodities by freight factors is of some interest and will indicate the general response of trade in these commodities to changes in transport cost.

We have alluded to many of the difficulties that restrict the development of detailed freight-factor statistics. It will be useful to bring these together at this point.

1. Few countries collect and publish statistics concerning the transportation content of the components of their international trade flows. Nor is this information available from private sources. Canada and the United States are no exception to this general rule. Only the most fragmentary statistics of this type are available. For this reason parts of this study emphasize railroad transportation, for which extensive statistical information was made available to the author by the railroads. Although the railroads are the most important carrier of transborder traffic, they still carry less than half of trade in both directions, measured in value terms. For water transportation considerable data are available. Much less information is available for highway transportation—the great unknown of the transportation world. Pipeline and air transportation are relatively unimportant for the purposes of this study.

2. A second problem involves classification anomalies. Stated briefly, the problem is that Canadian and U.S. transport and trade statistics are gathered according to different commodity classifications. There is no easy route to comparability, and the laborious adjustments on which much of the statistical material in this study are based are not perfect. This lack of comparability of transport and trade classifications affects both rate and cost analysis, which we have briefly touched on in this chapter, and the description of trade flows in terms of transportation, which will be the subject of the next chapter.

3. Finally, mention should be made of the variability of freight factors. There are two aspects of this. First is the variation over time. This is most apt to be significant when either commodity prices or transport costs fluctuate widely. The former fluctuation is not typical of many goods, and the latter is mainly confined to ocean transport.[32] We can be reasonably confident, then, that important freight-factor relationships will be stable. There is another type of variation, however. This arises from the enormous amount of averaging that analysis of freight rates demands. Part of the averaging is over unlike commodities forced together in one grouping of commodities and consuming locations. Thus, although it was suggested earlier in this section that the freight factor for lumber and plywood exports from Canada to the United States was 24, a lumber producer at

---

[32]Between 1950 and 1953 the annual average freight factor for lumber shipped from the Pacific coast of Canada to the Netherlands changed from 9 to 17 to 10 to 7, reflecting the impact of the Korean war on ocean freight rates. Karreman, *Methods*, Table 5, p. 15.

Quesnel in the B.C. interior could expect to pay $31.40 per ton to ship lumber to Birmingham, Alabama.[33] Adding this to the f.o.b. mill price of about $44[34] and dividing, we arrive at a freight factor of 42. Examples in the other direction could also be given.

For these reasons this study does not include formal and complete calculations of freight factors. Instead, reference to the transportation content of particular imports and exports will be made on an *ad hoc* basis where useful.

F. TERMINOLOGY AND DEFINITIONS

It is essential to set forth the way in which the term "transport cost" will be used in the rest of the study. So far the term has been used rather indiscriminately but has referred usually to the rates charged by transportation companies for the movement of freight. This is indeed the direct "cost" of transportation as seen by the transport user. But this meaning is inappropriate in a study that will be concerned with the effects of public and private transportation policies and practices. More correctly, transport cost refers to the value of the resources used to provide transport services. There are two varieties of cost involved. One is the cost to the transport firm of producing transport service; the other is the cost to the transport user of purchasing that service. The second category includes, net of the freight rate, the class of costs known as distribution costs. These include costs of holding inventory, packaging, storage, handling, and so on, that are involved in firms' logistics activities. In this study we will assume, unrealistically, that such costs are the same as between different modes of transport. Thus we exclude them from further consideration.

In most transport situations there is not a direct relationship between costs and the price charged to transportation users.[35] This makes it imperative that we differentiate the two, and so in future transport cost will refer to the costs of transport enterprises. The direct costs of transport users will be identified as transport "rates," "revenues," or "prices."

We have so far measured transport rates in terms of weight—dollars per ton—and for some types of analysis this is necessary. There will, however, be increasing reference to cents per ton-mile when speaking of freight rates. The ton-mile is the best available unit in which to measure transportation output, and comparisons of rates and costs are most meaningful when made in terms of this measure. Also, although transport costs are not proportional

[33]British Columbia, Department of Industrial Development, Trade, and Commerce, *Freight Rates in Effect January 1, 1967, on Lumber and Forest Products from British Columbia Points to Canadian and American Markets*, Victoria, Department of Industrial Development, Trade, and Commerce, 1967, p. 9.
[34]Calculated from DBS, *Sawmills and Planing Mills*, 1964 (1967), Table 13A, p. 23.
[35]Reasons for this divergence are set out in chap. 3.

to distance traveled, distance *is* a major determinant of transport costs and transport prices. This is especially so when comparisons are being made within a restricted commodity group so that other influences on transport cost levels may be assumed to be more or less equal.

Previous study of transport sector harmonization in trade groupings

A. INTRODUCTION

The subject of this study is not novel and has been treated in connection with other trade groupings. The barriers to free trade caused by lack of harmonization of public and industry transport policies have received extensive study in the European Economic Community and, before that, in the European Coal and Steel Community. This question has also been approached in connection with the Latin American Free Trade Association.

The Canadian-American Committee's proposed plan for a North American free trade area included the following clauses:

14. The abolition of tariffs and quotas will not by itself provide reciprocal free trade which is meaningful. The partners must also modify policies and practices affecting the production, transport and marketing of products to the extent that they give an unfair advantage to domestic products in either the Canadian or U.S. sectors of the continental market.
15. The partners will take appropriate steps to control the discriminatory effects of such government aids to freely traded products as:
   a) measures resulting in assistance to exports to the partner;
   b) measures manifestly and artificially giving domestic production a competitive advantage over the production of similar products in the partner country;
   c) *national transport policies resulting in rates or conditions manifestly favoring domestic products*;
   d) measures favoring government procurement of domestic products over products originating in the partner country.[36]

The effects of discriminatory government aids working through the transport sector are felt, of course, whether trade between two countries is free or carried on subject to protection. But it is in a free trade area that transport policies which discriminate against imported goods are most pernicious.

Thus, the removal of one of the impediments established at political boundaries—the tariff—will not automatically lead to the rationalization that might otherwise be expected. The protection of Canadian industry, for example, required not only the tariff but also policies relating to transportation, taxation, and industrial organization. These permitted the greater

[36]*A Possible Plan for a Canada-U.S. Free Trade Area,* staff report, Montreal and Washington, Canadian-American Committee, 1965, pp. 7–8 (emphasis added).

volume of output encouraged by the tariff to be sold in Canada. It is clear that transportation policies designed to encourage the distribution, within Canada, of Canadian goods will act as an impediment to a greater flow of trade between Canada and the United States, even if this flow is given impetus by lower tariffs. The same holds, of course, for policies of a similar nature that exist in the United States.

Transportation's close relationship to international trade and specialization has already been discussed. In one sense freight rates are analogous to tariffs; the higher the freight rates or tariffs between two countries, the more constricted is the flow of trade, and *vice versa*. Were freight rates based solely on transportation costs, the degree of constriction caused by their level would be quite acceptable, reflecting as it would some of the real opportunity costs of international trade. But rates rarely reflect cost very directly, and transportation is subject to so many varieties of public policy that the level of freight rates cannot validly be viewed as opportunity cost. Government influence over transportation ranges from detailed economic and safety regulation through subsidization to the public provision of large portions of the industry's fixed facilities. Many of these policies were not designed as protectionism, but they often have this effect. This is particularly true when public policies towards transportation differ between countries.

Canadian transportation policy, for example, has discouraged the development of transborder trucking.[37] Until this attitude is modified the gains that would accrue to both countries from an elimination of tariffs on industrial machinery, which is generally most economically transported by truck, could never be fully realized. Neither the rationalization of industrial location nor the simultaneous and resulting alteration of trade patterns could be carried out in an environment of transport favouritism for the Canadian trucking industry. This holds whether free trade in industrial machinery would mainly augment U.S.–Canada or Canada–U.S. trade flows. Either way, this Canadian impediment within the transport sector would, to some degree, inhibit the growth of international trade. Many aspects and problems of transport harmonization will become apparent in the following survey of European and Latin American experience.

B.   THE EUROPEAN COAL AND STEEL COMMUNITY

The importance of the transport sector to the effective working of a trade grouping has been recognized in studies of the European Coal and Steel Community.[38] This grouping, the forerunner of the European Economic

[37]See chap. 5 for a discussion of this policy. A similar impediment exists on the U.S. side of the border.
[38]See J. E. Meade, H. H. Liesner, and S. J. Wells, *Case Studies in European Economic*

Community, provided for free trade in coal and steel among six European nations—Belgium, France, Germany, Italy, Luxembourg, and the Netherlands. Since coal and steel are products with relatively high freight factors and since discriminatory national transport policies were rife, policy harmonization within the transportation sector was extremely important to the objectives of the Community.

In view of this, "only far-reaching changes . . . could have ensured the proper working of the common market."[39] But these changes have not been forthcoming; indeed, Liesner's appraisal of the ECSC's progress in this field is highly critical: "The achievements of the first eight years may therefore be summed up by saying that although some knotty problems have been successfully tackled, in relation to the task ahead the Community has only removed a few of the symptoms without curing the underlying malaise.[40]

The "underlying malaise" included six basic problem areas which may be described as follows:

1. *Discriminatory railway rates.*[41] These rates were set at different levels according to the country of origin or destination of the commodity being transported. Adjustment was achieved surprisingly easily, perhaps because, as Liesner suggests, they tended to have mutually offsetting effects on the various Community members.

2. *Broken freight rates.*[42] This involved treating international traffic as though its passage were in fact interrupted at the international boundary. The effect was to increase railway freight rates because additional (and non-existent) terminal costs thus became incorporated in international rates. Effective elimination of this impediment was achieved in 1957, an accomplishment that Jean Monnet, the ECSC President, hailed as "tantamount to the opening of a second common market."[43]

3. *Special railway tariffs.*[44] Such tariffs provided for the application of lower freight rates to particular traffic. They were occasioned by regional development policy, competition from other modes of transport, or lower costs of railway transportation. These special tariffs were a feature of German and, to a lesser extent, French transport policy. Most of these tariffs have been modified, after long negotiation and, finally, litigation.

4. *Harmonization of national railway freight rates.*[45] This issue, as Liesner

Union: The Mechanics of Integration, London, Oxford University Press, 1962, pp. 336–405. The section on transport in the ECSC is by Liesner and is the most useful general treatment of this subject that is available. This volume also contains briefer references to the role of transportation in the Belgium-Luxembourg economic union, pp. 47–8, and the later Benelux economic union, pp. 185–94.
[39]*Ibid.,* p. 404.   [40]*Ibid.*   [41]*Ibid.,* pp. 341–51.
[42]*Ibid.,* pp. 351–70.   [43]*Ibid.,* p. 370.   [44]*Ibid.,* pp. 370–9.
[45]*Ibid.,* pp. 380–92.

describes it, involved "how far the existence of the common market requires changes in the general structure and level of railway rates in the member countries. . . ."[46] More specifically, harmonization concerned the adoption of uniform rate taper (reduction in rate per ton-mile as length of haul increases), of uniform proportions between the rates on the different ECSC products,[47] and of uniform rates for shipments where only shipping procedures differed. The fundamental question here, and indeed in the other three problem areas thus far discussed, is the basis for national transportation policy. When rail freight rates bear a close relationship to cost (as in the Netherlands), their impact on location decisions and trade flows will be quite different than if rates are based on gratifying regional political and social needs (as in Germany). The example given here clearly demonstrates this—German iron ore is greatly favoured relative to German coal when German freight rates on these commodities are compared with the more rational Dutch rates. Non-harmonization remains the rule in the ECSC and still plagues attempts to rationalize the transport sector in the more comprehensive EEC.

5. *Charges for water transport.*[48] There were substantial differences within the Community between water freight rates on domestic and international traffic. Coupled with this discriminatory rate structure was a system of flag privileges—preferences for national flag vessels and barges. Neither practice has proved amenable to significant improvement. Liesner suggests that shipping industry pressure and the governments' reluctance to amend the Rhine Statute of 1868, which prohibits government control of international rates, are responsible.

6. *Regulation of road transport.*[49] Although only about 10 percent of the Community's commodities were carried by truck, this mode of transport dominated the movement of some products and was, moreover, growing rapidly. Three probable impediments to the objectives of the ECSC existed in road transport. These were the lack of published freight-rate tariffs, the existence of suppressive measures designed to restrict competition between truckers and railroads, and the conflict between vehicle size and weight maximums in different countries. Virtually nothing has been done to remedy these anomalies.

Examination of these six areas shows that harmonization of transport policy is a complex matter that is vulnerable to frustration by various vested

---

[46]*Ibid.*, p. 380.
[47]For example, for a 300-kilometer haul the relationship between coal rates (100) and iron ore rates varied within the Community as follows: Belgium 80, France 88, Germany 44, Italy 87, Luxembourg 54, and Netherlands 100. *Ibid.*, Table 13, p. 383.
[48]*Ibid.*, pp. 392–7. [49]*Ibid.*, pp. 397–403.

interests. The *status quo* has often been preferred in the ECSC experience, not because its conditions were desirable, but rather because change was unthinkable. Yet some harmonization was achieved, especially in railway transport, and Liesner's pessimistic assessment may be too gloomy. At least some of the most obvious (and probably the most substantial) transportation barriers to rationalization of the coal and steel industries of the ECSC members have been removed. The contrast with the lack of this type of progress in the wider European Economic Community is striking.

C. THE EUROPEAN ECONOMIC COMMUNITY—TRANSPORT POLICIES OF THE
    MEMBER STATES

The European Economic Community was established by the Treaty of Rome in 1957. This treaty had much more to say about transportation than had its 1952 predecessor, the Treaty of Paris, which established the European Coal and Steel Community. The Treaty of Paris required only that transportation policies and practices could not be allowed to distort the coal and steel markets; commercial transport policy was left outside the jurisdiction of the Community.[50] The Treaty of Rome, however, states in Article 74 that "the objectives of the Treaty shall be pursued by the Member States within the framework of a common transport policy."[51] The implementation of this "common transport policy" is elaborated in the article immediately following. Article 75 of the Treaty reads as follows:

1. ... the Council shall establish:—
   (a) common rules for international transport to or from the Territory of a Member State or passing across the territory of one or more Member States;
   (b) conditions for admitting non-resident carriers to the national transport within Member States; and
   (c) any other appropriate provisions.
   In so doing, the Council shall have a regard to the special aspects of transport. . . .[52]

The remaining nine articles of the Transport Title qualify and expand the instructions given to the Council of Ministers, the main legislative body of the Community, in Articles 74 and 75. They permit transport subsidies in the interests of transport coordination and the provision of non-economic but

[50]N. S. Despicht, "Transport and the Common Market—II," *Institute of Transport Journal*, XXXI, March 1966, p. 323.
[51]Quoted in N. S. Despicht, *Policies for Transport in the Common Market*, Sidcup, Kent, Lambarde Press, 1964, p. 192. The "objectives" are earlier in the Treaty stated to be the following: "a harmonious development of economic activities, a continuous and balanced expansion, an increased stability, a more rapid improvement in the standard of living, and closer relations between its member states." *Ibid.*, p. 193.
[52]*Ibid*. The article then sets forth the procedures for action by the Council of Ministers with respect to transport.

socially desirable services, protection of carriers for financial reasons, special assistance to depressed regions, and the exclusion of sea and air transport from the provisions of the Treaty.[53]

Domestic transport policies in the various EEC countries are substantially different. It is desirable, therefore, to pause in this review of European experience with transport policy harmonization and summarize the attitudes towards transportation that exist among the six members of the EEC.

This summary is most conveniently approached by beginning with the country with the most "laissez-faire" approach to transportation, the Netherlands, and finishing with the heavily restrictive regime of West Germany.[54] Dutch transport policy allows virtually total commercial freedom to the nationalized railway system. For motor carriers there is regulation of rates and capacity, but it is probably the most enlightened system in the world, being based on sophisticated measures of vehicle utilization and operating efficiency. As in all European countries water transport in the Netherlands is stringently regulated. Rates are fixed, there is some control of entry, and traffic bureaus actually allocate traffic among different carriers.

In Belgium transport policy (broadly defined) is not as free. The qualification is necessary because the striking feature of Belgian transportation is the weight of social obligations imposed on the national railway. The railway operates at a substantial deficit because of the large number of very low special rates which the government obliges it to make available. Entry into Belgian trucking is regulated somewhat along Dutch lines, but the details of the regulation have less economic rationale. At present trucking rates are not controlled. Water transportation has the familiar rate-control, entry-restriction, and traffic-allocation features.

Italian railroads are operated as a quasi-department of government, and as might be expected, freight rates are very low and operating deficits very high. There is no regulation of motor carrier rates in Italy, but entry is controlled, although the controls have not been restrictive. Inland water transport is, of course, of little importance in Italy.

In France transport policy has been concerned with securing a "desirable" distribution of traffic. The desirability of alternative distributions does not depend on a single criterion, however. Instead, French transport policy is based on a peculiar mix of economic, political, and industrial considerations. The French national railway has a cost-based rate structure that has

[53]*Ibid.*, pp. 195–201.
[54]The discussion draws heavily on the material in Eric Schenker, "European Transport Policy and the Common Market," *Public Utilities Fortnightly*, LXXV, June 10, 1965, pp. 37–49. For more detailed information see Despicht, *Policies for Transport*, pp. 37–176, and Brian T. Bayliss, *European Transport*, London, Kenneth Mason, 1965, pp. 61–147.

advantages of simplicity and at least partial relation to the marginal costs of providing railway service.[55] It carries the virtue of simplicity too far, however, and also is weakened by the existence of social exceptions. The rates charged by French truckers are under close and rather unrealistic regulation by the government, and the system of capacity control in French trucking is notorious for its rigidity. National quotas are based on carrying capacity of the vehicles in service and have been effective in keeping 65 percent of freight traffic in France moving by railroad.[56] Water transport is controlled at least as closely as in other west European countries.

The philosophy of transport policy in West Germany is that "transport should be subordinated to the general needs of the economy."[57] Unlike the Dutch, who appear to feel that transportation as an industry has no special role to play in the economy, the Germans have tried to use their transport industries, particularly their railways, as major instruments of public policy. Thus German railways carry a large proportion of their traffic at unremunerative rates in furtherance of government policies for regional and industrial development. Competition between the railways and motor carriers is restrained by restricting entry under a quota system and by careful control of rates. Indeed, until very recently German truckers were forced to follow railway rate structures. As elsewhere, German water transport is closely regulated, although there is no control of entry.

Three things stand out in this summary, and each could be expected to pose grave difficulties for the establishment of a common transport policy in the EEC. First, except in the Netherlands, there is really very little freedom of competition among different modes of transportation. Yet without some freedom it is unlikely that effective rationalization of transport can ever be achieved.[58] Second, most EEC countries impose arbitrary and varying systems of capacity control on their trucking industries. Resolution of these differences would require a major exercise of intra-European goodwill. Finally, there are fundamentally significant differences in the approach to the railroads. In West Germany and Belgium the railways are made to act in the implementation of a wide variety of socio-economic policy objectives— some of these being, in fact, rather trivial. The distortions that this approach introduces into the transport sector are difficult to reconcile with the relatively economic orientation of the Dutch and French railways.

[55]The pricing policies of the French railways and public utilities have received considerable attention from economists. For a collection of writings of French experts in this field, see James R. Nelson, *Marginal Cost Pricing in Practice*, New York, Prentice-Hall, 1963.
[56]Schenker, "European Transport Policy," Table I, p. 39.   [57]*Ibid.*, p. 41.
[58]See D. L. Munby, "Fallacies in the Community's Transport Policy," *Journal of Common Market Studies*, I, May 1962, pp. 67–78.

As an aid to understanding the potential consequences of the national transport anomalies within the EEC, Table 3 shows the volume of international traffic among the six EEC countries. What we do not know, of

TABLE 3

INTERNATIONAL TRAFFIC IN THE EUROPEAN ECONOMIC COMMUNITY, 1960
(thousand tons)

From	To					
	Belgium	France	Germany	Italy	Luxembourg	Netherlands
Belgium	—	5,772	5,489	*	*	8,204
France	20,388	—	17,078	3,005	*	1,517
Germany	7,460	14,130	—	3,192	4,085	20,137
Italy	*	499	1,884	—	*	*
Luxembourg	*	*	1,503	*	—	*
Netherlands	10,457	2,772	40,548	*	*	—

Source: Brian T. Bayliss, *European Transport*, Table XLV, facing p. 140.
*Not available.

course, is what pattern these flows of goods would assume in the absence of the transportation anomalies that we have just discussed. In any event, it is apparent that the major flows of goods in volume terms are between the Netherlands and Germany in both directions, Germany and France in both directions, and France and Belgium, northbound. As we have observed, these products move under transport regulatory regimes of markedly different philosophy and execution.

D. THE EUROPEAN ECONOMIC COMMUNITY—EFFORTS AT TRANSPORT
POLICY HARMONIZATION

The administrative organizations of the Community have worked for ten years towards harmonization of national transport policies, with little success. The EEC Commission's[59] first major effort came to fruition in 1961 when the Schaus Memorandum on a common transport policy was issued. The Memorandum contained few definite proposals and was devoted mainly to an interpretation of the transportation proposals of the Treaty of Rome.[60] A more specific document was the Action Program of 1962. It presented a specific timetable for planning and implementing the harmonization of national transportation systems. Two proposals constituted the heart of the Action Program:

[59]The EEC Commission is a staff body which makes proposals relating to common economic policies.
[60]Despicht, *Policies for Transport*, pp. 214–15.

1. Studies should be made and improvements undertaken in these areas: access to the market, freight rates, harmonization of competitive conditions, and coordination of investment.
2. The common transport policy should be introduced in such a way as to avoid disturbing the national economies during their transformation into a Community economy.[61]

The Action Program was regarded by the Council of Ministers as very far-reaching, and no further action was taken on it or on subsequent related proposals by the Commission until June, 1965. At that time the Council agreed on this timetable for future Community action in the transport field:

1. Taxation of vehicles and transport operations to be standardized between 1966 and 1968.
2. Conformity of working conditions in the transportation industries to be established by 1969.
3. Rules for subsidies to be proposed by mid-1966.
4. Internal cross-subsidization to be eliminated between 1968 and 1972 (i.e., the institution of payment of direct subsidies for services performed as public obligations).
5. Capacity quotas for international trucking to be established by mid-1966.
6. "Market transparency"—the knowledge of all concerned of market prices and conditions—to be achieved by the mandatory publication of tariffs of rates. Tariffs on international traffic to be instituted first (1967–70), followed by tariffs on domestic traffic (1970–73).[62]

The preceding program may appear non-controversial, but little has been done towards its implementation. Most of the program remains to be acted on; and indeed, on those parts which have received detailed consideration, the Council had failed, by the end of 1966, to reach agreement. The disagreements, which came to a head over the institution of "forked" or "bracket" tariffs[63] under the market transparency objective, were so basic that the six EEC countries have decided to alter their approach to transport policy har-

---

[61]*Ibid.*, p. 216.
[62]N. S. Despicht, "Transport and the Common Market—I," *Institute of Transport Journal*, XXXI, Jan. 1966, pp. 278–80.
[63]These tariffs represented a key compromise of the opposing philosophies set forth above. A forked tariff prescribes a price range within which carriers may have freedom to set prices. It is a device to preserve some commercial freedom while preventing ruinous competition below the lower-range rate and monopolistic exploitation of shippers above the higher-range rate. The allowable range may be wide or narrow; if the former, then forked tariffs impose a minimum regulatory restraint; if the latter, then carriers have virtually no rate-making freedom at all.

monization. As Despicht describes it, they have now decided to "set about considering schemes for controlling access to the market and for rules of competition appropriate to the transport sector instead of giving priority to agreement on a forked tariff regime."[64] Here Despicht argues that it is the end result—the creation of a common market in transport—that matters and that the means by which this is obtained are unimportant. Be that as it may, the abandonment of what appeared to be a viable compromise is an ominous sign for the implementation of the Transport Title of the Treaty of Rome. It is perhaps true, as D. L. Munby contends, that the implementation of a common transport policy is impossible in the absence of substantial market freedom in the transport sector.[65] According to this argument the free interplay of economic forces would produce a much faster and more effective harmonization of the EEC transportation industries than would decades of laborious effort at modifying restrictive national regulatory policies.

E. THE EEC EXPERIENCE AND NORTH AMERICA

The purpose of this extended survey was to illuminate some of the ramifications that can be involved in schemes to harmonize transportation policies in different countries. These problems arise, of course, whether the harmonization is undertaken in the context of a customs union (like the EEC) or a free trade area or merely between two countries interested in increasing mutual trade.

The following comments seem appropriate in the rather uncertain North American context. First, no detailed consideration has ever been given to the questions that Hans Liesner has documented in his study of the ECSC. The possibility that public or industry policies and practices in transportation might discriminate, directly or indirectly, has generally been ignored.[66] It appears, however, that all but one (charges for water transport) of the six problems that Liesner identified in his ECSC study exist to some degree in North America. Second, there is more trade between Canada and the United States in both value and volume terms than between any two of the EEC countries. In terms of volume, which has the most significance for transportation, over 100 million tons of goods move in both directions between Canada and the United States annually as opposed to only 61 million between

[64]N. S. Despicht, "Transport and the Common Market—IV," *Institute of Transport Journal*, XXXII, Nov. 1966, p. 25. Part III of this series appeared in the Sept. 1966 issue of the *Institute of Transport Journal*.
[65]Munby, "Fallacies in the Community's Transport Policy."
[66]As, for example, in Francis Masson and J. B. Whitely, *Barriers to Trade between Canada and the United States*, Montreal and Washington, Canadian-American Committee, 1960.

the Netherlands and Germany.[67] In addition, there are far more independent government jurisdictions involved in making transport policy in two federal countries such as Canada and the United States than in the six EEC countries combined. Every state and province in North America acts as an independent agent in many policy areas that are of crucial importance to highway transport.

F. THE EUROPEAN FREE TRADE ASSOCIATION

In marked contrast to the emphasis of the Treaty of Rome, the Stockholm Convention establishing the European Free Trade Association is silent concerning transportation. Two articles of the Convention could, however, be applied to transport situations of the types that have concerned the EEC. The first of these is Article 14, which provides that publicly controlled companies must "bring to an end measures the effect of which is to afford protection that would be inconsistent with the Convention if it were achieved through tariffs, quotas, or subsidies."[68] Article 15, which deals with restrictive business practices, could also be applied to transportation. This article states that "agreements which have as their object or result the prevention, restriction, or distortion of competition within the free market" are incompatible with the Convention.[69]

There are two likely reasons for the lack of attention paid to the transport sector in the EFTA arrangements. For one thing, the EFTA members are interested, for the time being, in a strictly limited degree of economic cooperation, and few of the measures that would be necessary for fuller economic integration have been accepted.[70] Second, over three-quarters of trade among EFTA members before the signing of the Stockholm Convention moved by ocean transport.[71] This mode of transport is relatively free from, and impervious to, the explicit influence of public policy.

G. THE LATIN AMERICAN FREE TRADE ASSOCIATION

The enabling treaty for the Latin American Free Trade Association, unlike the Stockholm Convention, includes an article respecting transportation policies and practices. Article 51 of the Treaty of Montevideo states that:

[67]North American figure calculated from various DBS publications. EEC figure from Table 3—much of the traffic between the Netherlands and Germany is in transit from overseas origins or to overseas destinations.
[68]European Free Trade Association, *The Stockholm Convention Examined*, 2nd ed., Geneva, EFTA, 1963, p. 40.
[69]*Ibid.*
[70]For a brief comparative survey of EFTA and EEC, see Lea, *A Canada-U.S. Free Trade Arrangement*, pp. 50–3.
[71]Author's estimate based on Miriam Camps, *The European Free Trade Association: A Preliminary Appraisal*, London, Political and Economic Planning, 1959, Table 1, p. 36.

"Products imported or exported by a Contracting Party shall enjoy freedom of transit within the Area and shall only be subject to the payment of the normal rates for services rendered."[72] Although vague, as are many of the provisions of the Treaty, this article does establish broad guidelines for the nine LAFTA members.[73]

In fact, transportation matters have been of great concern in Latin American economic development and trade relations. Existing trade patterns are not oriented to trade within the Association—in 1962 only 7.5 percent of South American countries' exports and 10.3 percent of their imports were to and from each other.[74] This lack of intra-Association trade is reflected in (and perhaps caused by) a lack of transport facilities between Association members.[75] Thus the major concern has been with the development of Latin American merchant fleets, air transport facilities, and highways rather than with the lack of harmony between transport policies of different governments.[76] The lack of investment in transport facilities is not the only barrier to the economic integration of this region, however. "It can . . . be noted . . . that the use of some completed links [of the Pan-American highway] (and also of many of the international railroads) is distressingly low. In large measure, this failure to make use of existing facilities is a result of burdensome bureaucratic obstacles at the frontiers and of controls and restrictions on international commerce and passenger movement in general. The elimination of these artificial barriers is crucial for the attainment of the LAFTA objectives."[77]

H. PREVIOUS APPROACHES TO TRANSPORT POLICY HARMONIZATION IN NORTH AMERICA

The effect of differences in Canadian and U.S. transport policies on flows of trade between the two countries has received little study. Some fragmentary approaches will be noted here.

The governments of both have units responsible for international transportation. In Canada the Transportation and Trade Services Division of the Department of Trade and Commerce has the following areas of responsibility:

[72]As reproduced in Victor L. Urquidi, *Free Trade and Economic Integration in Latin America*, Berkeley, University of California Press, 1962, p. 157.
[73]Eight South American countries and Mexico.
[74]Robert T. Brown, *Transport and the Economic Integration of South America*, Washington, The Brookings Institution, 1966, Table 3-1, p. 32.
[75]Almost 90 percent of intra-Latin American trade is carried by ocean shipping, a reflection of the rugged geography of the area. Miguel S. Wionczek, "Latin American Free Trade Association," *International Conciliation*, Jan. 1965, p. 35.
[76]See Brown, *Transport and Economic Integration*, pp. 212–28 for recommendations concerning South American transportation in light of the opportunities of LAFTA.
[77]*Ibid.*, p. 228.

1. Economic research into transportation matters affecting export promotion programs and Canadian export trade in general.
2. Consultative service to firms encountering export transportation problems.[78]

The purpose of the research activities is to help the Department develop policies that will "encourage the development of a transportation environment in which export trade can flourish."[79] The Transportation and Trade Services Division, however, concentrates its activities in ocean transportation and so has little impact on Canada–U.S. trade.

Within the U.S. Department of Transportation there is an Assistant Secretary for International Affairs. This official has responsibility for the international transportation relations of the United States. There is also transportation activity within the U.S. Department of Commerce of the same export-promotion type that exists in Canada. Neither department spends much time or effort on U.S.–Canada trade.

There is, indeed, little intergovernmental contact of any type between Canada and the United States where transportation topics are concerned. Relations between the Canadian Department of Transport and the U.S. Department of Transportation are not close, and liaison is informal and infrequent although increasing. Similarly the Interstate Commerce Commission (U.S.) and the Board of Transport Commissioners (Canada), which had, until September, 1967, together been subjecting much intra-North American transport to economic regulation for over sixty years, had no formal (or even informal) working arrangements.[80] It remains to be seen whether the advent of the Canadian Transport Commission will change this.

A proposal was made just before the time of the ill-fated Reciprocity Treaty of 1911 that an "International Commerce Commission" be set up to coordinate regulation of railway traffic between Canada and the United States.[81] Nothing came of the proposal, despite the fact that the chairman of the Interstate Commerce Commission and the chief commissioner of the Board of Railway Commissioners (latterly the Board of Transport Commissioners) reported that: "the existing laws of the United States and of Canada are inadequate for the effective control of international carriers, as

[78]H. A. Hadskis, "Thinking Export?" *Canadian Transportation*, May 1967, p. 16.
[79]*Ibid.*
[80]We will return in later chapters to the nature of the control that each regulatory body has exercised over international transportation.
[81]See William J. Wilgus, *The Railway Interrelations of the United States and Canada*, New Haven, Yale University Press, 1937, appendix C, pp. 247–55 for the text of a proposed treaty setting up the Commission, together with supporting documents.

respects through rates and the establishment of through routes and other matters which are proper subjects of joint regulation and that such regulation would be mutually advantageous to the interests of both countries."[82] The two officials continued, in a manner perhaps typical of the flavour of U.S. dominance often associated with the 1911 free trade proposals: "It is equally plain that the regulation to which international carriers should be subjected is substantially similar to that provided for interstate carriers of the United States. . . ."[83] The recommendation, as we have said, languished. This may not be unfortunate, for an examination of the Treaty generates the suspicion that the International Commerce Commission was conceived of as an administrative convenience rather than as an instrument for improvement of the economics of regulation.

Conclusions

Harmonization of transport policy within North America has moved little further. There have, however, been some advances. Cooperation between states and provinces has eased the burden of double highway taxation, the St. Lawrence Seaway is administered jointly by both countries, there has been continuing expansion in the bilateral agreement controlling airline operations, and the development of international pipeline transportation has been, on the whole, well coordinated. Both Canadian and U.S. government bodies have admitted the important effect that ocean transportation can have in stimulating or discouraging export trade.[84] What is needed now is action to resolve the problems and obstacles that are discussed in the remainder of this study.

The organization of the remaining chapters of the study is as follows. Chapter 2 outlines in some detail the transport patterns of trade flows between Canada and the United States, and chapter 3 discusses transport

[82]*Ibid.*, p. 248.
[83]*Ibid.*
[84]In Canada the Restrictive Trade Practices Commission has investigated the practices of shipping conferences and concluded that, although these practices contravene the Combines Investigation Act, the public interest in the maintenance of ocean freight service for exports outweighs this offence. See Restrictive Trade Practices Commission, *Shipping Conference Arrangements and Practices*, Ottawa, Queen's Printer, 1965, esp. pp. 91–102. Several Congressional hearings in the United States have also dealt with this question. Among them are U.S., Joint Economic Committee, *Discriminatory Ocean Freight Rates and the Balance of Payments*, 88th Congr., 1st and 2nd sess., 1963–64, and U.S., Senate, Committee on Commerce, *Great Lakes-St. Lawrence Seaway Transportation Study*, 88th Congr., 1st sess., 1964.

policy in the two countries in general terms. The next three chapters are devoted to intensive investigation of instances of non-harmonization in each of the major modes of transportation. Chapter 7 examines the impact of freer trade between Canada and the United States on the transportation industries of Canada, with special reference to the Automotive Free Trade Agreement of 1965. Chapter 8 evaluates the over-all impact of transport policies on Canada–U.S. trade and presents conclusions and recommendations.

2. Transportation Aspects of the Flow of Goods within North America

Introduction

Transportation is and has been an important ingredient of national output in both Canada and the United States. Estimates of the "transportation content" of gross national product are difficult to construct and vulnerable to criticism, but Table 4 may serve as a substitute. It shows, for a number of years for both Canada and the United States, gross national product in constant dollars, total freight ton-miles, and the number of ton-miles required for each dollar of GNP. According to Table 4, more transportation has been required per unit of output in Canada than in the United States. The degree to which the Canadian economy is more transport-intensive— i.e., the degree to which ton-miles per dollar of GNP is greater in Canada than in the United States—has varied from 25 percent in 1950 to 61 percent in 1964 and has averaged 45 percent over the years included in Table 4.

This information is presented here because of its value in explaining differences in the approaches of Canada and the United States to transportation policy. It sheds little direct light on the transportation aspects of trade between Canada and the United States, except to develop the supposition that the transport content of this trade would be some sort of an average of the transport content of national output in each of the two countries.

More useful for a study dealing with the impact of transportation policy on Canada-U.S. trade would be statistics providing a commodity breakdown of this trade in terms of use of the various modes of transportation. That the attempt in this chapter to provide such statistics is not wholly successful may be blamed on two basic difficulties in developing such statistics. One is the lack of development of a classification of commodity trade that is meaningful and complete from the points of view of both production and transportation. The existence, in Canadian government statistics, of different systems of commodity classification for imports, exports, rail transport, road transport, and water transport[1] adds to the obstacles inherent in such an exercise. Another difficulty arises from the gaps in government transportation

[1]It should be emphasized that there are means of converting between classifications. However, it might also be added that government statisticians have a predilection for

TABLE 4

TRANSPORTATION AND GROSS NATIONAL PRODUCT, UNITED STATES AND CANADA

	United States			Canada		
	Total freight ton-miles[a] (billions)	GNP ($ billion)	Ton-miles per $ of GNP	Total freight ton-miles[a] (billions)	GNP ($ billion)	Ton-miles per $ of GNP
1940	651	227.2	2.87	62	14.71	4.21
1945	1,072	355.4	3.02	88	20.97	4.20
1950	1,094	355.3	3.08	91	23.56	3.86
1955	1,298	438.0	2.96	123	29.55	4.16
1960	1,342	487.8	2.75	133	34.85	3.82
1961	1,343	497.3	2.70	143	35.75	4.00
1962	1,409	530.0	2.66	152	38.12	3.99
1963	1,477	550.0	2.69	166	39.89	4.16
1964	1,536	577.6	2.66	185	43.19	4.28
1965	1,668	609.0	2.74	192	46.16	4.16

Sources: U.S. ton-miles, 1940–63: Bureau of the Census, *Statistical Abstract of the United States*, 1965, Washington, U.S. Government Printing Office, 1965, Table no. 779, p. 559. U.S. ton-miles, 1964: ICC, *Annual Report*, 1966, Washington, U.S. Government Printing Office, 1966, p. 53. U.S. ton-miles, 1965: *Transport Economics*, July 1967, p. 4. U.S. GNP: *Economic Report of the President*, 1966, Washington, U.S. Government Printing Office, 1966, Table C-2, p. 210.
Canada ton-miles: DBS, *Daily Bulletin*, February 13, 1967, p. 4. Canada GNP, 1940–63: calculated from DBS, *Canada Year Book*, 1966, p. 1018. Canada GNP, 1964: calculated from *Canadian Statistical Review*, May 1966, Table 9, p. 4. Canada GNP, 1965: calculated from DBS, *Canadian Statistical Review*, April 1967, Table 9, p. 4.
[a]Includes ton-miles performed by rail, road, water, air, and oil pipeline. Excludes gas pipeline ton-miles.

statistics. In this study we have generally made use of Canadian govern- ment statistics because they are more complete and more suitable than U.S. statistics. However, there is still a lack of information on the value of Canadian imports from the United States transported by each of the various modes. In addition, there are no reliable statistics on the physical volume of exports and imports via highway transportation. Finally, while it is not important for this chapter, we might add that *no* published statistics reveal, by commodity, the freight charges paid in the course of trade between Canada and the United States.

Canadian exports to the United States by mode of transport

Tables 5–30 show the value of Canadian exports to the United States accord- ing to the mode of transport by which they crossed the border. This is pre- sumed to be the mode which predominated in their movement from Canadian

frequent amendment of commodity classifications and that U.S. and Canadian trade and transportation statistics do not use the same systems of classification.

seller to U.S. buyer. The value of exports in each commodity group is shown for five years—1960, 1962, 1964, 1965, and 1966—in order to reveal recent trends in export trade with the United States. The modal breakdown of this trade is available only for 1964 and 1965. It should be noted that export values for 1960 are based on a different commodity classification than that used for later years and that perfect adaptation was not possible for all commodity groups.

TABLES 5–30
VALUE OF VARIOUS CANADIAN EXPORTS TO THE UNITED STATES
AND MODE OF TRANSPORTATION

	Value† ($000)	Percentage by water	Percentage by highway	Percentage by rail	Percentage by air	Percentage by pipeline
5. MEAT (includes export commodity classes 11, 13, 15)						
1960	28,527					
1962	29,784					
1964	34,498	*	92	7	*	—
1965	55,860	*	94	5	*	
1966	77,321					
6. FISH (includes classes 31, 33, 35, 37, 39, 41–43, 46, excl. 4680)						
1960	93,541					
1962	105,251					
1964	119,010	34	56	10	*	—
1965	138,971	36	54	10	*	—
1966	138,545					
7. DISTILLED ALCOHOLIC BEVERAGES (includes class 173)						
1960	73,998					
1962	80,760					
1964	97,033	*	65	35	*	—
1965	110,744	*	62	37	*	—
1966	123,079					
8. IRON ORE AND SCRAP (includes class 251)						
1960	107,578					
1962	184,847					
1964	302,265	96	*	4	*	—
1965	291,673	92	*	7	—	—
1966	308,650					
9. NICKEL ORE AND SCRAP (includes class 255)						
1960	7,944					
1962	10,452					
1964	34,524	*	66	34	—	—
1965	39,582	—	66	34	—	—
1966	28,653					
10. ORE AND SCRAP OF LEAD, ZINC, AND PRECIOUS METALS (includes classes 254, 256, 257)						
1960	26,564					
1962	30,251					
1964	34,063	11	5	84	*	—
1965	52,301	11	11	78	*	—
1966	62,951					
11. RADIOACTIVE ORES AND CONCENTRATES (includes class 259)						
1960	237,008					
1962	152,424					
1964	37,263	*	4	96	—	—
1965	19,348	1	11	88	*	—
1966	19,037					

TABLES 5–30 continued

	Value† ($000)	Percentage by water	Percentage by highway	Percentage by rail	Percentage by air	Percentage by pipeline
12. PETROLEUM AND NATURAL GAS (includes class 264)						
1960	112,501					
1962	305,640					
1964	360,402	—	*	*	—	100
1965	384,498	—	*	*	—	100
1966	430,630					
13. ASBESTOS (includes class 271)						
1960	53,903					
1962	57,449					
1964	62,996	4	4	92	—	—
1965	65,195	6	5	89	*	—
1966	64,974					
14. LUMBER, OTHER SAWMILL PRODUCTS, AND PLYWOOD (includes classes 331, 333–35)						
1960	304,126					
1962	360,364					
1964	407,805	18	7	75	*	—
1965	412,957	19	9	73	*	—
1966	367,658					
15. WOODPULP (includes class 340)						
1960	256,170					
1962	298,167					
1964	346,017	11	1	81	*	7
1965	371,428	12	1	80	*	7
1966	390,760					
16. PAPER FOR PRINTING (includes class 351)						
1960	639,251					
1962	639,753					
1964	698,291	40	5	55	*	—
1965	748,432	39	5	56	—	—
1966	842,486					
17. CHEMICALS (includes classes 400–402, 404–5, 408, 414)						
1960	6,315 (incomplete)					
1962	45,655					
1964	43,417	7	35	57	1	—
1965	53,577	10	32	57	1	—
1966	58,314					
18. FERTILIZERS (includes class 416)						
1960	46,941					
1962	57,284					
1964	67,757	3	9	87	—	—
1965	95,598	5	9	87	*	—
1966	114,064					
19. PRIMARY AND MANUFACTURED IRON AND STEEL (includes 442–9)						
1960	60,668					
1962	78,142					
1964	134,544	20	33	48	*	—
1965	153,689	22	34	44	*	—
1966	171,052					
20. ALUMINUM AND ALLOYS (includes 451)						
1960	52,545					
1962	102,014					
1964	118,898	*	6	94	*	—
1965	162,124	*	7	93	*	—
1966	183,809					
21. COPPER AND ALLOYS (includes 452)						
1960	74,159					
1962	56,086					
1964	69,564	—	14	86	*	—
1965	69,497	*	20	80	*	—
1966	116,923					

TABLES 5–30 *concluded*

	Value† ($000)	Percentage by water	Percentage by highway	Percentage by rail	Percentage by air	Percentage by pipeline
22. LEAD, ZINC, AND PRECIOUS METALS, INCLUDING ALLOYS (includes 453, 455, 457)						
1960	35,227					
1962	39,604					
1964	43,294	*	21	79	*	—
1965	53,822	*	28	69	4	—
1966	60,682					
23. NICKEL AND ALLOYS (includes 454)						
1960	80,653					
1962	163,403					
1964	140,868	*	56	44	*	—
1965	167,186	*	52	48	*	—
1966	163,732					
24. AGRICULTURAL MACHINERY—NOT INCL. TRACTORS (includes 541–3, 545, 549)						
1960	76,032					
1962	76,544					
1964	120,348	*	23	77	*	—
1965	134,028	*	21	79	*	—
1966	155,947					
25. MOTOR VEHICLES AND TRAILERS (includes 58019 and 58049. Modal shares include motor vehicle parts, see Table 26)						
1960	463					
1962	2,444					
1964	21,481	1	92	7	*	—
1965	81,085	*	92	8	*	—
1966	466,093					
26. MOTOR VEHICLE PARTS (includes 58050 and 58099. For modal shares see Table 25.)						
1960	15,117					
1962	12,528					
1964	75,306					
1965	150,166					
1966	374,832					
27. AIRCRAFT AND PARTS (includes 600)						
1960	32,311					
1962	106,992					
1964	186,475	*	26	4	70	—
1965	163,950	*	33	6	60	—
1966	167,013					
28. COMMUNICATIONS AND LABORATORY EQUIPMENT (includes 630, 700)						
1960	20,502 (incomplete)					
1962	55,551					
1964	67,033	*	60	11	29	—
1965	89,805	*	58	8	33	—
1966	142,530					
29. TOTAL—24 COMMODITY GROUPS						
1960	2,441,044					
1962	3,051,389					
1964	3,623,152	21	17	47	4	11
1965	4,065,516	19	21	46	3	10
1966	5,029,735					
30. TOTAL—ALL EXPORTS						
1960	2,932,171					
1962	3,608,439					
1964	4,271,059	20	23	44	4	10
1965	4,840,456	18	27	43	3	9
1966	6,027,722					

Sources: 1960 and 1962 export values: DBS, *Trade of Canada*, II, *Exports*, 1961–1962 (1966); 1964 export values and transport information: DBS, *Exports by Mode of Transport*, 1964 (1966); 1965 export values and transport information: DBS, *Exports by Modes of Transport*, 1965 (1967); 1966 export values: DBS, *Trade of Canada*, *Exports by Countries*, January-December 1966 (1967).
*Less than 1 percent.
†f.o.b. point of consignment for export.

The 24 commodity groups include 83–85 percent of Canadian exports to the United States in each of the years included in the above tables. Their selection and composition were based on a subjective evaluation of the significance of various groups in terms of transportation characteristics and production cohesiveness. Taken as a whole, the 24 groups generally reflect the same transportation pattern that exists for all commodity trade from Canada to the United States. As a comparison of Tables 29 and 30 shows, they under-represent the importance of highway transport and over-represent the importance of rail transport. This must be kept in mind in the analysis of these statistics.

Railroads carried 44 percent of Canada's exports to the United States in 1964 and 43 percent in 1965. The railroads dominate in 13 of the 24 commodity groups, including such major exports as paper for printing, woodpulp, lumber, aluminum, agricultural machinery, and fertilizers. The one percentage point decline from 1964 to 1965 in their share of the value of Canada's exports to the United States is probably, in itself, not significant.

Of Canada's U.S.-bound exports, 27 percent were carried by truck in 1965, an increase from 23 percent in 1964. Highway transport is predominant in 6 of the 24 commodity groups. Among these are nickel and alloys, communications and laboratory equipment, and, of great and growing significance, motor vehicles and parts. Fully 92 percent of shipments of vehicles and parts from Canada to the United States moved by truck in both 1964 and 1965. The 1964–65 increase in trucking's share of Canada-U.S. trade may be attributed to its strong position in this commodity group and in other groups which also expanded rapidly between those two years, notably meat and communications and laboratory equipment.

Water transportation accounted for 18 percent of Canadian exports to the United States in 1965, a drop of 2 percent from 1964. Iron ore and scrap exports were almost entirely carried by vessel, and a substantial share of paper for printing was also transported in this way. Apart from these commodity groups, lesser values of fish, lumber, and iron and steel comprised the major Canada-U.S. traffic of water carriers. The 2 percent decline from 1964 to 1965 may be attributed to the reduced share of water carriers in the transportation of iron ore and scrap during a time when total exports in this commodity group declined slightly.

Virtually 100 percent of Canada's exports of crude petroleum moved via pipeline. The pipelines' share of Canada-U.S. trade declined slightly between 1964 and 1965 (from 11 percent to 10 percent).

Only 3 percent of Canada's exports to the United States moved via air transport in 1965, a slight drop from 1964. Over three-quarters of the value of these exports in 1964 was accounted for by the commodity group "aircraft

and parts." A substantial portion of exports of communications and laboratory equipment also moved by air.

The six-year changes in Canadian exports to the United States reveal
trends that are significant for the relative roles of the various forms of transport. Over this period ten of the commodity groups have increased in value by
more than $100 million. The increases by group are as follows:

	($ million)
Motor vehicles and trailers	466
Motor vehicle parts	360
Petroleum and natural gas	318
Paper for printing	203
Iron ore and scrap	201
Aircraft and parts	135
Woodpulp	135
Aluminum and alloys	131
Primary and manufactured iron and steel	110
Communications and laboratory equipment	108

Motor vehicles and parts together have contributed 32 percent of the 1960–66
$2.59-billion increase in exports within the 24 commodity groups. In 8 of the
above 10 groups exports have expanded more rapidly over the 1960–66
period than in the 24 groups as a whole. The exceptions are paper for printing and woodpulp; in both groups export growth has lagged far behind the
24-group average.

The absolute and relative growth patterns have significance for the importance of the different transport media in Canadian exports to the United
States. Of the 8 fast-growth groups, highway transport dominates in 3, rail
transport in 2, and each of the other modes in 1. Moreover, significant shares
of two other of these commodity groups (iron and steel and aircraft and
parts) are also exported via highway transport.

Rough estimates may be made of the impact of these trends on the shares
of the various modes, despite the unavailability of pre-1964 and 1966 statistics.[2] Using the 1964 modal shares by commodity group and applying them
to the 1960 export values, it is estimated that for-hire and private motor
carriers accounted for 15 percent of the 1960 exports in the 24 groups. For
all exports to the United States the highway transport share is estimated to be
about 21 percent of total value in 1960. Applying 1965 shares by commodity

---

[2]Statistics are available for the last nine months of 1963, but the seasonal bias inherent
in partial-year data makes them unusable for this purpose. 1966 statistics of this type
are as yet unpublished.

group to 1966 export values shows a dramatic increase in the importance of highway transport in Canadian exports to the United States. Of exports in the 24 groups, 30 percent are estimated to have moved via highway transport, and 36 percent of *all* Canadian exports to the United States in 1966 were transported by highway. According to these approximations,[3] as far as exports are concerned, highway transport has doubled in importance since 1960.

Canadian imports from the United States by mode of transport

Tables 31 to 65 show the value of Canadian imports from the United States according to the predominant mode of transport. In several ways and for several reasons these tables are not as complete nor as accurate as those presented for exports. First, accurate and complete values of imports in each group are available for 1964 and 1965 only. In its 1966 import statistics the Dominion Bureau of Statistics made major errors involving the commodity detail of imports from the United States.[4]

TABLES 31–65

VALUE OF VARIOUS CANADIAN IMPORTS FROM THE UNITED STATES
AND MODE OF TRANSPORTATION

	Value† ($000)	Percentage by water	Percentage by highway	Percentage by rail	Percentage by air
31. MEAT (includes import commodity classes 1109–1599)					
1960	21,038				
1962	14,488				
1964	27,450	15	48	37	1
1965	20,461				
1966	26,472				
32. CORN AND OTHER UNMILLED CEREALS (includes import commodity classes 6129–6199)					
1960	20,556				
1962	50,867				
1964	36,928	68	11	22	*
1965	36,352				
1966	41,094				
33. FRESH AND FROZEN FRUIT AND VEGETABLES (includes 7103–7299, 9105–9299)					
1960	108,853				
1962	120,184				
1964	128,913	1	25	74	*
1965	140,505				
1966	148,997				

[3]Actually, the application of 1964 modal shares to 1960 exports probably overstates the 1960 share of highway transport. This would more or less offset the probable overstatement of the 1966 highway transport share resulting from the use of 1965 modal shares. The conclusion of an approximate doubling of trucking's share in the value of Canadian exports to the U.S. seems viable.

[4]For a report of the causes of this, see Clive Baxter, "Classic Boob in Trade Statistics," *Financial Post*, June 24, 1967, p. 1.

TABLES 31–65 *continued*

	Value† ($000)	Percentage by water	Percentage by highway	Percentage by rail	Percentage by air
34. SOYBEANS AND OTHER SEEDS (includes 21230–21299)					
1960	34,530				
1962	39,373				
1964	58,707	79	15	6	*
1965	56,899				
1966	62,917				
35. COTTON (includes 24410–24499)					
1960	46,106				
1962	53,098				
1964	62,043	*	*	100	*
1965	53,363				
1966	31,958				
36. IRON ORE AND SCRAP (includes 25120–25199)					
1960	65,188				
1962	67,282				
1964	90,807	70	11	19	—
1965	94,190				
1966	73,273				
37. COAL AND COKE (includes 26105–26189, 43530, 43549)					
1960	87,222				
1962	83,871				
1964	98,554	81	7	12	—
1965	144,214				
1966	162,038				
38. LUMBER, OTHER SAWMILL PRODUCTS, AND PLYWOOD (includes 33104–33599)					
1960	37,400 (est.)				
1962	35,400 (est.)				
1964	40,312	1	23	76	*
1965	41,494				
1966	42,773				
39. COTTON FABRICS (includes 37302–37398)					
1960	53,305				
1962	45,843				
1964	43,170	*	71	29	1
1965	36,032				
1966	44,105				
40. CHEMICALS (includes 40003–41399)					
1960	‡				
1962	100,100 (est.)				
1964	118,901	11	17	71	1
1965	138,572				
1966	130,072				
41. PETROLEUM PRODUCTS (includes 43109–43999, excl. 43530, 43549 and 43941)					
1960	54,954				
1962	52,340				
1964	42,761	49	30	21	*
1965	45,384				
1966	45,063				
42. PLASTICS (includes 42302–42599)					
1960	88,363				
1962	84,200				
1964	92,725	*	83	16	1
1965	102,490				
1966	118,674				
43. PRIMARY AND MANUFACTURED IRON AND STEEL (includes 44219–44989)					
1960	133,324				
1962	104,211				
1964	176,695	2	36	62	1
1965	181,291				
1966	184,715				
44. ALUMINUM AND ALLOYS (includes 45105–45149)					
1960	8,950				
1962	14,700				
1964	34,504	*	82	17	1
1965	42,782				
1966	62,485				

TABLES 31–65 *continued*

	Value† ($000)	Percentage by water	Percentage by highway	Percentage by rail	Percentage by air
45. GLASS AND PRODUCTS (includes 47303–47399, 85063, 85064, 86730, 95032, 95036, 96179)					
1960	33,361				
1962	39,800 (est.)				
1964	43,207	*	28	71	1
1965	46,024				
1966	51,588				
46. GENERAL-PURPOSE ENGINES AND PARTS (includes 50209-50299)					
1960	25,473				
1962	27,430				
1964	34,776	*			5
1965	46,539				
1966	49,855				
47. ELECTRIC GENERATORS AND MOTORS (includes 50309–50379)					
1960	13,500 (est.)				
1962	16,300 (est.)				
1964	23,014	*			9
1965	26,905				
1966	32,294				
48. OTHER GENERAL-PURPOSE INDUSTRIAL MACHINERY (includes 50405–51099)					
1960	—				
1962	—				
1964	195,535	*			3
1965	236,442				
1966	268,894				
49. MINING, EARTHMOVING, AND CONSTRUCTION MACHINERY (includes 52101–52299)					
1960	—				
1962	—				
1964	200,907	1			3
1965	194,719				
1966	245,000				
50. METALWORKING MACHINERY (includes 52303–52396)					
1960	—				
1962	—				
1964	107,141	1			1
1965	127,835				
1966	149,585				
51. TEXTILE-INDUSTRY MACHINERY (includes 52706–52799)					
1960	16,541				
1962	29,449				
1964	47,723	*			2
1965	38,515				
1966	42,942				
52. SPECIAL MACHINERY FOR OTHER INDUSTRIES (includes 52515–52669, 52802–52999)					
1960	—				
1962	—				
1964	108,234	*			6
1965	108,417				
1966	128,172				
53. AGRICULTURAL MACHINERY (includes 54109–54699)					
1960	87,144				
1962	98,346				
1964	140,479	*			*
1965	148,417				
1966	176,284				
54. TRACTORS AND PARTS (includes 55103–55199)					
1960	108,503				
1962	112,749				
1964	149,628	*			*
1965	180,597				
1966	202,527				
55. MOTOR VEHICLES AND TRAILERS (includes 58104–58799)					
1960	96,899				
1962	82,558				
1964	75,416	*	81	19	*
1965	181,458				
1966	421,153				

TABLES 31–65 *concluded*

	Value† ($000)	Percentage by water	Percentage by highway	Percentage by rail	Percentage by air
56. MOTOR VEHICLE PARTS (includes 50401, 58804–58999, 68166)					
1960	—				
1962	—				
1964	631,400	*			2
1965	813,559				
1966	1,046,663				
57. AIRCRAFT AND PARTS (includes 60151–60599)					
1960	134,974				
1962	195,801				
1964	118,437	*	85	*	15
1965	174,091				
1966	196,983				
58. COMMUNICATION EQUIPMENT (includes 63372–63999)					
1960	72,722				
1962	110,042				
1964	102,919	*			19
1965	125,222				
1966	196,072				
59. ELECTRICAL CONTROL EQUIPMENT (includes 68326–68879)					
1960	—				
1962	—				
1964	50,645	*			18
1965	56,710				
1966	43,456				
60. MEDICAL, OPTICAL, AND SCIENTIFIC INSTRUMENTS (includes 70613–70999)					
1960	—				
1962	—				
1964	99,705	*			19
1965	120,467				
1966	148,042				
61. BUSINESS AND OFFICE MACHINES AND PARTS (includes 77104–77199)					
1960	41,266				
1962	64,522				
1964	76,456	*	87	5	9
1965	86,753				
1966	131,266				
62. MAGAZINES AND BOOKS (includes 89104–89349)					
1960	62,768				
1962	67,100 (est.)				
1964	87,716	1			1
1965	101,518				
1966	110,202				
63. PHOTOGRAPHIC EQUIPMENT AND SUPPLIES (includes 91111–91999)					
1960	35,719				
1962	40,797				
1964	52,173	*			6
1965	68,768				
1966	79,269				
64. TOTAL—33 COMMODITY GROUPS					
1960	—				
1962	—				
1964	3,397,981	8	51	37	3
1965	4,016,985				
1966	4,894,883				
65. TOTAL—ALL IMPORTS					
1960	3,686,625				
1962	4,299,769				
1964	5,164,285	7	51	38	4
1965	6,044,831				
1966	7,135,860				

Sources: import values for 1960: DBS, *Trade of Canada*, III, *Imports*, 1959–1960 (1966) using conversion tables in DBS, *Trade of Canada*, III, *Imports*, 1962–64 (1968); for 1962: DBS, *Trade of Canada*, III, *Imports*, 1962–1964 (1968); for 1964: DBS, *Trade of Canada*, *Imports by Countries*, January–December 1965 (1966); for 1965 and 1966: DBS, *Trade of Canada*, *Imports by Countries*, January–December 1966 (1967); transport information developed using DBS sources and U.S. Bureau of the Census, *U.S. Exports: Commodity, Country, and Method of Transportation*, monthly issues, January–December 1966, Washington, U.S. Government Printing Office, 1966 and 1967.

*Less than 1 percent.   †Generally f.o.b. point of shipment in the U.S.

It is in the modal shares, however, that these import statistics are most deficient. This is regrettable—the development of this information is the purpose of these series of tables—but unavoidable.[5] The 1964 estimates of the share of each mode of transport in Canada's imports from the United States are therefore constructed from a variety of sources. These include statistics of U.S. exports to Canada by water, air, and other modes of transportation; Canadian railroad freight traffic statistics; Canadian import statistics; Canadian shipping statistics; and a certain amount of subjective evaluation.[6] Where these have failed, no modal share information is presented. However, a discussion of the probable importance of the various modes for the omitted commodity groups follows the tables.

One last word concerning the effect of these procedures is necessary. The share of water and air transportation is based, essentially, on 1966 U.S. data (all that was available for any year), as is the over-all land transportation share. The split of land transportation between rail and highway depends on 1964 Canadian transportation statistics by commodity group. All in all, the procedure is somewhat uncertain and the transport-share statistics that follow should be treated with caution.

Canada's imports from the United States are more diversified than her exports to that country. Thus the 33 import commodity groups include only about two-thirds of Canada's imports from the United States in each of the years used in the above tables. The coverage is less complete than was used for exports but is believed to be adequate.

The transportation shares obtained from U.S. statistics are used to develop the following breakdown for U.S.-Canada trade in 1966:

	%
Land transport	89.1
Water transport	7.4
Air transport	3.5
	100.0

This compares with the following Canadian statistics for Canada–U.S. trade in 1965:

	%
Land transport	79.3
Water transport	17.6
Air transport	3.1
	100.0

[5]The DBS is planning publication of an import companion to its *Exports by Mode of Transport*, but it is not yet available.
[6]The procedure and assumptions used for most of the 18 import groups for which

The differences between the two transportation patterns arise from the greater use of water transport in the export of such Canadian commodities as iron ore and newsprint. It is not possible to provide an over-all breakdown of the land transport share of Canadian imports from the United States between rail and highway transport. However, the combination of educated guesses with the estimates presented in some of the preceding tables will be helpful. For 18 of the 33 groups estimates of the shares of all modes of transport are given. These accounted for about 40 percent of the imports in the 33 commodity groups in both 1964 and 1966, and about 25 percent, in both years, of *all* Canadian imports from the United States. Applying the respective transportation shares to imports in each of these 18 groups in 1964 and 1966, we develop the following results:

	1964	1966
	%	%
Water transport	20	16
Highway transport	38	51
Rail transport	40	31
Air transport	2	2
	100	100

---

modal share estimates were developed is as follows: U.S. trade statistics provided modal share information on a land-water-air basis for 1966. The U.S. commodity classification was adapted to our import groups, and land-water-air shares developed on this basis. It was assumed that these shares remained constant between 1964 and 1966, an assumption that may be shaky for those import groups where water and air transport are significant. The problem then became one of splitting the share of land transportation into its component rail and highway shares. This was done using 1964 railroad traffic statistics and the ICC's value per ton by freight commodity class (FCC) data. For example, as regards Table 31 (meat), 6,740, 1,942, and 3,149 tons of meat arrived in Canada from the United States by rail in the 3 corresponding FCC groups. The values per ton in these groups were $872, $620, and $1,068, respectively. Therefore, rail-borne meat imports in 1964 were valued at $10,444,000. The value of all meat imports by land transport was 84.6 percent (from 1966 U.S. statistics) times $27,450,000 (1964 import value from Canadian trade statistics), which equals $23,795,000. The rail share was therefore 44 percent of land imports and 37 percent of all meat imports, while the highway share was 56 percent and 48 percent, respectively.

This procedure assumes parity between the U.S. and Canadian dollar. Since the U.S. dollar was at a premium in 1964, the share of imports assigned to railroad transport is understated. In the case of meat, for example, rail-borne imports totaled $11,280,000 in Canadian funds. Truck-carried imports, treated here as a residual, have been overstated. However, this error acts to compensate another that is inherent in the estimating procedure. This second error originates in the assumption that, within each freight commodity class, traffic carried by rail and truck has equal unit value. In fact it probably does not—truck-carried unit values should be higher, and our treating them as equal understates the value of truck-carried imports. So these two errors are offsetting, at least in direction.

Within this limited selection of imports the growth of highway transport is striking. It must be re-emphasized that these are crude estimates developed from a variety of sources of varying accuracy. Nevertheless, the pattern, within these 18 commodity groups, seems clear.

Highway transport is the most important mode of transportation for 7 of these 18 groups, rail transport for 6, and water transport for 5. Four of the groups that are dominated by highway transport—plastics, motor vehicles and trailers, aircraft and parts, and business and office machinery—are important components of Canada's total imports from the United States, each accounting for over $100 million in 1966. Of the railroad-dominated import groups, 3 (fruits and vegetables, primary and manufactured iron and steel, and chemicals) amounted to over $100 million in 1966. Only 1 import group (coal and coke) that moved predominantly by water was in this class in 1966. Rapid growth has been experienced in all 4 of the major import groups that are mainly imported by truck, while for the other modes the combination of rapid growth and large volume only occurs with water transport's imports of coal and coke.

Air transport was not the dominant mode for any commodity group. It did, however, carry more than 15 percent of the following commodity groups: aircraft and parts; communication equipment; electrical control equipment; and medical, optical, and scientific instruments. Although air transport is less important in U.S.-Canada trade than in Canada-U.S. trade, a much wider variety of products are transported via this mode northbound. Three-quarters (by value) of Canada-U.S. air cargo traffic is accounted for by aircraft and parts, while in the opposite direction this proportion is only .06.

The preceding discussion of the rail-truck split in land transportation omits the bulk of Canadian imports from the United States. There is another 39 percent of the total value of this trade included in the 15 omitted commodity groups (Tables 46–54, 56, 58–60, 62, 63) and a further 34 percent for which commodity groups have not been developed. About this last group we can do little, except to point out that much of it consists of a wide array of consumer goods. Most of these imports arrive by land, and we would expect more to arrive by motor carrier than by railroad. Unfortunately, we are unable to be more explicit, and the 55–45 split of land transport between highway and rail that we will use later is only a rough estimate.

We can, however, venture further in the case of the 15 important commodity groups for which transport shares were not estimated. For the industrial machinery groups in Tables 46 to 52, inclusive, probably 80 percent of the land transport is provided by motor carriers and only 20 percent by railroads. For medical, optical, and scientific instruments, for magazines and books, and for photographic equipment and supplies the truck-rail proportion is probably on the order of 90-10. Tractors and parts and agricultural machinery are estimated, together, to be imported 55 percent by highway transport and 45 percent by rail transport. In the import of motor vehicle parts, railroads predominate; about 65 percent of the land arrivals of these imports are by rail and 35 percent by truck. The imports by land transport of the communications equipment and electrical control equipment are difficult to allocate between the two modes, but the best estimate would assign 80 percent of the value of these imports to truck transport and 20 percent to rail transport.

Combining these rough estimates and applying them to 1964 and 1966 imports in these 15 commodity groups, we can suggest that, in both years, about 60 percent of the value of these imports arrived by truck, 35 percent by rail, and 5 percent by air. We may consolidate these figures with the more accurate modal shares presented in the tables earlier in this section (for 1964, 38 percent highway, 40 percent rail, 20 percent water, and 2 percent air) and with previous speculation concerning the transportation preferences of the remainder of Canada's imports from the United States. Having done this, we conclude that, in terms of value, 51 percent of Canada's imports from the United States were transported by truck in 1964. Railway transport accounted, therefore, for about 38 percent of the 1964 value of Canada's imports from the United States. This accounts for the modal share figures given in Table 65. Applying 1964 modal shares to the 1966 commodity structure of Canada's imports from the United States, we estimate that highway transport accounted for 55 percent of imports in the 33 commodity groups and 54 percent of total imports in 1966.

Transport preferences of exports and imports compared

This section deals briefly with transport patterns within commodity groups that are common to both export and import trade. There are 10 of these groups,[7] and although we would hardly expect transport preferences to be identical for imports and exports, an examination of preferences may indicate the impact of transport policy differences on certain portions of North American trade. Public and industry policy, along with location of buyer and seller and commodity variations within these commodity groups, would

[7]Meat; iron ore and scrap; lumber, plywood, and other sawmill products; chemicals; primary and manufactured iron and steel; aluminum and alloys; agricultural machinery; motor vehicles and trailers; motor vehicle parts; and aircraft and parts.

be expected to have some effect on the mode of transport selected for the majority of trade transactions within a particular commodity group.

Five anomalies present themselves upon examination of exports and imports in these 10 groups.

1. The greater importance of water transport in exports of primary and manufactured iron and steel and of lumber, plywood, and other sawmill products. This may be explained by the location of Canadian producers on the Great Lakes (iron and steel) and on the Pacific coast (lumber).
2. The dominance of railroads in transporting aluminum and alloys for export to the United States. Once again, locational differences may be used to explain this. U.S. producers are located close to their Canadian customers and ship by truck; Canadian producers are located at a distance from their U.S. customers and ship by rail at very low freight rates.
3. Railroads predominate in the export of agricultural machinery to the United States, whereas imports in this commodity group are mainly carried by truck. The commodity composition of trade within this group is very similar in both directions, and we must turn to location or transport policy to explain the anomaly in transport preference. Location provides a partial answer—but an incorrect one. Exports of agricultural machinery mainly move between Ontario and the U.S. Midwest, while imports move between the U.S. Midwest and the Prairie provinces and, to a lesser extent, Ontario. Given a longer length of haul on imports, we would expect, other things being equal, to find rail transport used more. The reverse is true, and the reason must lie in some regulatory or rate influence.
4. Motor vehicles and parts are mainly exported by truck. The railroads are the main mode of import for parts, with trucks predominating in the import of motor vehicles. The anomaly exists, then, only for motor vehicle parts. Location has little impact here, since origins and destinations of both exports and imports are similar. The traditional traffic flow in the automotive industry has been that parts travel north, and the railroads have always carried most of this. Their failure to participate as fully in the southbound flow of parts and, concomitantly, the failure of trucks to dominate northbound traffic have their origin in several government and industry policies and practices.
5. Exports of aircraft and parts are mainly moved via air transport, while for imports highway transport is more important. The reason for this appears to lie in a commodity variation within this group. A large proportion of exports of aircraft and parts consists of whole aircraft that are presumably moved to the United States under their own power. Canadian imports of aircraft and parts include a relatively larger quantity of assem-

blies, engines, and parts—products which make greater use of highway transport.

Volume patterns in Canada-U.S. transportation: rail

The emphasis in our analysis to this point has been on the *value* of commodities moved as exports and imports via the various modes of transport. This view has been appropriate because value determines the importance of different commodities in trade. It directs our attention to transport factors that are important in this context. Thus we have not gathered statistics on the 1.4 million tons of crushed stone that Canada imported from the United States in 1966, but we *have* considered imports of business and office machines and parts, which probably amounted to, in 1966, no more than 11,000 tons. The gravel, however, was worth only $3.6 million, whereas the business machines were valued at $131.3 million.

The effect of this approach has been, of course, to stress the importance of a mode of transport, trucking, that carries, in physical terms, far less of Canada's trade with the United States than either railroads or water carriers. The emphasis has been deliberate; trade difficulties involving transportation are significant only if the trade involved is significant. But analysis of these difficulties requires a shift in emphasis.

Table 66 shows the volume of rail traffic from the United States to Canada. Seven commodity groups were selected; for all of these, total arrivals by rail in 1964 were valued at more than $60 million. In volume terms rail imports in these groups amounted to almost 1.8 million tons in 1964. This was 18.7 percent of total railway traffic (in tons) northbound between the United States and Canada.[8]

Over the eight-year period represented in Table 66, the volume of rail traffic from the United States to Canada in the 7 commodity categories rose by 28 percent. From 1962 through to 1966 the increase was 53 percent, and between 1964 and 1966 traffic rose by 11 percent. Different commodity categories fared quite differently over the eight years, however. Motor vehicle parts, fruit and vegetables, and agricultural machinery have trended upward, whereas iron and steel has declined and the other

[8]The largest volumes of this traffic are accounted for by lumber and bulk commodities. 1964 U.S.-to-Canada volumes in the most important of these groups were as follows: phosphate rock 1,123 (thousand tons), scrap iron and steel 522, bituminous coal 498, industrial sand 413, coke 411, anthracite coal 364, lumber and plywood 311, clay and bentonite 304, fertilizers 240. These together accounted for another 44.6 percent of railway freight moving from the United States to Canada. DBS, *Railway Freight Traffic*, 1964 (1965).

TABLE 66

VOLUME OF SELECTED COMMODITIES IN U.S.-CANADA RAILROAD TRAFFIC
(thousand tons)

	1958	1960	1962	1964	1965	1966
Fresh and frozen fruit and vegetables[a]	497	555	486	526	543	644
Cotton[b]	87	96	105	124	110	90
Chemicals[c]	178	153	129	144	202	174
Primary and manufactured iron and steel[d]	397	303	131	413	301	203
Agricultural machinery[e]	55	68	64	83	89	103
Industrial machinery[f]	111	95	80	123	115	124
Motor vehicle parts[g]	209	227	287	343	497	628
Total	1,534	1,497	1,282	1,756	1,857	1,966

Sources: DBS, *Railway Freight Traffic*, various years and 1966 quarters.
[a]Includes Freight Commodity Classification (FCC) nos. 57, 61, 79, 81, 85, 87, and 89; excludes some of the commodities included in Table 33.
[b]Includes FCC nos. 33 and 35; all commodities in Table 35 are included.
[c]Includes FCC no. 527; excludes some of the commodities included in Table 40.
[d]Includes FCC nos. 577 and 583; excludes some of the commodities included in Table 43.
[e]Includes FCC nos. 591 and 593; all commodities in Table 53 are included.
[f]Includes FCC nos. 595 and 597; includes all the commodities included in Tables 46 through 52 and some of the commodities included in Table 60 and 63.
[g]Includes FCC no. 623; includes most of the commodities included in Table 56.

three categories have had mixed experiences. In the case of these latter four, the railways' traffic has moved in an opposite direction to the general trend of imports as shown in Tables 31–65.

Little, however, can be made of this conclusion. U.S.-to-Canada rail traffic does not consist only of Canadian imports from the United States; some imports from other countries are also included. Also, an increase in the *value* of imports is not necessarily accompanied by an increase in the *volume* of imports. Changes in the actual commodities involved in trade within the commodity groups and in the locational orientation of trade flows may also introduce contradictory influences. Finally, the commodity classifications used in Tables 31–65 and Table 66 are not strictly comparable, as is obvious from the notes to Table 66.

The volume of rail traffic in the other direction, from Canada to the United States, is shown in Table 67. The eight commodity groups were selected according to their importance in rail-carried exports to the United States. In all eight, 1964 rail-borne exports were valued at more than $59 million. The most important group was newsprint; 1964 rail exports of this commodity were valued at $384 million. The eight groups included

TABLE 67
VOLUME OF SELECTED COMMODITIES IN CANADA-U.S. RAILROAD TRAFFIC
(thousand tons)

	1958	1960	1962	1964	1965	1966
Lumber and plywood[a]	2,612	3,004	3,640	3,785	3,652	3,452
Fertilizers[b]	778	869	1,034	1,553	2,132	2,680
Aluminum and alloys[c]	143	72	188	260	349	385
Nickel and alloys[d]	45	34	61	47	61	55
Primary and manufactured iron and steel[e]	79	118	181	430	283	304
Agricultural machinery[f]	102	83	77	110	119	145
Woodpulp[g]	1,708	1,876	2,372	2,526	2,638	2,793
Newsprint[h]	3,113	3,181	3,096	3,133	3,427	3,611
Total	8,580	9,237	10,649	11,844	12,661	13,425

Sources: see Table 66.
[a]Includes Freight Commodity Classification (FCC) nos. 411 and 415; excludes some of the commodities included in Table 14.
[b]Includes FCC no. 539; all commodities in Table 17 are included.
[c]Includes FCC no. 555; excludes some of the commodities included in Table 19.
[d]Includes FCC no. 571; includes commodities additional to those included in Table 22.
[e]Includes FCC nos. 573, 577, and 583; excludes some of the commodities included in Table 18.
[f]Includes FCC nos. 591 and 593; all commodities in Table 23 are included.
[g]Includes FCC no. 653; all commodities in Table 15 are included.
[h]Includes FCC no. 657; excludes some of the commodities included in Table 16.

traffic of 11,844,000 tons in 1964, about 62 percent of total Canada-U.S. railway traffic in that year.[9] The concentration of rail export tonnage is much more marked than is the case with imports. Value and volume are also more closely associated.

Between 1958 and 1966 Canada-U.S. railway traffic in these eight commodity categories increased by 56 percent. From 1962 to 1966 this traffic increased by 26 percent, and between 1964 and 1966 growth was 13 percent. All commodity groups, except perhaps nickel, have shared in this increase. Fertilizer traffic (mainly potash) has almost quadrupled, and the traditional rail-borne forest products exports have shown fairly steady, if unspectacular, growth.

The same caveats that were made in the case of northbound railway traffic after Table 66 apply here. Exports to other countries routed through U.S. ports, price changes, and commodity variation make it difficult to say anything about the trends in railway tonnages in relation to trends in

[9]Other major southbound commodities in 1964 were as follows: asbestos 678 (thousand tons), sulphur 587, stone and rock 410, iron ore 352, and zinc ore and concentrates 261. *Ibid.*

export values. Nevertheless, the trends in Table 67 are much more closely related to those in the pertinent parts of Tables 5 to 30 than is the case with Table 66 and Tables 31 to 65. The relative dominance of rail transportation in Canadian exports to the United States is at the root of these divergent patterns.

Volume patterns in Canada-U.S. transportation: water

The next series of tables shows trends in the commodity composition of water-borne traffic between Canada and the United States over the period 1956 to 1965. The tables also show the origins and destinations of this traffic by port areas. This type of information was not included in the railway tabulations for two reasons. First, it is generally irrelevant to the economics and regulation of railway transportation between the two countries. Second, much rail traffic that is shown arriving in one province from the United States is actually destined for points in other provinces. This is even more the case with traffic shown *leaving* one province for the United States. Many B.C. rail-borne lumber exports, for example, actually leave Canada in Ontario and are so treated in DBS railway statistics. For water transport, however, this disguising of actual origins and destinations is negligible. In addition, the nature of water transportation—its economics and sensitivity to government policy—very much depends on which port areas are involved in origin and destination.

Exports from Canada to the United States via water transport are shown in Tables 68 to 73. The six commodity groups selected all accounted for over $26 million worth of water-borne exports in 1964.[10] They comprised 75 percent of the total volume of Canada-U.S. water traffic in that year and almost 90 percent of the total value of Canadian exports to the United States by water. The five origin and destination combinations generally account for 99 percent or more of the volume of water-borne traffic between the two countries.

Over the nine-year period covered in the preceding tables, there have been marked changes in the structure of Canada's water-borne exports to the United States. Total volume has increased by almost 60 percent. Most notable is the increase in traffic moving between Canadian Atlantic ports

[10]It is believed that the six groups correspond very closely to the respective commodity groups in Tables 5–30. The corresponding table numbers are as follows (export values by water in 1964 are given in brackets): fish—Table 6 ($40 million); iron ore and scrap—Table 10 ($290 million); lumber, other sawmill products, and plywood— Table 14 ($73 million); woodpulp—Table 15 ($38 million); paper for printing— Table 16 ($279 million); primary and manufactured iron and steel—Table 18 ($27 million).

TABLES 68–73

VOLUME OF SELECTED COMMODITIES IN CANADA-U.S.
WATER-BORNE TRAFFIC, SELECTED YEARS
(thousand tons)

	Atlantic-ᵃ Atlantic and Gulf	Atlantic-ᵇ Great Lakes	Great Lakes-ᶜ Great Lakes	Pacific-ᵈ Pacific	Pacific-ᵉ Atlantic and Gulf	Total, all origins and destinations
68. YEAR 1956						
Fish	60	4	*	2	—	66
Iron ore and scrap	7,150	2,1919	4,757	1	—	14,099
Lumber, plywood and						
other sawmill products	*	—	—	209	141	371
Woodpulp	78	49	—	16	—	143
Paper for printing	762	162	327	438	4	1,722
Primary and manufactured						
iron and steel	23	70	222	*	—	316
Total, all traffic	12,466	2,744	7,516	2,997	162	26,075
69. YEAR 1958						
Fish	59	3	—	5	—	66
Iron ore and scrap	4,946	1,259	2,751	1	—	8,957
Lumber, plywood and						
other sawmill products	*	—	9	291	691	1,001
Woodpulp	61	14	106	123	49	354
Paper for printing	708	299	262	333	8	1,573
Primary and manufactured						
iron and steel	3	21	176	1	—	207
Total, all traffic	8,784	1,992	5,350	1,984	755	18,945
70. YEAR 1960						
Fish	71	4	—	1	—	76
Iron ore and scrap	3,658	4,019	3,942	—	—	11,620
Lumber, plywood and						
other sawmill products	—	—	7	301	822	1,149
Woodpulp	41	8	110	144	31	334
Paper for printing	734	274	349	524	2	1,910
Primary and manufactured	9	35	246	*	3	311
iron and steel						
Total, all traffic	9,036	4,568	7,346	2,656	865	24,616
71. YEAR 1962						
Fish	59	—	—	1	—	59
Iron ore and scrap	8,959	5,745	4,345	—	—	19,049
Lumber, plywood and						
other sawmill products	—	—	9	219	972	1,221
Woodpulp	97	24	119	148	24	411
Paper for printing	727	298	351	579	*	1,982
Primary and manufactured						
iron and steel	34	85	465	3	*	590
Total, all traffic	14,640	6,311	8,190	2,703	998	33,000
72. YEAR 1964						
Fish	75	*	—	1	—	75
Iron ore and scrap	10,293	12,213	5,317	2	—	27,825
Lumber, plywood and						
other sawmill products	*	—	*	98	1,215	1,330
Woodpulp	80	12	123	179	11	406
Paper for printing	896	343	295	625	3	2,191
Primary and manufactured						
iron and steel	*	161	277	*	—	446
Total, all traffic	16,911	13,010	9,006	2,637	1,258	43,066
73. YEAR 1965						
Fish	96	—	—	1	—	96
Iron ore and scrap	9,327	11,701	4,444	—	—	25,473
Lumber, plywood and						
other sawmill products	*	—	*	95	1.311	1,419
Woodpulp	76	6	104	254	9	448
Paper for printing	915	289	418	703	3	2,374
Primary and manufactured						
iron and steel	48	234	345	*	—	633
Total, all traffic	15,786	12,696	7,679	3,135	1,258	40,694

Sources: DBS, *Shipping Report* for various years: 1956, Part I; 1958, Part I; 1960, Part I; 1962, Part I; 1964, Part I; and 1965, Part I.
ᵃCanadian Atlantic ports (Montreal and east) to U.S. Atlantic and Gulf ports.
ᵇCanadian Atlantic ports (Montreal and east) to U.S. Great Lakes ports.
ᶜCanadian Great Lakes ports to U.S. Great Lakes ports
ᵈCanadian Pacific ports to U.S. Pacific ports.
ᵉCanadian Pacific ports to U.S. Atlantic and Gulf ports.   *Less than 500 tons.

and U.S. Great Lakes ports through the St. Lawrence Seaway. There has also been a striking increase in traffic moving between Canadian Pacific ports and U.S. Atlantic and Gulf ports. This traffic was, however, unusually low in 1956 because of high ocean freight rates resulting from the Suez disturbance. Some increase in traffic between the Atlantic ports of both countries has also occurred. Over the two remaining pairs of port areas traffic volumes have remained more or less constant.

Growth in volume of exports has occurred in all commodities. The greatest absolute growth has been, of course, in iron ore traffic (up by over 11 million tons between 1956 and 1965, and 16.5 million tons between 1958 and 1965). In relative terms the growth of Canada-U.S. water traffic has been even greater in the cases of woodpulp (mainly between Canadian and U.S. Great Lakes ports and Canadian and U.S. Pacific coast ports) and iron and steel[11] (mainly to U.S. Great Lakes ports from Canadian Atlantic and Great Lakes ports).

Details of water traffic northbound from the United States to Canada are given in Tables 74 through 79. Only five commodity groups are included[12]; each of them accounted for more than $20 million worth of water-borne imports from the United States in 1964. In volume terms the five groups include 86 percent of 1964 northbound U.S.-Canada water traffic, which totaled almost 27.9 million tons. About 95 percent of this traffic is accounted for by the four origin and destination combinations.

The movement of one commodity group—coal and coke—over one route (between U.S. and Canadian Great Lakes ports) clearly dominates in northbound water traffic between the two countries. The relative importance of this commodity in actual water-borne trade volume between the United States and Canada is, in fact, greater than shown in the above tables. This is because DBS statistics include large volumes of unmilled cereals and soybeans moving between the United States and Canada that are in fact transshipped at ports, mainly on the lower St. Lawrence River, for overseas export. It is estimated that in 1964 two-thirds of the soybean traffic and five-sixths of the unmilled cereals traffic on the Great Lakes–

[11]As mentioned earlier, lumber traffic (most of which moves between Canadian Pacific and U.S. Atlantic and Gulf ports) was unusually low in 1956 because of the Suez crisis.

[12]It is believed that the five groups correspond very closely to the respective commodity groups in Tables 31–65. The corresponding table numbers are as follows. Import values by water in 1964 are given in brackets.
Unmilled cereals, Table 32 ($25 million)
Soybeans and other seeds, Table 34 ($46 million)
Iron ore and scrap, Table 36 ($64 million)
Coal and coke, Table 37 ($80 million)
Petroleum products, Table 41 ($21 million)

TABLES 74–79

VOLUME OF SELECTED COMMODITIES IN U.S.-CANADA

WATER-BORNE TRAFFIC, SELECTED YEARS

(thousand tons)

	Great Lakes-[a] Great Lakes	Great Lakes-[b] Atlantic	Atlantic-[c] and Gulf Atlantic	Pacific-[d] Pacific	Total, all origins and destinations
74. YEAR 1956					
Unmilled cereals	157	71	*	*	233
Soybeans and other seeds	275	8	—	*	284
Iron ore and scrap	5,222	3	—	—	5,226
Coal and coke	14,390	1,393	74	13	15,870
Petroleum products	825	5	626	900	2,481
Total, all traffic	23,558	1,606	1,430	1,287	28,424
75. YEAR 1958					
Unmilled cereals	341	98	*	*	443
Soybeans and other seeds	423	—	—	—	423
Iron ore and scrap	3,491	15	—	*	3,535
Coal and coke	9,863	713	70	—	10,646
Petroleum products	741	2	484	450	1,734
Total, all traffic	16,393	977	1,220	689	19.729
76. YEAR 1960					
Unmilled cereals	277	746	*	3	1,026
Soybeans and other seeds	420	207	*	—	627
Iron ore and scrap	4,996	19	—	—	5,025
Coal and coke	10,125	678	154	5	10,961
Petroleum products	237	7	253	486	1,046
Total, all traffic	17,655	1,712	1,081	797	21,638
77. YEAR 1962					
Unmilled cereals	553	1,759	16	—	2,335
Soybeans and other seeds	407	354	—	—	761
Iron ore and scrap	5,086	15	—	—	5,108
Coal and coke	10,270	707	260	—	11,240
Petroleum products	79	22	30	436	616
Total, all traffic	18,088	2,952	1,077	974	23,488
78. YEAR 1964					
Unmilled cereals	271	2 315	*	—	2,589
Soybeans and other seeds	525	591	—	—	1,116
Iron ore and scrap	5,387	—	*	—	5,388
Coal and coke	13,119	651	313	—	14,125
Petroleum products	57	25	117	528	787
Total, all traffic	21,149	3,874	1,204	1,250	27,859
79. YEAR 1965					
Unmilled cereals	294	2,630	*	—	2.930
Soybeans and other seeds	471	650	—	—	1,121
Iron ore and scrap	4,961	—	*	—	4,976
Coal and coke	14,471	734	478	—	15,683
Petroleum products	17	19	199	640	905
Total, all traffic	22,198	4,266	1,374	1,595	29,932

Sources: DBS, *Shipping Report* for various years: 1956, Part I; 1958, Part I; 1960, Part I; 1962, Part I; 1964, Part I; and 1965, Part I.
[a]U.S. Great Lakes ports to Canadian Great Lakes ports.
[b]U.S. Great Lakes ports to Canadian Atlantic ports (Montreal and east).
[c]U.S. Atlantic and Gulf ports to Canadian Atlantic ports (Montreal and east).
[d]U.S. Pacific ports to Canadian Pacific ports.
*Less than 500 tons.

Atlantic route in fact fell into this category.[13] Thus for 1964 U.S.-Canada water traffic should be reduced by 1.9 million tons of unmilled cereals and

[13]Estimate based on a comparison of values from Tables 32 and 34 with volumes shown in Table 78 in light of 1964 prices. Evidence from a U.S. source for earlier years supports this. See U.S. Department of Agriculture, *Changing Shipping Patterns on the St. Lawrence Seaway with Emphasis on United States Grain Exports*, Marketing Research Report no. 621, Washington, 1963, Table 12, p. 12.

.4 million tons of soybeans and other seeds.[14] This type of shipment began, incidentally, after completion of the St. Lawrence Seaway.

Traffic has increased between all four of the origin and destination pairs shown in the tables. 1958 seems a better year for beginning comparisons than 1956 because of the sharp decline in traffic between 1957 and 1958. Almost 7 million tons of northbound Great Lakes–Great Lakes traffic, mostly coal and coke,[15] disappeared in that year. The increase between the Great Lakes ports of the United States and the Atlantic ports of Canada consists entirely, however, of grain destined for overseas export. Traffic moving along the Atlantic coast between U.S. and Canadian ports has also shown sluggish growth. The largest absolute growth in northbound traffic has occurred between the Great Lakes ports of both countries, although 1965 volumes were below 1956 levels. The fastest rate of growth (131 percent between 1958 and 1965) has occurred in water traffic moving between U.S. Pacific and Canadian Pacific ports.

After exclusion of overseas traffic, only one of the five commodity groups, soybeans and other seeds, has maintained growth over this period. Unmilled cereals destined for Canada and iron ore have remained stagnant, and petroleum products have declined sharply since 1956 with the loss of Great Lakes–Great Lakes and Atlantic and Gulf-Atlantic traffic. Recovery has been occurring, however, since 1962. Northbound water traffic in coal and coke has finally regained a volume about on a par with that of 1956.

Volume patterns in Canada-U.S. transportation: highway

Statistical information concerning the volume of highway transportation between Canada and the United States is sparse and conflicting. What follows is an attempt to resolve the conflicts and provide some basis for later discussion of the trade impediments resulting from highway transport policy.

The origins of statistical problems in highway transport lie in the nature of the industry. Statistics for rail transport are provided by railway companies, and in the case of water transport, statistics are collected by customs

[14]A partly analogous statistical situation exists on the West Coast. Traffic moving by water from Skagway, Alaska, to Vancouver (not shown separately) is treated as though it originated in the United States. In fact, this traffic's origin is in the Yukon Territory, and it moves through the United States in bond. About 225,000 tons was involved in 1964.

[15]Between 1957 and 1958 coal consumption in Canada dropped by 6.1 million tons. Dominion Coal Board, *Annual Report*, 1964–65 (1966), p. 31. Appropriate Canadian subsidy arrangements ensured that the bulk of this decline was borne by imports from U.S. coal producers.

officers acting as agents of the Dominion Bureau of Statistics. Highway transport statistics are collected, however, by a series of stratified sample surveys of all trucks registered in Canada. About 7 percent of the total Canadian truck population is included. The approach used has one obvious flaw as far as transborder trucking is concerned—U.S.-registered trucks that are engaged in transportation between the two countries but are not registered in a Canadian province are excluded from the sample, and their transport activities from the statistics. Other grave weaknesses stem from the sampling procedure and begin with the probably low quality of responses to the DBS "Truck Traffic Questionnaire." There is, however, little to be gained from proceeding with an evaluation of DBS highway transport statistics.[16] It is sufficient to reiterate that the industry is a difficult one from which to gather the kinds of information essential to full understanding of its economics and that the Dominion Bureau of Statistics has not yet been able to meet the challenges presented.

Three divisions of the DBS prepare statistics dealing with transborder trucking. The statistical procedures described in the preceding paragraph are carried out by the Transportation and Public Utilities Division and are used to prepare statistics showing volume, revenue, and traffic patterns for intra- and extra-provincial highway transport. The Balance of Payments and Financial Flows Division presents statistics showing the number of Canadian and foreign (almost entirely U.S.) commercial vehicles entering Canada at each of 140-odd ports of entry. The External Trade Division shows, in its import and export statistics, some volume information. For exports this information is available, for some commodities, by mode of transport.

Table 80 shows the trends, since 1958, in the volume of for-hire and private truck transportation between the various Canadian provinces and the United States in both directions. The pattern shown in Table 80 is one of growth, but the trends are decidedly erratic. There are at least a dozen annual and biennial changes in traffic that are so extreme as to require special explanation. In few cases can such explanation be developed. The existence of these mysterious major variations calls into question the correctness of each year's statistics, and it is perhaps best to conclude our analysis of Table 80 simply by noting the obvious substantial growth in trucking between Canada and the United States between 1958 and 1964.

The rest of this section concentrates on 1964. According to *Motor*

[16]This is the case particularly in view of the planned revision of the collection, coverage, and format of these statistics. For a discussion of highway statistics in Canada, see D. W. Eldon, "Review of Federal Transportation Statistics," Royal Commission on Transportation, *Report*, Vol. III, Ottawa, Queen's Printer, 1962, pp. 409–544.

TABLE 80

VOLUME OF HIGHWAY TRANSPORTATION BETWEEN CANADA AND THE
UNITED STATES, SELECTED YEARS
(thousand tons)

	1958	1960	1962	1963	1964
A. For-Hire					
Atlantic to U.S.	9	7	22	51	31
from U.S.	5	14	6	2	5
Quebec to U.S.	131	162	164	226	273
from U.S.	148	135	116	219	130
Ontario to U.S.	149	338	461	347	742
from U.S.	213	293	400	275	194
Manitoba to U.S.	12	3	5	8	7
from U.S.	21	25	11	8	3
Saskatchewan to U.S.	7	7	4	7	14
from U.S.	3	7	5	—	11
Alberta to U.S.	11	11	22	17	39
from U.S.	5	14	26	17	19
British Columbia to U.S.	101	132	394	111	185
from U.S.	77	136	107	72	87
Canada to U.S.	420	660	1,072	767	1,291
from U.S.	472	614	671	593	449
B. Private					
Atlantic to U.S.	29	127	123	114	252
from U.S.	7	34	31	29	16
Quebec to U.S.	272	100	242	191	133
from U.S.	4	133	79	139	106
Ontario to U.S.	229	106	238	166	300
from U.S.	201	144	276	293	292
Manitoba to U.S.	5	12	26	5	7
from U.S.	—	7	8	12	—
Saskatchewan to U.S.	—	—	8	20	4
from U.S.	2	—	5	12	13
Alberta to U.S.	—	1	2	70	1
from U.S.	3	12	8	—	—
British Columbia to U.S.	1	73	114	69	33
from U.S.	31	50	20	16	22
Canada to U.S.	536	419	753	635	730
from U.S.	248	380	427	501	449
C. Total					
Atlantic to U.S.	38	134	145	165	283
from U.S.	12	38	37	31	21
Quebec to U.S.	403	262	406	417	406
from U.S.	152	288	295	358	236
Ontario to U.S.	378	444	699	513	1,042
from U.S.	414	437	676	578	486
Manitoba to U.S.	17	15	31	13	14
from U.S.	21	32	19	20	3
Saskatchewan to U.S.	7	7	12	27	18
from U.S.	5	7	10	12	24
Alberta to U.S.	11	12	24	87	40
from U.S.	8	26	34	17	19
British Columbia to U.S.	102	205	518	180	218
from U.S.	108	186	127	88	109
Canada to U.S.	956	1,079	1,825	1,402	2,021
from U.S.	720	994	1,098	1,094	898

Source: DBS, *Motor Transport Traffic: Canada,* various issues.

Transport Traffic: Canada, 2 million tons moved south between Canada and the United States and 898,000 tons moved north. An unpublished commodity breakdown of this traffic, undifferentiated as to direction, is shown in Table 81.

TABLE 81
TOTAL TRUCK TRAFFIC BETWEEN CANADA AND THE UNITED STATES
BY MAJOR COMMODITY GROUPS, 1964
(thousand tons)

	For hire	Private	Total
Live animals	2	6	8
Food, feed, beverages, and tobacco	303	202	505
Crude materials, inedible	456	511	967
Fabricated materials, inedible	592	303	895
End products, inedible	262	98	360
General freight*a*	125	58	183
Total	1,740	1,178	2,918

Source: Unpublished DBS data.
*a*A group comprised of otherwise unclassified traffic.

Comparison of Table 81 with the other sources of statistics mentioned above uncovers large anomalies. There were 1.2 million commercial vehicles that entered Canada from the United States in 1964.[17] Assuming that the average load was 2.5 tons[18] and that only 60 percent of the trucks were loaded, we estimate that 1.7 million tons of goods entered Canada by highway transport in 1964. This is almost double the *Motor Transport Traffic: Canada* figure. Even wider discrepancies occur when we use commercial vehicle entries by province to check the highway transport statistics. According to *Motor Transport Traffic: Canada* only 3,000 tons of freight moved into Manitoba from the United States in 1964. Yet there were almost 40,000 border crossings by commercial vehicles, a volume of traffic that should have involved at least 100,000 tons of goods.

Turning to foreign trade statistics we find similar anomalies. Major discrepancies, incidentally, do *not* exist between rail and water traffic statistics and foreign trade statistics. Quantity statistics are available for 16 of the 24 export commodity groups used in Tables 5 to 30. These show

[17]DBS, *Travel between Canada and the United States*, calendar year and December, 1965 (1966), Table 1, p. 11, and Table 3, p. 15.
[18]Estimate developed by estimating composition of commercial vehicle entries in terms of average payload. "Commercial vehicles" include trucks ranging from half-ton pickups to tractor-trailer combinations. Trucks with a gross vehicle weight of less than 8,000 lbs. (60 percent of the U.S. truck fleet) are excluded from the 2.5 ton estimate—i.e., they are assumed to have entered empty—in the interests of conservatism.

that just over 1.3 million tons of exports to the United States in 1964 moved by truck.[19] This is well within the 2.0-million-ton figure shown in Table 80. There are, of course, the 8 commodity groups for which quantity information is not available. But these *might* have accounted for only 700,000 tons of exports by truck in 1964, since at least some of them are composed of low-volume, high-value manufactured products. There is, however, a considerable *volume* of export trade with the United States not shown separately in Tables 5 to 30. Just five of these excluded commodities accounted for over 950,000 tons of 1964 exports by truck.[20] Within at least one of the commodity groups shown in Table 81 there is an even more striking discrepancy. Imports *and* exports of live animals totaled 8,000 tons in 1964 according to Table 81. Yet 200,000 head of cattle alone were exported in 1964. Since this was not the only trade in live animals between the two countries in that year and, even if it were, since the average cow weighs far more than 80 pounds, a gross error obviously exists here.

The actual volume of truck traffic moving from Canada to the United States in 1964 was probably on the order of 3 million tons, a figure 50 percent greater than that provided in DBS highway transport statistics. The underestimation of transborder truck traffic is much greater in the case of northbound traffic.

According to the DBS this traffic totaled 898,000 tons in 1964. Using our estimated value of truck-borne imports ($2.5 billion), we arrive at an average value per ton of $2,790. This is far too high, considering the mix of Canadian imports from the United States moving by truck.[21] The corresponding figure for exports, developed in the same way, is $360.[22] We would have expected the value per ton for imports to be higher, but not by this much.

Revelation of the degree of underestimation involved in the DBS figure of 898,000 tons is not difficult. Imports of fruit and vegetables (Table 33)

[19]DBS, *Exports by Mode of Transport*, 1964.
[20]Cereals 75,000 tons, fruit and vegetables 140,000 tons, hay and feeds 200,000 tons, pulpwood 415,000 tons, and coal 125,000 tons. *Ibid.*
[21]According to the Interstate Commerce Commission, in 1959 only 10 of the 262 commodity groups in the freight commodity classification had such high values per ton. The high-valued groups were as follows: business and office machines; military vehicles, n.o.s.; airplanes, aircraft, and parts; guns, small arms, and parts, n.o.s.; cotton factory products; cloth and fabrics, n.o.s.; boots, shoes, and findings, n.o.s.; luggage and handbags, n.o.s.; manufactured tobacco, n.o.s.; and cigarettes. ICC, *Freight Revenue and Wholesale Value at Destination of Commodities Transported by Class I Line-Haul Railroads*, 1959, Washington, 1961. The average value of manufactured products was $281 per ton.
[22]Truck export value of $1,076,085,000 and volume of 3 million tons (see above).

totaled 930,000 tons in 1964.[23] Twenty-five percent of the value of imports entered Canada by truck. We may assume, for this commodity group, that there are few intermodal differences in value/volume relationships. Therefore, over 230,000 tons of fruit and vegetables moved northbound by truck between the United States and Canada in 1964. Imports of coal and coke (Table 37) amounted to 15.7 million tons in 1964. By value, 7 percent of this was imported by truck. Reducing this proportion to 4 percent to account for value/volume relationships, we still have almost 630,000 tons of truck traffic. Iron ore and scrap imports (Table 36) amounted to 6.3 million tons in 1964. Eleven percent of this traffic moved by truck, a volume of 690,000 tons. These three groups amount to 1.5 million tons.

Within just three commodity groups we have exceeded the DBS estimate by over 600,000 tons. Two of these are admittedly atypical in their low value in relation to weight, but it is apparent that there is a serious disagreement between the import statistics and the highway transport statistics. We are very much disposed to believe the former and would estimate the northbound volume of goods moved by truck at between 2.5 million and 3.5 million tons in 1964.

One minor task remains. The provincial breakdown of values of exports transported by truck is of interest because regulation differs among the provinces. The statistics[24] shown in Table 82 are believed to be a correct representation of the influence of various provincial regulatory regimes on the value of exports by truck. Similar statistics could not be developed for imports, but it is believed that the pattern would be similar.

Each of the commodity groups shown in Table 82 accounted for more than $28 million worth of exports to the United States by truck in 1964. Also, each corresponds to a separate part of Tables 5 to 30. The dominant position of Ontario, which accounts for 64 percent of export value in Table 82, is striking. This would be expected on the basis of the provincial statistics of Table 80. Further comparison of these two tables suggests that the highway transport policies of the Prairie provinces are, taken singly, unimportant to trade. The low export value for British Columbia does not quite agree with the volume statistics of Table 80 but may be partly explained by low-value exports of such commodities as peat moss. In any case, it is clear that Ontario and Quebec are the key provinces as far as the influence of highway transport policy on trade is concerned. The dominance of these provinces, and particularly Ontario, has increased since 1964 with increased highway transport associated with the Automotive

[23]DBS, *Imports by Countries*, January–December, 1965.
[24]Available by region only for the Atlantic and Prairie provinces.

TABLE 82

VALUE OF EXPORTS BY TRUCK OF SELECTED COMMODITY GROUPS, BY REGIONS, 1964
(million dollars)

	Atlantic	Quebec	Ontario	Prairies	B.C.
Meat	0.4	10.3	18.1	4.1	1.2
Fish	38.3	4.9	8.4	11.4	4.4
Distilled alcoholic beverages	—	18.5	41.6	1.4	3.3
Lumber, other sawmill products, and plywood	4.0	10.2	9.4	0.2	5.8
Paper for printing	—	16.9	19.4	0.1	0.2
Primary and manufactured iron and steel	0.2	5.1	38.7	1.0	0.7
Nickel and alloys	—	0.2	80.7	1.1	—
Agricultural machinery	—	0.2	20.0	7.6	—
Motor vehicles and parts	—	2.8	99.7	4.3	0.9
Aircraft and parts	1.2	34.8	15.8	1.5	0.3
Communications and laboratory equipment	—	16.4	29.3	0.2	1.1
Total, 11 groups	44.1	120.3	381.1	32.9	17.9

Note: Values include a small amount of exports by truck destined to countries other than the United States.
Source: DBS, *Exports by Mode of Transport*, 1964 (1966).

Free Trade Agreement. In 1965 domestic exports of the value of $1.4 billion moved by highway transport, $1.3 billion of them destined for the United States. Of the total domestic exports by truck, 63 percent were cleared from Ontario.[25]

Pipeline and air transportation between the United States and Canada

Only fragmentary information is available on volumes of air freight and air express moving between Canada and the United States. Commodity detail is non-existent. Thus, the description of air transportation of Canadian exports to and imports from the United States in earlier sections of this chapter will have to suffice.

Pipeline transportation is more important than air transportation in Canada-U.S. trade, but it is totally concentrated in moving Canadian exports to the United States. Moreover, only two commodities are exported by pipeline, and for these there is virtually no competition from other modes of transport. But it is the circumstances of policy-making for pipeline transport that encourages us to omit further discussion, despite a

[25]DBS, *Exports by Mode of Transport*, 1965.

relative abundance of statistical material relating to export locations and volumes. Decisions regarding international operations are made with reference to detailed proposals regarding the marketing of petroleum or natural gas. Because of these peculiarities, pipelines seem to lie somewhat outside the scope of the present study.

Conclusions

The statistical information presented in this chapter provides a suitable base for the analysis in succeeding chapters of this study. Information concerning the scope and detail of the transportation aspects of trade between Canada and the United States is essential to an examination of the impact of transport policy on this trade. It is also useful for its own sake, since statistical information of this type has not been previously developed.

3. Transport Policy in Canada and the United States

Introduction

Included in chapter 1 was a brief survey of transport policy in the different countries of the European Economic Community. This was used as a base for the subsequent discussion of transport policy harmonization in the EEC. Chapter 3 provides a more comprehensive review of transport policy in Canada and the United States to precede the analysis, in the next three chapters, of problems in transportation and trade between the two countries.

Specific features of transport policy in either country are not analyzed profoundly here but, where necessary, in the following chapters. Rather, a broad outline of the philosophy and practice of national transport policy in each country is provided. Differences at this level between the two countries are of sufficient consequence to make such an outline valuable.

The product of public policy towards transportation is a system of transport regulation. Economic and safety regulation is typical of the transportation sector the world over. There are many reasons for the eagerness with which governments regulate the transport operations falling within their jurisdictions. They may be enumerated as follows:

1. A fear of monopoly abuses of various types or, for some modes, a fear of "excessive" competition.
2. A belief that transportation is a key determinant of the relative prosperity of national and regional economies.
3. The convenience of using the transport sector to fulfil various non-transport objectives of national policy.
4. The sheer difficulty of making radical changes in an established system of regulation.

Canada and the United States are both excellent examples of countries where these four tendencies to elaborate and perpetuate transport regulation are present in good measure.

By itself regulation *could* be of minor importance in inhibiting trade, if it were flexible enough to be adjusted to changing conditions in an often dynamic sector of the economy and if regulatory policies and practices in two potential trading partners were more or less harmonized. Unfortunately, neither of these conditions is fulfilled in the case of Canada and the United States. Regulation of the transportation sector is cumbersome and uneven in both countries, but in different ways in each.

Like many types of public policy, transport policy is not readily identifiable. There is often a substantial gulf between word and action and promise and performance. Moreover, there is, in both Canada and the United States, more than one source of pronouncements on transportation policy. Given this multiplicity, which source is to be believed?

In Canada this question can be answered with a reasonable degree of confidence. We will assume that current Canadian transport policy is represented by the National Transportation Act of 1967,[1] supported by the statements of government officials in Parliament and before Parliamentary committees. The 1961 report of the Royal Commission on Transportation must also be considered, although its conclusions do not, of themselves, constitute public policy. The potential gap between statement and practice in transport policy remains.

The proper origin of transport policy in the United States is less easily discernible. As the following abbreviated list of U.S. sources indicates, transport policy in that country has many voices, which, incidentally, rarely speak in unison.

1. The Interstate Commerce Act.[2]
2. The Department of Transportation Act of 1966.[3]
3. Other transportation-related statutes.[4]
4. Congressional hearings on assorted transportation proposals and investigations.
5. Transportation messages to Congress of President Kennedy in 1962 and President Johnson in 1966.
6. A transportation policy statement in the 1966 *Annual Report of the Council of Economic Advisers.*
7. A host of private and semi-official assessments.

The following discussion is briefer than would be required to resolve completely the conflicts among these transport policy sources and to analyze their impact on (or assessment of) actual public policy towards transportation.

[1]14–15–16 Eliz. II, 595–670.   [2]49 U.S. Code.   [3]Public Law 89–670.
[4]Including particularly the Shipping Act of 1916, the Merchant Marine Act of 1936, and the Civil Aeronautics Act of 1938.

Canadian transport policy

A recent study of the economics and regulation of U.S. transportation contained the following statement of the objectives of transport policy: "The oft-stated objective of public transportation policy is to meet the transportation needs of the economy with a minimum expenditure of economic resources."[5] Identification of these needs and selection of their least-cost satisfaction is an involved process. Equally involved is the translation of this philosophy into specific and meaningful statements of policy. Transportation is recognized as an important force in national economic, social, and political well-being, but there is great controversy over the nature of this importance and the policies that should be adopted because of it. The traditional importance of transportation in Canadian national policy is well indicated in the following quotation:

The responsibility for creating a national economy and the conditions in which it could survive lay with the state. Extending far beyond the basic constitutional framework of government, internal security, and justice, this responsibility embraced also the construction, in partnership with private enterprise, of the east-west transport system; the erection of tariff barriers behind which an industrial complex could develop; and the promotion of immigration and a flow of investment capital from Europe. The over-all objective of the policy was to make possible the maintenance of Canadian political sovereignty over the territory north of the American boundary. . . .[6]

The development of a transportation system required specific government decisions concerning initial investment in the system, promotion and extension of the existing system, and regulation of its relationships with the country's producers and consumers. Beginning with railways and inland water transportation in the nineteenth century, this pattern has been repeated in this century in highway, air, and pipeline transport.

The federal government has played a far more important role in transport policy than have the provincial governments. The terms of the British North America Act have required this. Section 91 of the Act reserves for the federal Parliament legislative power involving "the Regulation of Trade and Commerce," "ferries between a Province and any British or Foreign Country or between Two Provinces," and matters not specifically assigned to the provinces in Section 92. In Section 92 the provinces are

[5]John R. Meyer, *et al.*, *The Economics of Competition in the Transportation Industries*, Cambridge, Mass., Harvard University Press, 1959, p. 242.
[6]Hugh G. J. Aitken, "Defensive Expansionism: The State and Economic Growth in Canada," *The State and Economic Growth*, ed. Hugh G. J. Aitken, New York, Social Science Research Council, 1959, p. 103.

given legislative authority over "Local Works and Undertakings," *except* the following:

1. Those that connect the provinces with each other or with foreign countries.
2. Those that have been declared by the federal Parliament "to be for the general Advantage of Canada or for the Advantage of Two or more of the Provinces."

Under this authority the federal government has dominated regulation and promotion in rail, water, air, and pipeline transport. Only in highway transport have the provinces exerted significant influence on policy. Highways and highway-use regulations have been, with a few exceptions, a matter for the provinces, as has the regulation of intra- and extra-provincial trucking. The authority over the latter derives from federal delegation in the Motor Vehicle Transport Act of 1954.

But in most extensions of public policy in transportation, there has been a disinterest in selection of the best alternatives. Anderson has described and explained this phenomenon in this way:

In the Canadian past, great national aspirations were reflected in national policy, of which transportation policy was a part. At no time was it discernible that careful economic criteria were the parameters of transportation policy. Transportation, which meant primarily railway transportation, was intended to serve the national interest and, in so doing, was expected to be extensively endowed by the public purse in capital construction and protected sufficiently to see the private investor adequately rewarded. Imperfectly as it might appear in terms of an economic analysis, the transportation function was well defined in relation to national policy.[7]

Instead of transport policy based on economic criteria, Canada has had transport policy founded on increasingly obsolete and meaningless political criteria. Many of these criteria have become totally irrelevant to the national destiny of Canada, yet their satisfaction has continued to be a prop for the outworn platitudes that have comprised government policy in transportation. To quote Anderson again:

In this generation transportation policy has contributed nothing of and by itself to the promotion of national purposes, either economic or political.

Every government since 1930 has been marked, to this date, by vacillation, by refusal to acknowledge change in transportation, and by diehard and fool-hardy adherence to transportation concepts which did honor to the original

---

[7]F. W. Anderson, "Research and Public Policy Issues: Some Canadian Comparisons," *Transportation Economics*, New York, National Bureau of Economic Research and Columbia University Press, 1965, p. 447.

policy makers in their day, but which only compound the difficulties of Canada in this.[8]

Our purpose, though, is to delineate Canadian transport policy, not to criticize it. Also, many of the most unpalatable features of policy have now been eliminated, thanks mainly to the Royal Commission on Transportation, of which Anderson was director of research. The Commission's report expressed the objective of national transportation policy in these terms:

Public policy in Canada should seek to create an efficient transport system. This we define as the objective of the National Transport Policy.

This objective we regard as of more importance than the preservation of any single mode of transport, or of any particular company offering the services of transport. Should it be apparent that a firm providing services of transport is unable to live under a policy which seeks to attain maximum efficiency, we state that the consequences of technology or economics must not be set aside to preserve any historical or preconceived ideas about the proper composition of the transportation industry.[9]

Three "elements of National Transportation Policy necessary to work toward efficiency in transportation"[10] were set forth by the Commission. These were as follows:

1. General reliance on market competition to keep the transportation industry efficient.
2. Regulation of a type and extent necessary to produce the results of competition in situations where pervasive competition was absent.
3. The equality of direct and indirect subsidization of transport firms and transport users.

The essence of the Commission's approach has been embodied, following a five-year period of procrastination, in the National Transportation Act of 1967. The Act's statement of national transportation policy deserves quotation in full because of its inherent novelty in Canadian legislation of any type and because of its potential impact on the nation's transportation system.

It is hereby declared that an economic, efficient and adequate transportation system making the best use of all available modes of transportation at the

---

[8]F. W. Anderson, "A Critique of Canadian Policy Developments," *Transportation Research Forum: Papers, Third Annual Meeting*, Oxford, Ind., Richard B. Cross, 1962, p. 3.
[9]Royal Commission on Transportation, *Report*, Vol. II, Ottawa, Queen's Printer, 1961, p. 8.
[10]*Ibid.*, pp. 8–9.

lowest total cost is essential to protect the interests of the users of transportation and to maintain the economic well-being and growth of Canada, and that these objectives are most likely to be achieved when all modes of transport are able to compete under conditions ensuring that having due regard to national policy and to legal and constitutional requirements

(a) regulation of all modes of transport will not be of such a nature as to restrict the ability of any mode of transport to compete freely with any other modes of transport;

(b) each mode of transport, so far as practicable, bears a fair proportion of the real costs of the resources, facilities and services provided that mode of transport at public expense;

(c) each mode of transport, so far as practicable, receives compensation for the resources, facilities and services that it is required to provide as an imposed public duty; and

(d) each mode of transport, so far as practicable, carries traffic to or from any point in Canada under tolls and conditions that do not constitute

    (i) an unfair disadvantage in respect of any such traffic beyond that disadvantage inherent in the location or volume of the traffic, the scale of operation connected therewith or the type of traffic or service involved, or

    (ii) An undue obstacle to the interchange of commodities between points in Canada or unreasonable discouragement to the development of primary or secondary industries or to export trade in or from any region of Canada or to the movement of commodities through Canadian ports;

and this Act is enacted in accordance with and for the attainment of so much of these objectives as fall within the purview of subject matters under the jurisdiction of Parliament relating to transportation.[11]

Examination of the proceedings of the House of Commons Standing Committee on Transport and Communications[12] and the debates in the Commons itself[13] reveals that the government's view of the intent of the National Transportation Act follows closely the principles enunciated by the Royal Commission on Transportation. Emphasis on the "new" competitive environment in Canadian transportation is found at many places in this record, and the desire to develop new policy and new regulatory institutions and procedures to match is obvious.

[11]*Ibid.*, sec. 1. The only predecessor of this statement was contained in Section 336 of the Railway Act (RSC, c. 234), which section has now been repealed. It read as follows: "It is hereby declared to be the national freight rates policy that, subject to the exceptions specified in subsection (4) [a very broad group], every railway company shall, so far as is reasonably possible, in respect of all freight traffic of the same description, and carried on or upon the like kind of cars or conveyances, passing over all lines or routes of the company in Canada, charge tolls to all persons at the same rate, whether by weight, mileage, or otherwise."

[12]House of Commons, Standing Committee on Transport and Communications, *Minutes of Proceedings and Evidence*, no. 23, October 6, 1966, to no. 41, November 24, 1966, Ottawa, Queen's Printer, 1966.

[13]House of Commons, *Debates*, December 20, 1966, to January 27, 1967, Ottawa, Queen's Printer, 1966–67.

Canadian transport policy includes a number of notable features that provide a contrast with U.S. policy.

1. One internally consistent statement of national transport policy.
2. A simplified and rationalized system of railway rate regulation in response to the widespread emergence of viable competition in transportation.
3. Decentralized and uncoordinated regulation of motor carriers.
4. The existence of carrier and shipper subsidies in railway transportation.
5. Acceptance of a high degree of concentration and a growing incidence of intermodal consolidation in the transportation industries.
6. The powerful influence of provincial governments on the federal government's exercise of its powers and, hence, their influence on the determination of national transport policy.

One feature that is common to both countries is a desire to protect their respective domestic transportation industries from direct foreign competition. Thus it is that trucking companies must overcome severe regulatory and licensing hurdles to engage in freight transport in the other country[14]; that similar rights for airlines have never been negotiated[15]; and that neither nation allows the ships of the other to engage in cabotage. The situation in rail transportation is inherently different and probably should be considered less restrictive.

U.S. transport policy

Any survey of U.S. transport policy must begin with the preamble to the Interstate Commerce Act. Here the following declaration of national transportation policy is set forth:

It is hereby declared to be the national transportation policy of the Congress to provide for fair and impartial regulation of all modes of transportation subject to the provisions of this Act, so administered as to recognize and preserve the inherent advantages of each; to promote safe, adequate, economical, and efficient service and foster sound economic conditions in transportation and among the several carriers; to encourage the establishment and maintenance of reasonable charges for transportation services, without unjust discriminations, undue preferences or advantages, or unfair or destructive competitive practices; to cooperate with the several States and the duly authorized officials

---

[14]This practice is known as "cabotage."
[15]The most recent Canada-U.S. air transport agreement, signed in January, 1966, states in Article IV that "an airline designated by one Contracting Party may not take on at one point in the territory of the other Contracting Party traffic destined for another point in the territory of such other Contracting Party."

thereof; and to encourage fair wages and equitable working conditions;—all to the end of developing, coordinating, and preserving a national transportation system by water, highway, and rail, as well as other means, adequate to meet the needs of the commerce of the United States, of the Postal Service, and of the national defense. All of the provisions of this Act shall be administered and enforced with a view to carrying out the above declaration of policy.[16]

This declaration has proved difficult to apply, at least to the satisfaction of the regulated industries. Practically all students of U.S. transportation policy share this dissatisfaction. The difficulties arise out of the basic conflict between the call "to recognize and preserve the inherent advantages of each [mode]" and the requirement "to promote . . . economical and efficient service . . . ." Such optima as the latter requirement are naturally difficult to achieve under the constraint of preserving the intermodal status quo.[17]

A later, briefer, and more consistent statement of policy is contained at the beginning of the Department of Transportation Act of 1966. Section 2 (a) of that Act reads as follows: "The Congress hereby declares that the general welfare, the economic growth and stability of the Nation and its security require the development of national transportation policies and programs conducive to the provision of fast, safe, efficient, and convenient transportation at the lowest cost consistent therewith and with other national objectives, including the efficient utilization and conservation of the Nation's resources." It is unlikely, however, that this statement will ever have the impact of its confused companion which introduces the Interstate Commerce Act. In the first place, it merely states that policies should be developed that are based on economic and other criteria. This has far less force than a statement applying to actual procedures and practices. Second, the Interstate Commerce Commission is unlikely to use it as a guide, and it is the ICC that is the prime vehicle for U.S. transportation policy. The ICC's role is less primary than in the past, though, for unregulated competition has a great influence on the regulated segments of U.S. transportation, and government investment in transport facilities has a growing effect on both. Changes in U.S. federal government policy towards transportation (which is relatively even more dominant vis-à-vis the states than is the case in Canada)[18] would require Congressional amendment of the Interstate Commerce Act.

[16]49 USC, preceding sec. 1.
[17]This was the basic criticism of the "Doyle report" concerning the present policy statement. See *National Transportation Policy*, preliminary draft of a report to the Senate Committee on Interstate and Foreign Commerce, 87th Cong., 1st sess., 1961, pp. 36–9.
[18]Judicial interpretation of Article I, Section 8, of the U.S. Constitution (which gives Congress power "to regulate Commerce . . . among the several States . . .") has

There have been two presidential transportation messages since 1962, both of which have aimed at reform of federal transport policy. President Kennedy's message of April 5, 1962,[19] adopted a view of policy that is well summed up in the following paragraph.

The basic objective of our nation's transportation system must be to assure the availability of the fast, safe and economical transportation services needed in a growing and changing economy to move people and goods, without waste or discrimination, in response to private and public demands at the lowest cost consistent with health, convenience, national security and other broad public objectives. Investment or capacity should be neither substantially above nor substantially below these requirements—for chronic excess capacity involves misuse of resources, and lack of adequate capacity jeopardizes progress. The resources devoted to provision of transportation service should be used in the most effective and efficient manner possible; and this, in turn, means that users of transport facilities should be provided with incentives to use whatever form of transportation provides them with the service they desire at the lowest total cost, both public and private.

No significant legislative action was stimulated by this message, which was designed, in the regulatory area, to decrease the incidence and improve the equity of existing transport regulation.

President Johnson's message of March 2, 1966,[20] was more successful. In it he emphasized the importance of transportation in the social and economic life of the United States and proposed the creation of a Department of Transportation to reduce the ineffectiveness of the existing dispersion of transportation activities throughout the federal government. This reorganization was approved and the new Department established, although it has less scope than was originally requested. The actual effect of the new Department of Transportation on national transport policy remains to be observed and evaluated.

In any case, the effect on regulation can only be indirect. The Department can, of course, propose legislative changes to the President and can also intervene in ICC proceedings. But the former seems unlikely to produce rapid change, and the latter is at best of uncertain strength.

The policy followed by the Interstate Commerce Commission in regulating rates (its most important activity in terms of economic impact) has been said to have the following features:

1. Each case determined on its own merits (*sui generis*).
2. No rates allowed to fall below some determination of cost.

---

given the federal government control over all interstate and international transportation. State influence in these primary areas of transport is essentially limited to highway-use taxes and regulations.

[19]H. Doc. no. 384 (87th Cong., 2nd sess.).   [20]H. Doc. no. 399 (89th Cong., 2nd sess.).

3. Encouragement of differential pricing (price discrimination) based on commodity differences.
4. Sharing of traffic among competing modes.
5. Rate stability because of regulatory procedures.[21]

This brief summary of the ICC's attitude to transport—which attitude is, incidentally, mainly the product of the provisions of the Interstate Commerce Act—suggests that this aspect of policy will show minimal response to change in the transportation environment.[22] There is a definite bias in favour of the existing regime, a bias that we would see reinforced if we were to examine the ICC's control of entry of firms into transportation.

It is not surprising that most independent students of U.S. transportation have urged a reduction in regulation. The views of John Meyer and his colleagues are fairly representative: "The clear orientation of the previous policy recommendations is toward a substantial reduction in government regulation of transportation and heavy reliance on the forces of market competition to insure services and rates in the best interest of the public. Indeed, for those sectors of transportation into which entry is quite easy, a category which includes virtually every carrier outside of the railroads and pipelines, the previous recommendations suggest virtually complete reliance on competitive forces."[23]

The identification of appropriate freight-rate policies

Controversy among transport economists concerning the appropriate level of freight rates dates back at least to the time of World War I. It is not intended here to join again in that controversy, but it is necessary to say something concerning the correct basis for freight rates.

Two polar views can be cited on this question. On the one hand, there are those who contend that freight rates should be set entirely on a demand basis, presumably with the proviso that some minimum cost be recouped. Such value-of-service pricing employs price discrimination; most rate differences do not reflect, directly, cost differences but, instead, differences in demand elasticity—in willingness to pay. The other view is that freight rates

[21]George W. Wilson, "The Effect of Rate Regulation on Resource Allocation in Transportation," *American Economic Review*, LIV, May 1964, pp. 160–9.
[22]For a well-documented case of this, see Paul W. MacAvoy and James Sloss, *Regulation of Transport Innovation: The ICC and Unit Coal Trains to the East Coast*, New York, Random House, 1967.
[23]Meyer, *et al.*, *The Economics of Competition in the Transportation Industries*, p. 270.

should be based on marginal costs. According to this prescription the additional cost incurred in producing an additional unit of transportation service would determine the price charged for that unit of service.

The value-of-service approach disturbs economists because of its potential for promoting, via the divergence of rates from costs, the misallocation of resources both within the transportation industries and in the economy generally. The marginal-cost approach, however, is unthinkable to transportation practitioners because it is so far removed from current rate policies, which are in the main value-of-service, and because it seems inevitably frustrated by certain institutional and financial factors. For example, transport firms with excess capacity must, if they base their rates on marginal cost, operate at a loss, at least in the short run.

The two approaches diverge most substantially in railroad transportation. In the other modes of transport the typical divergence between marginal and average costs is much smaller, for a variety of reasons. In this study we will make little use of direct cost/rate comparisons—the lack of suitable transport cost data forces this decision. Where such comparisons are necessary and feasible, we will adopt the point of view that rates which are substantially above variable or incremental costs[24] are undesirable. Such lack of precision is to be regretted, but the current state of transport-cost information really leaves no alternative.[25]

Canadian and U.S. transport policy and international transportation

The quotation that ended the section on U.S. transport policy is reminiscent of official Canadian policy in its recognition of the rise of competition in transportation. The crucial difference is that this is by no means *official* U.S. policy. The closest that an official U.S. pronouncement has come to the new Canadian policy is in the 1966 report of the Council of Economic Advisers.[26] The CEA in effect called for cost-oriented rates, the relaxation of control over entry and abandonment, and a quick policy response to technological change and market opportunity. But these improvements will not come

[24]These are substitutes for the economists' "marginal cost." These measures of costs would be close approximations in highway transport and more remote approximations in rail transport; the other modes would range in between. For a discussion of transport cost terminology, see George W. Wilson, *Essays on Some Unsettled Questions in the Economics of Transportation*, Bloomington, Ind., Foundation for Economic and Business Studies, 1962, pp. 31–8.

[25]In Canada the problem is one of sheer lack of such information. In the United States the difficulties are more qualitative in nature—cost data are available, but their suitability for economic analysis is often suspect.

[26]See pp. 126–9.

quickly, and U.S. policy seems likely to continue to be oriented to traditional viewpoints and procedures.

The new emphasis in Canadian federal policy towards transport is on efficiency and on the role of the transportation industries in serving the nation's economic needs. Where vital social needs diverge from economic needs, subsidies are provided to allow the former to be met without financial damage to the carriers involved. Protection of modes and firms is downgraded, and shippers are expected, in the vast majority of cases, to be able to obtain protection through the existence of alternative transport services. So, even though Canadian transportation industries have quite a high level of concentration, competition between modes is relied on to avoid monopoly abuse within any one mode. The above is, at least, the version of policy for all transport modes except trucking; and this industry, although provincially regulated, cannot really escape the force of the competitive approach.

The United States has a more complex and comprehensive system of regulation of transport. There is a built-in resistance to change of this system that may well be the key feature of U.S. transport policy. Both Congress and the Interstate Commerce Commission itself approach change very cautiously. Neither is likely to favour a significant shift to the sorts of principles inherent in the new Canadian policy. Rather, the existing system seems likely to endure, and along with it the emphasis on preservation of the various transport industries. Competition will be given a free rein only insofar as it originates in unregulated transportation (mainly private and exempt trucking).

The basic anomaly between the two countries' policies exists in rail transportation and in competition between railways and the other modes of transport. Here Canadian policy encourages intermodal competition, and U.S. policy restricts it. In air transportation the situation is reversed. This, however, has little impact on air transport between the two countries, since this is controlled by direct negotiation between the Canadian and U.S. governments. Water transport provides few policy differences within or between Canada and the United States. Pipeline transportation may perhaps be ignored in this study for the reasons outlined in chapter 2. In highway transport, Canadian policy—as chaotically defined by the provincial governments—seems to allow trucking companies considerable freedom in their operations. But this freedom ends at each of the provincial boundaries. Extra-provincial trucking in Canada (including international trucking) has been given far less encouragement to develop than in the United States. The details of this anomaly and its trade effects are explored in a later chapter.

4. Railway Transportation and Canada-U.S. Trade

Introduction

Chapter 2 showed the importance of rail transport in North American commodity trade. In 1964, 44 percent of the value of Canada's exports to the United States moved by rail, as did 38 percent of the value of Canadian imports from the United States. Railroads carried at least 5 percent of 23 of the 24 export commodity groups (all except petroleum and natural gas) and of each of the 18 import commodity groups for which a railroad share could be most accurately estimated. Moreover, railroads have a pervasive influence on transportation in all regions and sectors of both Canada and the United States. Railroads compete with all modes of transport for traffic, being able to offer a variety of service and price attributes that ranges across practically the entire transport-demand spectrum. Public policy towards railroad transport is thus probably the key variable in analyzing the impact of transport policies on North American trade, since rail transport is responsible for the largest share of the total value of trade within North America.[1] This importance is reinforced by the centralization of railroad policy formulation in both countries.

Canadian railway transport policy

A. THE CANADIAN RAILWAY INDUSTRY

In 1965 the twenty-nine railroads operating in Canada had rail operating revenues of $1,510 million.[2] Invested capital totaled $5,031 million, and income before fixed charges was $108.2 million. There were 154,832 people

[1]In 1964 rail accounted for $3.8 billion of total trade between Canada and the United States. Highway transport's share was $3.6 billion. In 1965 highway transport had moved into a slight lead (using 1964 modal shares for 1965 imports), and by 1966 this lead would undoubtedly have widened. See chap. 2 for further discussion.
[2]Statistics in this paragraph from Dominion Bureau of Statistics, *Railway Transport*, 1965, Part II, *Financial Statistics*, and Part VI, *Employment Statistics*, Ottawa, Queen's Printer, 1966.

employed by the railroads. The industry is highly concentrated; in 1965 Canadian National Railways accounted for 51 percent of the rail operating revenues, 73 percent of the invested capital,[3] 26 percent of the income before fixed charges, and 56 percent of the employees. For the Canadian Pacific Railway Company the percentages were 38 for revenue, 19 for capital, 42 for rail income before fixed charges, 123 for total net income, and 38 for employees.

This degree of concentration gives to Canadian railway transportation the characteristics of duopoly. With 90 percent of the market controlled by two firms and the remaining 10 percent spread among twenty-seven other railroads, none of which has much more than 3 percent of the market, the two large railways effectively dominate Canadian railway transport. Their dominant position comes into clearer focus when we consider the widespread operations of the two major railways. Almost every Canadian economic region and every commodity produced in this country is affected by these two giants. Very little of the Canadian economy, in regional and commodity terms, is affected by any one of the smaller railroads.

Our discussion of Canadian public policy towards railway transport will begin with an examination of the role of U.S.-owned railways in Canadian transportation. From there we will move to a discussion of the regulation of rates, service and finances, and intermodal competition under the Railway Act and the new National Transportation Act.

Six U.S. railroads owned and operated 554 route miles in Canada in 1965.[4] Most of this mileage consisted of "bridge" lines handling traffic from Detroit to Buffalo through southern Ontario. Most of the traffic on these lines originated and terminated in the United States. The other important U.S.-owned mileage in Canada was in British Columbia, where the Great Northern Railroad Company operated over 100 miles of transborder railroad carrying imports and exports between Canada and the United States. Service is also provided into Manitoba. These railroads are treated for policy and regulatory purposes as though they were Canadian-owned. The mileage operated by U.S. railroads in Canada has decreased over the last several decades. It is a moot point whether, had this trend been reversed, such equitable treatment would have been continued.

---

[3]The correctness of the valuation of capital invested in railways is open to question. Particularly is this so for Canadian National—the railway's management has been trying to obtain a capital reorganization for several years.
[4]DBS, *Railway Transport*, 1965, Part III: *Equipment, Track and Fuel Statistics* (1966). Another 688 miles of railroad was operated by U.S. railroads, mainly over lines owned by U.S. railroad companies. Association of American Railroads, *Railroad Mileage by States*, December 31, 1965, Washington, Association of American Railroads, 1966.

B. REGULATION OF RAIL FREIGHT RATES

Under the new National Transportation Act, railway freight rates are controlled by the Canadian Transport Commission.[5] Railroads must file tariffs with the Commission,[6] and the Commission may require proof that the rate is compensatory. A compensatory rate is one that "exceeds the variable cost of the movement of the traffic concerned as determined by the Commission."[7] A companion to this rate "floor" is the "ceiling" prescribed in the new Section 336 of the Railway Act. A shipper who has no alternative means of common carrier transport may ask the Commission to set a maximum rate on his traffic. The rate is to be set at 250 percent of the variable cost of carrying the traffic. The shipper is then required, once the maximum rate has been fixed, to ship all his goods by rail.[8]

The provisions outlined in the preceding paragraph do not apply to less-than-carload freight traffic,[9] grain and flour exported from the Lakehead, Churchill, and Pacific coast ports,[10] and grain and flour exported from ports east of Montreal.[11] Nor do they apply to traffic to and from the United States.[12] Special transitional protection is provided for some traffic moving to, within, and from the Maritime provinces[13] and on traffic moving across northern Ontario between western and eastern Canada in either direction.[14]

Mention should also be made of agreed charges. This type of rate would be lawful under the amended Railway Act, but was first introduced in Canadian transportation in the Transport Act,[15] which is still in effect. An agreed charge is a special low rate which railroads make available to shippers selected by them in exchange for a guaranteed annual percentage (usually about 90 percent) of the traffic of shippers. All competing rail carriers must consent to or join in the agreed charge, and shippers who feel the charge unjustly discriminates against them may apply to the Commission for their own agreed charge or charges.[16] Rates of the agreed-charge type are not generally lawful in the United States, and the Transport Act restricts their application to traffic between Canadian points.

There is little provision for control of intermodal competition in Canadian

[5]14–15–16 Eliz. II, c. 69, Parts I and V. Part V of this Act, dealing with freight rates, consists of amendments to the Railway Act, RSC, c. 170.
[6]14–15–16 Eliz. II, c. 69, sec. 48.
[7]Ibid., sec. 53.
[8]Ibid.
[9]New Section 317 of the Railway Act (ibid., sec. 44) provides for maximum rate control when the tariff rate is ". . . such as to take undue advantage of a monopoly situation. . . ."
[10]Ibid., sec. 50.   [11]Ibid.   [12]Ibid., sec. 53.
[13]Ibid.   [14]Ibid., sec. 74.   [15]RSC., c. 271.
[16]Ibid., sec. 32, as amended.

railroad freight-rate regulation. Only two provisions exist. One of the new amendments to the Railway Act requires that railroads make available the same facilities at the same rates to independent for-hire trucking companies as they do to their own trucking subsidiaries.[17] A second reference to inter-modal competition is contained in a 1961 amendment to the Transport Act. This allows trade associations of motor carriers to protest to the Minister of Transport agreed charges that are unjustly discriminatory or place a motor carrier at an unfair disadvantage. The Minister may refer the complaint to the Commission for investigation.[18]

C.   OTHER REGULATORY POLICIES

There are no explicit controls of intermodal acquisitions or mergers in Canada. Thus it is that probably the three largest trucking complexes in Canada are owned by the two major railways and Canada Steamship Lines, Ltd., the largest water carrier in the country. The railways' entry into truck-ing occurred over the bitter protests of trucking-industry organizations, but this opposition has become rather muted in recent years, perhaps after recognition of a *fait accompli*.

The Railway Act contains provisions respecting railway finance, mergers and acquisitions, and safety facilities and regulation. The Commission's approval must be obtained before the commencement of any railroad con-struction.

It is probably appropriate in this survey of Canadian railroad regulation to refer to the position of Canadian National Railways. This railway is treated as any other in the statutory expressions of government transporta-tion policy. However, it is a Crown corporation, and thus its activities are subject to a certain measure of control by the government and an often hysterical degree of scrutiny by members of parliament generally. This mani-fests itself in the daily question period and, to a lesser extent, during the appearances of Canadian National executives before the Commons Com-mittee on Transport and Communications. The point is that this railway, which accounts for over half of railway operating revenues in Canada, is subject in various formal and informal ways to aspects of transportation policy that may never be written into law. Attempts to study the form and substance of the Canadian National's relationship with the government have been made,[19] but these cannot reveal the full impact of this relationship.

[17]14–15–16 Eliz. II, c. 69, sec. 45. This refers to piggyback operations.
[18]9–10 Eliz. II, c. 63, sec. 1.
[19]See L. D. Musolf, *Public Ownership and Accountability: The Canadian Experience*, Cambridge, Mass., Harvard University Press, 1959.

D. PROMOTION AND SUBSIDIZATION

From regulation we move to promotion of railroads in Canada to see how Canadian policy has encouraged, morally, administratively, and financially, the development of this mode of transport. The scope of railroad promotion in various periods of Canadian history is well known. Cash subsidies, land grants, loan guarantees, duty remissions, and guarantee of monopoly rights have all played a part in the development of the Canadian railroad industry. (The reasons for this promotion were pointed out in chapter 3.)

The structure of promotional policy towards railways in Canada is undergoing a sharp change now under the influence of the National Transportation Act. The act provides for subsidy payments declining in equal annual amounts from $110 million in 1967 to $12 million in 1974. The subsidies are to be allocated by the Canadian Transport Commission. Subsidy payments will be discontinued in 1975,[20] except for payments under three special categories. Subsidies will be paid to the railways for operating unprofitable branch lines,[21] for providing unprofitable passenger service,[22] and for providing reduced rates on grain and flour moving to ports east of Montreal for export.[23] Four other railway subsidies exist outside the National Transportation Act and will be continued. Under the Maritime Freight Rates Act,[24] rates on traffic moving within "select territory" (the Atlantic provinces and Quebec east of Quebec City) are reduced by 20 percent, and rates on traffic moving *from* select territory to Canadian destinations are reduced by 30 percent.[25] The MFRA subsidy, which is paid directly to the railways, totaled $14.5 million in the fiscal year ending March 31, 1967.[26] The deficit of Canadian National Railways may also be considered a railway subsidy. Exclusive of losses on east coast ferry and steamship services, Canadian National received payments of $25 million from the government to cover its fiscal year 1966/67 deficit.[27]

Two other railway subsidies are tied to shipments of particular commodities. The transportation of coal is subsidized under various Orders-in-Council

[20]For details of these "normal payments," see 14–15–16 Eliz. II, c. 69, sec. 74.
[21]*Ibid.*, sec. 42.
[22]*Ibid.*
[23]*Ibid.*, sec. 50.
[24]RSC, c. 174.
[25]Originally conceived of as a device to widen the market of Maritime producers, the Maritime Freight Rates Act has contributed over time less and less to this end. A recent study of the Act was highly critical of the procedures, impact, and objectives of this subsidy. See the Economist Intelligence Unit, *Atlantic Provinces Transportation Study*, Vol. V, *Legislation and Public Policy*, Ottawa, Queen's Printer, 1967, pp. 1–93.
[26]Canada, *Estimates for the Fiscal Year Ending March 31, 1968*, Ottawa, Queen's Printer, 1967, p. 530.
[27]*Ibid.*, p. 526. The deficit has run as high as $67.5 million, in the 1960 calendar year.

in order to make high-cost Canadian coal competitive with imported coal and alternative fuels.[28] These "subvention payments" are made directly to railways (and to water carriers) and amounted to $33.3 million in the 1966/67 fiscal year.[29] Most of the payments are made in respect of coal mined in Nova Scotia and transported to central Canada—in recent years the subvention has amounted to between $5 and $6 per ton.[30]

The final formal transportation subsidy is the feed-grain subsidy, administered by the Department of Forestry and Rural Development and paid directly to consignees. The subsidy "contributes in varying amounts to equalizing the cost of Prairie feed grains used for livestock and poultry feeding in other areas across Canada."[31] In the 1966/67 fiscal year $21.7 million was paid to feed dealers and livestock and poultry feeders.[32]

One quasi-subsidy remains to be discussed. This is the subsidy inherent in the frozen rates on the rail movement of grain and flour for export—the Crow's Nest grain rates. Under present authority of Section 328 of the Railway Act, rates on this traffic are set at 3 cents per hundredweight below the level of rates in effect in 1897. The amount of subsidy implicit in this statutory requirement is difficult to fix. The 1961 Royal Commission on Transportation made attempts in this direction,[33] but their findings were not included, in spirit or in detail, in the recent National Transportation Act. Some idea of the shortfall between railroad revenues under the Crow's Nest rates and revenues under "normal" rates can be obtained from comparing U.S. and Canadian rates on export grain. In a recent study, U.S. rates were found to be 3.3 to 4.1 times as high as Canadian rates on grain moving east for export and 2.5 to 3.9 times as high on grain moving west for export.[34] Assuming a reasonable degree of competition for this U.S. traffic (a safe

[28]See Dominion Coal Board, *Annual Report*, 1964–65, pp. 71–2, for a summary of these Orders.
[29]*Estimates*, 1967, p. 113. The figure includes payments to water carriers.
[30]Dominion Coal Board, *Annual Report*, 1964–65, p. 23. The prospects are for increased subsidies being required. For a thorough analysis of coal-mining assistance policies, see J. R. Donald, *The Cape Breton Coal Problem*, Ottawa, Queen's Printer, 1966.
[31]Royal Commission on Transportation, *Report*, Vol. II, Ottawa, Queen's Printer, 1961, 1966, p. 120.
[32]*Estimates*, 1967, p. 194.
[33]Royal Commission on Transportation, *Report*, Vol. I, 1961, 1966, pp. 28–30. The shortfall on variable costs in 1958 was estimated at $6 million. A further $16.3 million was determined to be an appropriate contribution to fixed costs. See also E. P. Reid, "Statutory Grain Rates," Royal Commission on Transportation, *Report*, Vol. III, 1962, pp. 368–407.
[34]John Lorne McDougall, "The Relative Level of the Crow's Nest Grain Rates in 1899 and in 1965," *Canadian Journal of Economics and Political Science*, XXXII, Feb. 1966, pp. 52–3.

assumption), we may conclude that the abolishing of the Crow's Nest rates would have added about $154 million to the revenues of Canadian railroads in 1965, *if there had been no diminution of traffic because of the higher rates.*[35]

Transportation policy in Canada is now, at the federal level, generally oriented to the creation of an efficient system of transportation. This orientation is particularly clear in the new statutory provisions concerning the regulation of railway freight rates. The direction of thrust in the application of these provisions by the Canadian Transport Commission remains to be seen. The competitive orientation is less clear when we examine policy in the realm of promotion—especially as exemplified in the five subsidies that have just been discussed. In general these subsidies represent an intrusion of special regional considerations—political and economic—into the model of a competitive transportation system conceived of by the 1961 Royal Commission and delivered in the National Transportation Act.

U.S. railway transport policy

A.   THE U.S. RAILWAY INDUSTRY

As of June 30, 1966, there were 569 line-haul and terminal and switching railroads in the United States.[36] Investment in the line-haul railroads amounted to $35.5 billion at the end of 1965, and in the same year income before fixed charges was $1.35 billion. For the 76 Class I line-haul railroads (those having annual operating revenues of $5 million or more) which dominate the industry, 1965 operating revenues were $10.6 billion. The Class I railroads had 639,961 employees in 1965.

The degree of concentration in the U.S. railroad industry is much less than in its Canadian counterpart. In 1965, the largest Class I railroad, the Pennsylvania, accounted for just under 10 percent of total Class I operating revenues, and the other firms' market shares ranged down from this. When we examine the degree of regional concentration in the U.S. railroad industry, we retain the impression that even on this level the industry is less concen-

[35]In 1965 Canadian railroads received $76,970,000 from transporting grain and flour under the Crow's Nest rates. (Developed from Board of Transport Commissioners, *Waybill Analysis: Carload All-Rail Traffic*, 1965, Ottawa, Queen's Printer, 1966, Table 1, p. 3.) The estimate has been developed on the assumption that in the absence of the statutory requirement these rates would have been three times as high.
[36]All figures in this paragraph are from Interstate Commerce Commission, *80th Annual Report*, June 30, 1966, Washington, U.S. Government Printing Office, 1967, appendix H, pp. 145–64.

trated than is the case in Canada. Future mergers between railroads will increase the concentration of economic power[37] but are unlikely to transform the present pattern to the point where it is comparable with the Canadian situation.

The two major Canadian railroads owned and operated, mainly through subsidiary companies, 6,719 miles in the United States in 1965.[38] The operations were mainly oriented to traffic between the two countries, although these Canadian-owned lines were of greater local importance than their U.S.-owned counterparts in Canada. For the purposes of regulation the U.S. government affords non-discriminatory treatment to Canadian-owned and -controlled railroads.

B. REGULATION OF RAIL FREIGHT RATES

Regulation of railroad rates is carried out by the Interstate Commerce Commission under the authority of Part I of the Interstate Commerce Act.[39] Four sections are of greatest importance.

1. Section 15(1) empowers the Commission to prescribe maximum or minimum rates whenever the proposed or actual rate is "unjust or unreasonable or unjustly discriminatory or unduly preferential or prejudicial. . . ."

2. Section 15a(2) sets forth the "Rule of Rate Making." It reads as follows:

In the exercise of its power to prescribe just and reasonable rates, the Commission shall give due consideration, among other factors, to the effect of rates on the movement of traffic by the carrier or carriers for which the rates are prescribed; to the need, in the public interest, of adequate and efficient railway transportation service at the lowest cost consistent with the furnishing of such service; and to the need of revenues sufficient to enable the carriers, under honest, economical, and efficient management to provide such service.

The next subsection goes on to apply this rule to intermodal competition.

In a proceeding involving competition between carriers of different modes of transportation subject to this Act, the Commission, in determining whether a rate is lower than a reasonable minimum rate, shall consider the facts and circumstances attending the movement of the traffic by the carrier or carriers to which the rate is applicable. Rates of a carrier shall not be held up to a particular level to protect the traffic of any other mode of transportation, giving due consideration to the objectives of the national transportation policy declared in this Act.

3. According to Section 4(1) of the Act, rates may not be higher for a shorter haul than for a longer haul that includes the shorter haul. Actual

---

[37]Twenty-two merger applications were pending before the ICC on June 30, 1966. Many of these were, however, conflicting. *Ibid.*, p. 113.
[38]Association of American Railroads, *Railroad Mileage by States*.   [39]49 U.S. Code.

competition from water carriers may provide an exemption to this requirement, at the Commission's direction.
4. Section 5a provides for exemption of railroad tariff bureaus from the
anti-trust laws of the United States. Rate agreements between railroads are
permitted, subject to certain rather unrestrictive conditions.

C. OTHER REGULATORY POLICIES

A wide range of other matters pertaining to railroads is also included in the
Interstate Commerce Act. The Commission is given authority over construction, abandonment, and discontinuance of railroad lines and operations, mergers and acquisitions, and securities and finance. The new Department of Transportation has regulatory responsibility for safety.

D. PROMOTIONAL POLICIES

There is in the United States a long history of promotion of railroad transportation.[40] This aspect of national policy waned before the end of the nineteenth century, however, and since that time railroads have received little, if
any, tangible promotion from the U.S. government. Only two promotional
policies have been implemented recently. One was the loan guarantee program authorized in the Transportation Act of 1958 (Part V of the Interstate
Commerce Act) and terminated in June, 1963. Under this program $244
million worth of loans[41] for railroad capital and maintenance expenditures
were guaranteed by the ICC. The other promotional policy involves financial
assistance to, and investment in, railroads providing commuter passenger
service and high-speed intercity passenger service. Governments at all three
levels—local, state, and federal—have been involved with expenditures
totaling hundreds of millions of dollars over the last few years. It could also
be argued, of course, that the legacy of past promotional efforts, which were
generous and extensive, remains with the railroads.

E. CONTROL OF INTERMODAL COMPETITION

One aspect of policy towards railroads in the United States remains to be
discussed. This concerns relationships between railroads and other modes of
transport. We have already quoted Section 15a(3) of the Interstate Commerce Act, which seems to exclude from consideration in rate proceedings
the effect of the rate on other modes of transportation. But the statement of
national transportation policy, which was discussed in the last chapter, is
given precedence over Section 15a(3) and it requires the Commission "to

[40]For a complete treatment of this subject, see Carter Goodrich, *Government Promotion of American Canals and Railroads*, New York, Columbia University Press, 1960.
[41]ICC, *Annual Report*, 1966, Table 6, p. 115.

recognize and preserve the inherent advantages of each [mode]." As interpreted by the Commission and by the U.S. Supreme Court, the intermodal application of the "Rule of Rate Making" has generally involved using the average total cost of the competing mode of transport as the floor for railroad rates.[42] In cases where railroad marginal (or variable) costs are lower than those of the competing mode, the application of these principles assures objection to most proposals for lower freight rates. For this and other reasons most of the Commission's rate workload consists of protests to rate reductions filed by competing carriers, usually from a different mode of transport.

Concerning another facet of intermodal relationships, the acquisition or establishment, by railroads, of operations in competing modes, the Interstate Commerce Act does not prohibit such diversification, except in the case of water carriers.[43] However, the Act does limit the expansion of railroads into trucking by requiring the Interstate Commerce Commission to find, prior to approving railroad purchase of a motor carrier, that "the transaction . . . will enable . . . [the railroad] to use service by motor vehicle to public advantage in its operations. . . ."[44] This has been applied to mean that railroads may engage only in such trucking activities as are incidental to their rail operations.

Canadian and U.S. railroad transport policies compared

A comparison of Canadian and U.S. policies towards rail transportation must begin by noting the marked differences between the railroad industries of the two countries. Canada exhibits a marked degree of market concentration; the United States, relatively little. This pattern both reflects and compels policy—explicit and implicit.

The regulation of railroad rates in the United States has its basis in law rather than economics. Such phrases as "just and reasonable rates" have no specific meaning in economics; they originate in common-law concepts of the responsibilities and privileges of common carriers and, farther back, in the medieval concept of the "just price." Canada has had such legally oriented rate regulation but found it unworkable and has abandoned it in favour of a system that largely depends on competition to achieve economic equity.[45] It also depends, to a degree that cannot be ascertained, on the

[42]See, for example, *ICC* v. *New York, New Haven and Hartford Railroad Co.*, 372 U.S. 744 (1963).
[43]Sec. 5(14) of the Interstate Commerce Act. 49 USC, sec. 5(14).
[44]Sec. 5(2)(b).
[45]The National Transportation Act does contain a section, added during the Act's consideration by the House of Commons, that allows the Canadian Transport

influence of the Canadian government on the pricing actions of Canadian National Railways.

In the United States, policies of general promotion of railroad transportation now exist only in history. These promotional activities were important in their time but ceased very quickly when railroads in the United States lost their status as struggling infant industries and became grasping, exploiting, and monopolistic. Canadian railroads still benefit from government promotional policies. This promotion is now not so much in the interest of national development as of the provision of below-cost transportation for regions and industries that are believed to need such encouragement. The $223.9 million in subsidies in respect of railroad transportation in the 1966/67 fiscal year[46] represents the cost of this policy—a not inconsequential 2.5 percent of total federal budgetary expenditures.

The United States has followed policies of prohibiting railroad diversification into other modes of transport and of restricting price competition between the railroads and other modes of transport. Canadian transport policy has permitted extensive purchase of trucking companies by railroads and vigorous price competition, where desired by the railroads.

Over-all, Canadian policy has encouraged the development of railroad transportation, while U.S. policy has been, in recent years, *directly* neutral.[47] Canada has twice as much railroad mileage per capita as the United States, and this higher degree of development is both cause and consequence of Canada's transportation policies.

International railroad transportation between Canada and the United States

Two questions will be discussed: the impact of domestically oriented policies, as outlined in the previous two sections, on transborder rail transportation; and the regulation of railroad rates on traffic moving between Canada and the United States. Most of this section will be concerned with the second question, but the first deserves some attention both because it is obviously

Commission to investigate a rate that "may prejudicially affect the public interest" (Sec. 16). This provision is an afterthought in terms of both timing and philosophy, and it seems unlikely, although possible, that the Commission will investigate many freight rates on the grounds that they "create an unfair disadvantage."
[46]*Estimates*, 1967. The amount is the sum of the subsidies mentioned earlier in this chapter plus $129.4 million for subsidies no longer paid and replaced by the declining subsidy under the National Transportation Act. No allowance for the Crow's Nest grain rates is included.
[47]"Directly" because the indirect effects of government policies towards other modes of transport in the United States have probably been anti-expansionary for the railroads.

related to the second and because it is difficult to identify the effects of each
policy aspect separately.

A.   THE IMPACT OF DOMESTIC POLICY

It has been concluded that Canadian policy has been more expansionary
towards railroads than has U.S. policy. Observing, as we did in the first
paragraph of this chapter, that, in 1964, 44 percent of the value of Canadian
exports to the United States moved by rail and only 38 percent of Canadian
imports from the United States, might we be able to develop some hypo-
theses? True, volume of traffic is of more consequence in this matter than
value, but the volume pattern is even more heavily weighted to southbound
rail traffic—almost two to one.[48] Perhaps this disparity is due to the relative
commodity mixes of exports and imports—more bulky and low-value goods
moving south and higher-value goods moving north. But, it might be argued,
the efforts of successive Canadian governments to develop railroad transportation have encouraged the growth of industries that use railroad transportation. Can it be, then, that Canadian railroad policies have played an
important role in determining the composition of the nation's output and
its trade with the United States?

Definite answers to such complex cause-and-effect questions are difficult,
but it seems unlikely that unqualified affirmatives should be given to these.
Reference to chapter 1 of this study will show that transportation's role in
determining trade patterns and preferences is quite variable. For the time
being, then, we will concentrate on the second question mentioned above,
the impact of specific transport policy on traffic moving by railroad across
the border.

One minor digression seems in order. Both Canada and the United States
have special statutory provisions applying to traffic originating and terminating at domestic points but passing through the other country en route. In
the United States, Section 6(2) of the Interstate Commerce Act requires
railroads to publish through rates for such traffic or have the freight pay
customs duties, as though it were of foreign origin, when it re-enters the
United States. No significant effect follows from this requirement, which is
apparently designed only to ensure public disclosure of freight rates. The
Canadian Railway Act contains a similar requirement.[49] It is, however, of
greater significance, since its purpose is to prevent traffic from eastern to
western Canada (or *vice versa*) from moving via U.S. railroads, except with

---

[48]In 1964, 18.6 million tons Canada-U.S. and 9.4 million tons U.S.-Canada. DBS,
Railway Freight Traffic, 1964.
[49]Sec. 438.

the approval of Canadian railroads (who would have to participate in a joint rate).

B. JURISDICTION OVER INTERNATIONAL RAILROAD TRANSPORT

In discussing transborder traffic, rates will be our first concern—problems associated with equipment and customs procedures will be left for later consideration. The regulation of international rates is made difficult because neither the Canadian nor the U.S. government has extraterritorial jurisdiction. Thus Part I of the Interstate Commerce Act applies to transportation of property by railroad "from or to any place in the United States to or from a foreign country, but only in so far as such transportation takes place within the United States."[50] Canadian law is less specific, and its application is to transportation *companies* rather than to transportation activities. Section 5 of the Railway Act states that the Act "applies to all persons, railway companies and railways, within the legislative authority of the Parliament of Canada." A more specific declaration, for our purposes, is made in the Act's next section, where application is extended to "every railway company operating or running trains from any point in the United States to any point in Canada. . . ."[51] Taken together, the statutes of the two countries would seem to confer authority on each government in respect of the intranational portion of international traffic.

C. FREIGHT-RATE REGULATION TO 1940

Such traffic is, however, not separable for regulatory purposes. This is particularly so in the case of rates, for much railway traffic between Canada and the United States moves under joint through rates which are published by the participating railroads and which specify origin and destination but do not reveal the portion of the rate which is applicable to transportation within any one of the two countries. Regulatory officials of Canada and the United States have tried to match their legislative mandates to the difficulties imposed by joint through rates for almost eighty years.[52] That only informal compromises have been forthcoming testifies to the magnitude of the problem.

   Until 1920 the Interstate Commerce Commission (operating under

[50] 49 USC, sec. 1(1)(b).
[51] RSC, c. 234, sec. 6(1)(b).
[52] A complete history of the question is available in Harry G. Christopher, "Through International Railway Freight Rates between the United States and Canada," unpublished M.Sc. thesis, University of Tennessee, June 1964. See also W. T. Jackman, *Economic Principles of Transportation*, Toronto, University of Toronto Press, 1935, pp. 662–84.

another version of Section 1 of the Interstate Commerce Act) generally asserted total jurisdiction over all traffic moving between Canada and the United States in both directions. The Commission's Canadian counterpart of the time, the Board of Railway Commissioners, complied in this intrusion of U.S. authority, although it did occasionally exercise its own powers over the Canadian portion of Canada-U.S. traffic.[53]

With its authority apparently amended to exclude transportation taking place outside the United States, the Commission began to restrict its activities. Through the 1920s only the U.S. carriers were held responsible for the unreasonableness of joint international rates and then only because they had failed to publish local (intra-U.S.) rates from the border to destination.[54] By its 1945 decision in *Carstens Packing Co.* v. *Great Northern Railway Co. et al.*,[55] the Commission extended its power to rule on the reasonableness of joint international rates to cases where local U.S. rates *had* been published.

In the meantime, however, there had been a spate of concern about international rates on newsprint. Both the Interstate Commerce Commission and the Board of Railway Commissioners conducted inquiries into the level and structure of newsprint rates.[56] The decisions in the two cases were complementary and involved no clash between the two jurisdictions.[57]

D.   CURRENT U.S. POLICY REGARDING INTERNATIONAL RATES

Since the mid-1930s there has been little Canadian interest in the regulation of international rates. This is strange in some ways, because the volume of traffic moving between the two countries is very much greater now than in the depths of depression-induced protectionism. The Interstate Commerce Commission has, however, heard a few formal cases in the course of its regulation of rates on international traffic. Brief reference to these will be useful in illuminating present practice in international rate regulation.

The most recent of these cases is *Canada Packers, Ltd.* v. *Atchison, Topeka and Santa Fe Railway Co. et al.*,[58] which was finally decided by the U.S. Supreme Court on December 5, 1966. The case involved the payment

[53]Christopher, "Through International Railway Freight Rates between the United States and Canada," chaps. III and V.
[54]The leading case is *News Syndicate Co.* v. *New York Central Railroad Co. et al.*, 275 U.S. 179 (1927).
[55]264 ICC 164 (1945).
[56]*Newsprint Paper Investigation*, 197 ICC 738 (1933) and *Newsprint Case*, 24 Judgements, Orders, Regulations, and Rulings (JOR & R), p. 17.
[57]See Edward Margolin and William P. McLendon, *Transportation Factors in the Marketing of Newsprint*, Washington, U.S. Government Printing Office, 1952, pp. 37–41.
[58]313 ICC 759 (1961).

of reparations to Canada Packers in the amount of $1,690 because rates charged in 1948 by the Santa Fe and other railroads for transporting potash from New Mexico and California to eastern Canada had been declared unjust and unreasonable by the Commission. The $1,690 represented unpaid reparations claimed for the Canadian portion of the transportation. The rates were judged to be unlawful because they were too high relative to rates on potash moving from the same origins to points in the eastern United States. The Commission's decision was upheld by the District Court and reversed by the Court of Appeals for the Seventh Circuit, which said that the Commission was without jurisdiction to determine the reasonableness of freight rates for transportation taking place in Canada and hence was without power to order reparations with respect to the Canadian portion of the rate and journey. The Interstate Commerce Commission's view was that its position in this case was consistent with 46 years of regulatory practice regarding international rates and that it had not "in any manner directly interfered with the jurisdiction of any foreign government."[59] In its decision the Supreme Court accepted the Commission's argument. "It is not shown . . . that the long-standing construction of the statute by both the Commission and this Court has produced any particularly unfortunate consequences and Congress, which could easily change the rule, has not yet seen fit to intervene."[60]

Another recent case involved the transportation of sulphur from Alberta to the U.S. Midwest.[61] The jurisdictional question was disposed of with these findings:

1. On international traffic, U.S. railroads may publish rates to or from the international boundary, in which case they are answerable only for those rates, or they may participate in joint international rates.
2. If U.S. railroads follow the latter course, the Commission may order them to cease and desist from maintaining unlawful rates for international transportation.

[59]ICC, *Canada Packers, Ltd.* v. *Atchison, Topeka and Santa Fe Railway Co. et al.: Brief as Amicus Curiae*, pp. 11–14. The Commission also contended that "(1) the law of Canada recognizes the ICC's jurisdiction over an entire joint through rate, and (2) the agencies and courts of Canada exercise an identical concurrent jurisdiction over the entire joint rate when suit is brought in that forum." The first point is at variance with the facts; the *law* of Canada makes and has made no such blanket recognition, although Canadian *practice* has done so. The second point is essentially irrelevant; Canadian practice has been to allow such cases to be adjudicated by U.S. authorities.
[60]Supreme Court of the United States, *Canada Packers, Ltd.* v. *Atchison, Topeka and Santa Fe Railway Co. et al.*, no. 11-October Term, 1966, pp. 2–3.
[61]*Sulphur, Canadian Origins to East St. Louis, Ill.*, 326 ICC 288 (1966).

3. The Commission has no power to prescribe just and reasonable joint through international rates for the future and can only adjudicate the lawfulness of existing rates.[62]

As far as the facts of the case were concerned, the Commission found that the rates were compensatory (contrary to the argument of competing sulphur producers in the United States) and that they were not unreasonable by virtue of being unduly preferential to Chicago consignees of sulphur (as argued by a St. Louis sulphur buyer). The determination of the rate as "compensatory" was made, using U.S. costs, despite the fact that up to one-half the transportation took place in Canada, because: "So far as appears, there are no material differences in operating conditions as between the Western District and the movement from Canadian origins to the border."[63] However, in an illogical turn, a hearing examiner had earlier excluded evidence comparing the international rates with Canadian rates, declaring as follows: "Comparisons of assailed rates with rates to points in Canada have little meaning, in the absence of any knowledge as to how Canadian rates may have been made with relation to the statutory standards of lawfulness in the United States."[64] In accord with these and other considerations, the sulphur rates were allowed to stand as just and reasonable.

In connection with the inadmissibility of comparisons of international rates with Canadian rates, it might be pointed out that comparisons of international rates with U.S. rates have been fairly common practice. Recent examples of this have involved coke moving from Indiana to Ontario[65] and liquefied petroleum gas moving from and to, among other points, Alberta and the U.S. Midwest.[66]

E. CANADIAN POLICY REGARDING INTERNATIONAL RATES

To follow this partial review of recent ICC control of international freight rates, an examination of the activities of the now-defunct Board of Transport Commissioners in this regard will be useful. In the last five years only four Board decisions have dealt with international traffic. These have touched on the following matters:

1. The amendment of the currency exchange regulations tariff to provide

[62]For discussion of this see *Thermoid Co., Southern Division* v. *Baltimore & Ohio Railroad Co. et al.*, 303 ICC 743 (1958), affirmed in *Porter Co.* v. *Central Vermont Railroad Co.*, 366 U.S. 272.
[63]303 ICC 288, 297 (1962).   [64]326 ICC 288, 313 (1963).
[65]*Citizens Gas and Coke Utility of Indianapolis, Ind.* v. *Canadian National Railways et al.*, 325 ICC 527 (1965).
[66]*Liquefied Petroleum Gas in Jumbo Tank Cars—S.W.F.B., W.T.L., I.F.A., T-L.F.B. Terr.*, 319 ICC 31 (1966).

for the payment of a premium to Canadian shippers paying freight charges in U.S. dollars when the U.S. dollar is at a premium relative to the Canadian dollar.[67]

2. The application of the correct classification rating to complete window frames and sash.[68]

3. The application of the correct tariff on fruit and vegetable traffic from California to the Lakehead. This is a procedural issue of little regulatory significance.[69]

4. Proposed amendments to the Canadian car demurrage rules and demurrage charges in relation to, among other things, U.S. rules and charges.[70]

The reason for the lack of recent Canadian initiative in regulating international rates can be seen when we examine the factors that control the level of international rates. In its judgment of September 15, 1958, the Board of Transport Commissioners declared that "the predominant influence upon the level of the international . . . rates is the structure of rates within the United States."[71] Exception can hardly be taken to this finding—in fact, there exists a very recent example of the influence to which the Board referred. From November, 1966, to August, 1967, four separate freight-rate increases (applying, in part, to different traffic) were imposed by Canadian railways. None applied to rates on international traffic. In August, 1967, after the Interstate Commerce Commission had approved a 3 percent general rate increase (with exceptions) for U.S. railroads, an increase of identical magnitude was applied to international traffic.

Since, on the average, 40 percent of the revenue from carrying international traffic is paid to Canadian railways,[72] why should the U.S. rate level be the sole determinant of the level of international rates? The answer, according to the Board of Transport Commissioners, is that this is necessary to ensure the continued existence of joint through international rates.[73] In

[67]52 JOR & R 347.   [68]53 JOR & R 449.   [69]55 JOR & R 121.
[70]56 JOR & R 953. "Demurrage" is the daily rental fee for use of a freight car owned by another railroad.
[71]In the Matter of Freight Rates between Canada and the United States . . ., File no. 18540.99, p. 3. U.S. rates can also be influential in determining intra-Canadian rates. The Board decided, in another case heard the same year, that rates on lumber from British Columbia to eastern Canada were "tied to the Seattle rate" and moved "with the U.S. increases." General Freight Rates Investigation: Equalization of Rates on Lumber and Forest Products, File no. 47828.4, p. 40; also see p. 25.
[72]The exact percentage in any instance depends on the rate "division" that has been negotiated among the participating railroads. Rate divisions are treated as confidential railway information in Canadian regulatory practice and have not been subjected to regulation as they are in the United States. The 40 percent is used in the currency exchange regulations tariff mentioned above. See 52 JOR & R 347, 359.
[73]In the Matter of Freight Rates between Canada and the United States . . ., pp. 1–4.

the absence of these rates, international traffic would move under combinations of rates to and from the international border; and, it is argued, the resulting freight charges would be much higher. A slightly different reason for basing international rates on U.S. rate levels was given by the 1951 Royal Commission on Transportation:

Since a joint international rate is one unit, and not divisible at the boundary in so far as the shipper is concerned, the whole through rate must be advanced in both countries at the same time to keep the international rate on a parity with other rates within the United States. If this practice were not followed, the American shippers would be discriminated against within their own country by the lower international rates on shipments to or from Canada. This may best be shown by an example: If Canadian railways did not increase their rates on lumber from Vancouver to Boston simultaneously with the American railroads' increase on lumber from Seattle to Boston, mill owners at Seattle would complain of loss of markets and unjust discrimination. Railways in the United States, to protect shippers along their lines as well as to protect their own revenues, would then withdraw their concurrence in the joint international rate from Vancouver to Boston. The rate which would then apply from Vancouver to Boston would be the relatively higher one, namely, the sum of the local rates. Canadian shippers would be out of the Boston market and would be worse off than if Canadian railways had advanced their rates exactly as American carriers had done.[74]

In characteristically unimaginative fashion, the Commission neglects to trace the impact of the present practice on *Canadian* shippers competing with imports from the United States. What seems to be needed here is less awareness of "discrimination"—which can work both ways—and more attention to the economics of freight rates.

F.   A CRITIQUE OF DE FACTO U.S. REGULATION OF INTERNATIONAL RATES

It is appropriate at this point to make a few comments concerning the criteria by which the Interstate Commerce Commission judges international rates to be "just and reasonable." Two criteria are employed by the Commission—rate comparisons and cost information. Where the former are used, the emphasis is on the legal-moral approach to rate regulation. This standard need have no relationship to the economics of various rate proposals and, in fact, may only render partial justice. This results from the law's and the Commission's peculiar view of discrimination: "commodity discrimination is eulogized, place discrimination tolerated under special circumstances, and personal discrimination outlawed."[75] In any case, as we pointed out earlier, the ICC considers that rate comparisons involving Canadian rates are irrelevant. Concerning the second standard, the relationship of the rate to cost,

[74]Royal Commission on Transportation, *Report*, 1951, p. 103.
[75]George W. Wilson, "The Effect of Rate Regulation on Resource Allocation on Transportation," *American Economic Review*, LIV, May 1964, p. 167.

the willingness of the Commission to apply U.S. cost data to Canadian transportation is peculiar, considering their increasing emphasis on particularity,
especially regional particularity, in developing cost information within the
United States.[76] We will shortly develop statistics that show—on a global
and estimated basis—that railroad variable costs are about 20 percent
higher in Canada than in the United States. The existence of a disparity of
this magnitude would seem to indicate that the development of Canadian
cost information by *someone* would be an asset to future international rate
cases. Jackman's statement of 1935 seems worth quoting at this point:
". . . first, how could the Supreme Court or the Interstate Commerce Commission, knowing only the conditions in their own country, determine what
constitutes a reasonable joint international rate when neither tribunal can
come across the boundary to inquire into the conditions of the movement
in Canada; and, second, how can either of these tribunals ascertain what
is a reasonable joint rate by reference only to the portion of the haul in the
United States? It seems to us that, in assuming to have the above authority,
the tribunals concerned have gone beyond the realm of reason."[77]

The new National Transportation Act brings a new and potentially significant element of non-harmonization of transport policy in Canada and the
United States. This Act introduces a type of railroad rate regulation that
is, as was pointed out in an earlier section of this chapter, distinctly different
in philosophy from that which exists in the United States and which had
existed previously in Canada. Although international traffic is expressly
excluded from the main thrust of the new regulation,[78] one wonders how
long it will take for important anomalies to develop between rail freight rates
on products produced and sold in Canada and rates on products produced
and sold in Canada *and* in the United States. If rates on chemicals manufactured and sold in Canada are allowed to fall to the level of variable cost,
what would be the future of chemicals imported from the United States at
freight rates that were tied to the U.S. rate level and held by ICC regulation
at a level above variable cost?

Any discussion of the views of Canadian and U.S. regulatory authorities
concerning the role of cost in railroad rate-making must of necessity be
speculative. The cost-determination policies and practices of the Canadian

[76]To quote the Commission's 1966 *Annual Report* (p. 23): "Transportation costs
continue to be used more each year in proceedings before this Commission, with the
result that more knowledge and sophistication are acquired regarding the computation
and use of these costs. This trend leads to a demand for more specific costs and to a
greater reluctance to accept territorial or system average costs as an indication of the
cost of a specific traffic movement."
[77]Jackman, *Economic Principles of Transportation*, p. 675.
[78]Railway Act, sec. 336(13).

Transport Commission have yet to be revealed. Although some legislative direction is contained in the revised Railway Act,[79] the implementation of new costing methods remains to be carried out. An order of the Board of Transport Commissioners, issued during the interim period before the appointment of the Canadian Transport Commission, did set forth cost-finding regulations,[80] but these seem likely to undergo modification. Whatever form Canadian cost-finding takes, it seems certain to result in rate regulation much more closely related to marginal costs than the regulation developed under its U.S. counterpart.

The Interstate Commerce Commission has since 1962 been engaged in a lengthy investigation of cost.[81] The Commission has made an interim report,[82] and following this, a hearing examiner has recommended a report and order to the Commission.[83] While there is not space here to make detailed comments on this report, it seems safe to surmise that, if adopted, the ICC's new view of cost and, subsequently, its cost-finding procedures will please economists no more than do the present view and procedures.[84] Hemmed in by a contradictory statute and preoccupied with intermodal competition, the Commission would, if it accepted the recommended report, be affirming and perpetuating several regulatory cost-rate norms of decidedly non-economic quality. These were mentioned earlier in this chapter. What is important for us here is that the variation between the concept of the role of costs in rate regulation embodied in these proposals and the role implicit in Canadian law is quite substantial. A minimum railroad rate under U.S. regulation would probably be much higher than a minimum rate for the same traffic and the same cost structure as determined under Canadian regulation.

International rate-making procedures

Having examined the regulation of international rates, we will turn to the procedures by which the railroads *make* joint through rates on international traffic. These rate-making procedures necessarily precede the regulatory processes.

[79]Secs. 336(3), 387A, and 387B.
[80] Order no. 123994, April 5, 1967.
[81]*Rules to Govern the Assembling and Presenting of Cost Evidence*, Docket no. 34013.
[82]321 ICC 238, 1963.
[83]Docket no. 34013, "Rules to Govern the Assembling and Presenting of Cost Evidence, Report and Order Recommended by Jair S. Kaplan, Hearing Examiner," October 10, 1966, mimeo.
[84]For criticisms of current practice see, for example, John R. Meyer, *et al.*, *The Economics of Competition in the Transportation Industries*, Cambridge, Mass., Harvard University Press, 1959.

A. PROCEDURES AND STRATEGIES

Proposals for joint through-rate changes on traffic moving from Canada to the United States[85] originate with one of the Canadian railroads, either internally or at the request of a shipper or a group of shippers. From there the proposal is taken to the Canadian Freight Association—the railroads' rate-agreement organization—for approval. The Canadian Freight Association acts as a forum within which the railroads agree to set common prices for their services. Although the anti-competitive effects of such collusion seem to be an offence under Section 32 of the Combines Investigation Act,[86] the Act has never been applied, presumably because of the explicit regulation of railway freight rates under other statutes.

When the Canadian Freight Association has approved alteration of an international rate, the change must then receive the approval of an international rate bureau whose membership includes the two major Canadian railroads and any U.S. railroads who are affected, directly or indirectly, by the change. In the United States, rate bureaus, as was mentioned earlier in this chapter, have formal immunity to the anti-trust laws. This relief was provided in 1948 by the Reed-Bulwinkle Act, in response to the threat of anti-trust prosecutions by the Department of Justice.

International rate bureaus meet monthly, and their deliberations can be slow enough to delay significantly the introduction of a new rate. Moreover, outright rejection of rate proposals is far from unknown, particularly when a proposal tends to upset established producer/market relationships. U.S. railroads who feel that part of their existing traffic is threatened by a new inflow of goods from Canada, stimulated by more favourable freight rates, are not likely to concur in such rates. The potential implications of such attitudes as far as trade between the two countries is concerned will be examined later.

If the rate proposal is refused by the international bureau, the option of taking independent rate action is open to the Canadian railroad(s); in fact, this option is guaranteed under the 1948 amendment to the Interstate Commerce Act. There are, however, two considerations which limit the utilization of this alternative. First, if the circumstances of the shipment so require, agreement of one or more connecting railroads in the United States must be obtained. While Canadian railroads do penetrate the U.S. Northeast and Midwest through their U.S. subsidiaries, by far the greater part of the United States lies outside the areas served by their subsidiary lines. Second, there

[85]The procedure for rate changes on traffic moving from the United States to Canada is essentially the opposite of that to be described here.
[86]"Every one who conspires, combines, agrees or arranges with another person . . . to prevent, or lessen unduly, competition in the . . . transportation of an article . . . is guilty of an indictable offence. . . ."

seems to be a certain reluctance on the part of Canadian railways to engage in independent rate action, probably because of their understandable desire to preserve the power and influence of rate bureaus and because of the difficulties that dissenting railroads could cause when the railroads seek regulatory approval for the rate.

Before regulatory agencies enter the picture, however, one final step remains to be carried out by the railroads. This is the setting of rate divisions, the apportionment of the revenue among the various carriers that participate in transporting the traffic. Once agreement has been reached on divisions, the rates are filed with the Canadian Transport Commission and the Interstate Commerce Commission. The CTC requires that tariffs that increase rates be filed 30 days in advance of their effective date, while tariffs that reduce rates may become effective on issuance of the tariff and before filing with the Commission.[87] Under the Interstate Commerce Act the ICC requires 30 days' notice of all changes in rates.[88] The grounds for objection to new rates are much broader in the United States than in Canada. The Interstate Commerce Commission may, on its own motion or on complaint, suspend a new rate, pending investigation, for a period of up to 7 months beyond the proposed effective date.[89]

B.   TRADE EFFECTS OF INTERNATIONAL RATE-MAKING

Because of the procedures outlined above, in practice the *minimum* time required to alter international rates is estimated at 3 months. The *average* time needed to effect changes in international rates is in the order of 6 months.[90] This compares with an implementation time of days in Canada, at least where rate decreases are concerned. This would seem to give Canadian producers something of an unfair advantage in responding to the threat of increased competition from U.S. imports because of rate changes. It could also offer discouragement to exports to the United States, since the time and effort required to be expended on rate negotiations must appear to shippers to be excessive in comparison with the requirements for intra-Canadian rate negotiations.

In fact, the whole process of international rate-making should have an inhibiting effect on trade between Canada and the United States. The cum-

---

[87]Railway Act, sec. 333(2) and (3).
[88]Sec. 6(3).
[89]Interstate Commerce Act, sec. 15(7).
[90]Where the rate change is protested to the ICC, the delay is likely to be much longer. The average processing time for railroad "investigation and suspension" cases (where the lawfulness of proposed rates is determined) is 11.1 months. Investigations of existing rates take an average of 11.0 months to complete. Robert H. Haskell, "Why the Regulatory Lag?" *Transportation and Distribution Management*, 7, no. 2 Feb. 1967, p. 52.

bersome mechanism of adjustment, tolerated in the interests of preserving joint through international rates, imparts an inflexibility to the international rate structure. Not only does it take months to change rates (during which time market opportunities may easily vanish), but U.S. railroads can be expected to oppose proposals that will increase international traffic at the expense of domestic traffic. Increased exports from Canada to the United States will, therefore, be inhibited where they result in a significant dislocation of traffic patterns and volumes in the United States. This inhibition will have both commodity and geographical aspects. The influence of international rate-making procedures is thus to perpetuate, to some degree, the existing commodity mix and destination pattern of Canadian exports to the United States. The degree to which this influence is effective in any one case will depend on circumstances. Independent rate action can always be resorted to, informal "bargains" may be made in the course of international rate-bureau negotiations,[91] and freight charges are, for many export commodities, unimportant determinants of trade flows. The low freight factors of many manufactured products prevent us from identifying this freight-rate problem as a major reason for the failure of Canadian manufactured exports to the United States to show satisfactory growth.[92] But as was pointed out in the discussion of freight factors in chapter 1, a few cents on the dollar can, if competitive pressures are strong enough, make the difference between trade and no trade.

What are the effects of the international rate-making procedure on Canadian imports from the United States? First, the negotiations are apt to move faster, because only two Canadian railroads are typically involved. Nevertheless, the Canadian National and Canadian Pacific are, theoretically, in a strong position to exclude imports that diminish their traffic within Canada. Independent rate action by U.S. lines is unlikely to be feasible, unless the cooperation of one of these railroads can be obtained. Despite the undoubtedly greater *potential* for interference with northbound trade, such interference is minimal. The reason for this lies in the influence of trucking competition. Practically all major eastern Canadian markets are situated within trucking distance of U.S. producing locations—a contrasting situation to that in southbound trade. A clear example of the effectiveness of this influence is provided by Canadian railroad pricing strategy since the Automotive Free Trade Agreement of 1965. Although the Agreement has had a detrimental effect on the two major Canadian railroads,[93] they have made

[91]Voting on international rate proposals is, however, simultaneous and secret, and therefore such *quid pro quo* arrangements are inherently unstable.
[92]See M. G. Clark, *Canada and World Trade*, Economic Council of Canada, staff study no. 7, Ottawa, Queen's Printer, 1964, p. 13 and Table B-5, p. 54.
[93]See chap. 7 for further discussion.

no attempt to frustrate the increased north-south flow of parts and vehicle traffic, presumably because of the existence of an alternative mode of transport-trucking. While similar conditions are not universal in traffic from the United States to Canada, they are far more common than in traffic from Canada to the United States.

There are, of course, legal remedies available to Canadian shippers who feel they are being treated unfairly in international rate negotiations. Such shippers may protest to the Interstate Commerce Commission regarding rates that are "unjust or unreasonable, or unjustly discriminatory or unduly preferential or prejudicial . . . ."[94] This protection is, however, imperfect and uncertain. As was pointed out earlier in this chapter, Commission decisions under this section are not based on any firm rule or guidelines but are instead determined by often subjective consideration of cost information, competitive relationships, and rate comparisons. In short, it is fully possible for an international rate to retard Canadian exports to the United States and yet fail to be disallowed under Section 15(1) of the Interstate Commerce Act.[95]

The level of international rates

A.   HISTORICAL RATE RELATIONSHIPS IN NORTH AMERICA

We now turn to an examination of the level of international railroad freight rates. It is commonly believed that international rates are 10 percent higher than rates within the United States.[96] The basis for this belief is undoubtedly historical and dates back to the period when the preservation of the freight-rate structure—the relationships between rates—was of prime concern to regulatory agencies in both Canada and the United States. The class-rate scale was the basis for the freight-rate structure, and commodity and other rates were built into the structure in accordance with the level and taper of class rates.

[94]Interstate Commerce Act, sec. 15(1).
[95]For such a decision see *Consolidated Mining & Smelting Company of Canada, Ltd., et al. v. Baltimore & Ohio Railroad Company, et al.*, 286 ICC 313 (1952). The case involved rates on lead and zinc from British Columbia to the eastern United States. Although the rates were up to 15 percent higher than the rates from western U.S. smelters over similar lengths of haul, the Commission found them to be lawful. The decision was apparently based on the fact that "since 1945 the importation of zinc from Canada increased from 44,595 to 109,710 tons" (p. 322) and on the Commission's feeling that "international rates may be somewhat higher than those published for domestic movements of the same commodities without being unreasonable for the transportation within the United States" (p. 321).
[96]From various interviews and correspondence in connection with this study.

With the rise of intermodal competition these considerations have become less important and have, in fact, virtually disappeared in Canadian regulation. But even during the time that the preservation of the structure of freight rates was an important consideration, the 10 percent surcharge on international rates was only partially in existence. Class rates within "Official Territory" (16 Lake and northeastern states) *were* 10 percent higher than rates from eastern Canada to destinations in these states. But rates from Southern Territory to Official Territory were 35 percent higher than intra–Official Territory rates (25 percent higher than international rates); rates from Western Trunk-Line Territory (8 Plains states) were 37 percent higher (27 percent higher than international rates); and rates from Southwestern Territory were 49 percent higher (39 percent higher than international rates).[97] So, to speak of international rates as "10 percent higher" omits many significant competitive factors. Canadian producers shipping by rail to the major U.S. markets actually enjoyed a competitive advantage, in terms of lower freight rates, over producers located in at least parts of 25 states. Even comparing the Canada-official versus intra-official rates, the 10 percent "disadvantage" is shown to have been variable in either direction upon examination of class-related commodity rates.[98]

B.   1964 INTERNATIONAL FREIGHT RATES ON SELECTED COMMODITIES

Information concerning the 1964 level of international freight rates on the most important rail-carried Canadian exports to, and imports from, the United States has been obtained for this study. The statistics were supplied by Canadian National Railways and the Canadian Pacific Railway Company. Rather than use actual freight rates as the basis for analysis of international rate levels, it was decided to use revenue, tonnage, and origin and destination information provided by these two railroads. This procedure has two

[97]Frank L. Barton, "Principal International and Interterritorial Class-Rate Structures of North America," *Essays in Transportation in Honour of W. T. Jackman*, ed. Harold A. Innis, Toronto, University of Toronto Press, 1941, Table I, p. 39.
[98]For newsprint rates, see Margolin and McLendon, *Transportation Factors in the Marketing of Newsprint*, Table 22, p. 40; Table 26, p. 49; and Tables 39 and 40, pp. 81 and 83.

Sources: Traffic and revenue statistics for 1964 provided by Canadian National Railways and the Canadian Pacific Railway Company. Lengths of haul calculated from railroads' origin and destination information.
Note: Inaccuracies due to rounding cause minor discrepancies in the relationships between tons, length of haul, and revenues. Revenue per ton *should* equal revenue per ton-mile multiplied by length of haul. The largest discrepancies are of the order of 1 percent of revenue per ton.
"See Table 67 for the composition of these commodity groups.
[b]Canada figures are weighted averages (by tons shipped) and may include regional components not shown separately.

TABLE 83

INTERNATIONAL RAILROAD FREIGHT RATES ON SELECTED CANADIAN EXPORTS, 1964

Commodity	Region of origin	Average revenue per ton (dollars)	Average length of haul (miles)	Average revenue per ton-mile (cents)
Lumber and plywood[a]	Atlantic	15.55	759	2.05
	Quebec	20.45	1,418	1.44
	Ontario	16.96	1,331	1.27
	Prairies	20.99	2,010	1.04
	B.C.	26.56	2,432	1.09
	Canada[b]	25.00	2,218	1.13
Fertilizers	Atlantic	18.73	1,049	1.79
	Ontario	7.19	513	1.40
	Prairies	15.16	1,154	1.31
	B.C.	11.80	679	1.74
	Canada	13.29	1,042	1.28
Aluminum and alloys	Quebec	15.60	902	1.73
	B.C.	23.89	2,811	0.85
	Canada	22.68	2,520	0.90
Nickel and alloys	Ontario	22.20	841	2.64
	Prairies	36.69	2,235	1.64
	Canada	32.02	1,794	1.78
Primary and manufactured iron and steel	Ontario	10.03	448	2.24
	B.C.	14.96	1,163	1.29
	Canada	11.72	666	1.76
Agricultural machinery	Ontario	35.95	954	3.77
	Canada	36.18	954	3.79
Woodpulp	Atlantic	14.97	943	1.59
	Quebec	13.36	658	2.03
	Ontario	14.53	870	1.66
	Prairies	18.80	2,345	0.80
	B.C.	20.34	2,915	0.70
	Canada	16.53	1,594	1.04
Newsprint	Atlantic	20.15	874	2.31
	Quebec	19.62	694	2.83
	Ontario	17.14	948	1.81
	Prairies	16.95	937	1.81
	B.C.	16.22	1,223	1.33
	Canada	18.41	830	2.22

See facing page for sources.

important advantages: it protects the investigation from being influenced by "paper" rates—published rates under which no traffic moves—and it automatically provides information concerning the importance of different freight rates in relation to the volume of traffic moved under each.[99]

Seven import commodity groups and eight export commodity groups were selected. (These are the same groups for which traffic-volume statistics were presented in Tables 66 and 67, respectively, chapter 2.) The seven import groups accounted for 50 percent of the total value of rail-borne imports from the United States in 1964 (19 percent of total imports), while the eight export groups included 72 percent of the total value of rail-borne exports to the United States in 1964 (32 percent of total exports).

Tables 83 and 84 show the average 1964 railroad freight rates on selected traffic moving in both directions between Canada and the United States. A few explanations and cautions are in order before the data are analyzed. The average rates (revenues) are based only on traffic originated on the Canadian National and Canadian Pacific in the case of exports and on traffic terminated on these two railways in the case of imports. The major effect of this limitation is that some commodities (notably lumber and plywood exports and iron and steel exports) and one region (British Columbia) are only sparsely covered. Most rail-carried imports of fruit and vegetables from the United States into British Columbia, for instance, are delivered at Vancouver on the Great Northern Railway. The lengths of haul are short-line mileages, as opposed to straight-line mileages, which would be less, and "actual" mileages which, reflecting circuitous routing practices, would be

---

[99]For example, suppose we were comparing two rates on lumber, one from Kamloops, B.C., to Portland, Oregon, at $1.25/100 lbs. and the other from North Bay, Ontario, to Toledo, Ohio, at 40 cents/100 lbs. Both hauls are approximately 600 miles. Without knowing volume information, we cannot evaluate the significance of these two rates. If, however, we are told that in a certain year 1,000 tons of lumber moved from Kamloops to Portland and generated freight revenues of $25,000, while 20,000 tons of lumber moved from North Bay to Toledo and generated freight revenues of $160,000, we can compare the two freight rates precisely and develop an accurate measure of the average freight rate, which is 44 cents/100 lbs. The average revenue per ton is $8.80, and the average revenue per ton-mile is 1.47 cents.

Sources: Traffic and revenue statistics for 1964 provided by Canadian National Railways and the Canadian Pacific Railway Company. Lengths of haul calculated from railroads' origin and destination information.

Note: Inaccuracies due to rounding cause minor discrepancies in the relationships between tons, length of haul, and revenues. Revenue per ton *should* equal revenue per ton-mile multiplied by length of haul. The largest discrepancies are of the order of 1 percent of revenue per ton.

[a]See Table 66 for the composition of these commodity groups.

[b]Canada figures are weighted averages (by tons shipped) and may include regional components not shown separately.

TABLE 84

INTERNATIONAL RAILROAD FREIGHT RATES ON SELECTED CANADIAN IMPORTS, 1964

Commodity	Region of destination	Average revenue per ton (dollars)	Average length of haul (miles)	Average revenue per ton-mile (cents)
Fresh and frozen fruit and vegetables[a]	Atlantic	49.81	3,404	1.46
	Quebec	44.60	2,677	1.67
	Ontario	44.50	2,412	1.84
	Prairies	41.06	2,203	1.86
	Canada[b]	44.89	2,616	1.72
Cotton	Atlantic	31.90	2,413	1.32
	Quebec	25.07	1,610	1.56
	Ontario	23.90	1,199	1.99
	Canada	25.10	1,525	1.65
Chemicals	Quebec	26.17	794	3.30
	Ontario	21.32	840	2.54
	Prairies	41.77	1,271	3.29
	B.C.	32.93	2,312	1.42
	Canada	24.62	960	2.54
Primary and manufactured iron and steel	Atlantic	30.47	1,011	3.01
	Quebec	21.89	534	4.10
	Ontario	16.88	508	3.32
	Prairies	28.71	963	2.98
	B.C.	31.86	1,851	1.72
	Canada	23.61	774	3.05
Agricultural machinery	Quebec	42.40	975	4.35
	Ontario	28.80	535	5.38
	Prairies	47.68	1,313	3.63
	Canada	42.93	1,099	3.91
Industrial machinery	Atlantic	50.96	1,611	3.16
	Quebec	36.90	885	4.17
	Ontario	28.41	555	5.12
	Prairies	52.92	1,498	3.53
	B.C.	66.94	2,283	2.93
	Canada	42.78	1,155	3.70
Motor vehicle parts	Ontario	24.24	453	5.35
	Canada	24.87	467	5.32

See facing page for sources.

longer.[100] The inclusion of regional commodity detail in Tables 83 and 84 was on the basis of trade value; all the rail-carried exports and imports by region shown in the tables were estimated to have been worth more than $2 million in 1964. Regional export values in 1964 ranged up to about $190 million for lumber from British Columbia and newsprint from Quebec, while the most valuable import group in 1964 was automobile parts into Ontario at about $215 million.

Warning may be in order against the hasty development of conclusions to the effect that particular regions are discriminated against because the freight rate they pay on exports to and/or imports from the United States is unfairly high when compared to rates paid by other regions. No such conclusions are tenable without the consideration of other factors. We will present some analysis of these statistics with a view towards exploring the regional impact of the international freight-rate structure.

Three approaches to analysis of these international rates will be presented. First we will compare the level of these rates to rate levels for domestic traffic in Canada and in the United States. We will be interested in both the *general* level of international freight rates, in an attempt to evaluate the truism that "international rates are 10 percent higher than U.S. domestic rates," and in the specific level of rates on each commodity group. This first analytical approach will reveal any disparities between rail freight rates charged to domestic and to foreign suppliers of the same commodities. The second type of analysis will disclose any particular rail freight-rate disadvantages faced by producers or consumers in the different regions of Canada. The disadvantages, if any, will of course be supplementary to those inherent in regional locations. Finally, we will attempt to develop some conclusions with respect to the relationship between railroad rates on international traffic and the costs of carrying this traffic.

C.   COMPARISONS OF INTERNATIONAL AND DOMESTIC
     RAILROAD FREIGHT RATES

Statistics showing, for various commodity groups, the levels of international, Canadian, and U.S. freight rates are presented in Tables 84 and 85.

Before analyzing the contents of these tables, we should mention two difficulties. One is the source of the U.S. and Canadian rates. They are developed from a 1 percent sample of railroad waybills carried out by the regulatory agency in each country. The sample generated 23,791 waybills in

[100]Within the United States average circuity (the ratio of the difference between short-line miles and actual miles to short-line miles) has been estimated at 13 percent. There is considerable commodity and territorial variation around this average. Interstate Commerce Commission, *Explanation of Rail Cost Finding Procedures and Principles Related to the Use of Costs*, 1963, pp. 149–54.

TABLE 85

FREIGHT RATES ON SELECTED CANADIAN EXPORTS, 1964
(cents per ton-mile)

	International		United States		Canada	
	Rate	Length of haul (miles)	Rate	Length of haul (miles)	Rate	Length of haul (miles)
Lumber and plywood[a]	1.13	2,218	1.20	1,545	1.41	1,139
Fertilizers	1.28	1,042	1.25	597	1.17	779
Aluminum and alloys	0.90	2,520	1.41	995	2.00	492
Nickel and alloys	1.78	1,794	2.39	286	1.71	1,105
Primary and manufactured iron and steel	1.76	666	2.19	387	1.71	590
Agricultural machinery	3.79	954	3.63	770	4.17	1,206
Woodpulp	1.04	1,594	1.27	900	1.74	655
Newsprint	2.22	830	1.97	602	2.50	387

Sources: International rates: Table 83; U.S. rates: Interstate Commerce Commission, *Carload Waybill Statistics*, 1963. *Territorial Distribution, Traffic and Revenue by Commodity Classes*, Washington, ICC, 1965; Canadian rates: Board of Transport Commissioners, *Waybill Analysis: Carload All-Rail Traffic*, 1964, Ottawa, Queen's Printer, 1965.
Note: U.S. data are for 1963. A major change in the freight commodity classification in the United States has made U.S. 1964 statistics non-comparable with the international statistics, which were collected for 1964. Differences between the two years on an aggregate basis are quite minor. Revenue per ton-mile declined by 2.1 percent, and average length of haul declined by 0.6 percent. It is believed that differences between the two years for the commodity groups shown in this table are similarly minor. An exception is fertilizers, for which the average U.S. rate appears to have increased by about 20 percent between 1963 and 1964.
[a]See Table 67 for the composition of these commodity groups.

Canada in 1964 and 250,860 waybills in the United States in 1963.[101] Despite the absolute magnitude of these samples, we may question whether a 1 percent sample, lacking any stratification, is suitably accurate when applied to such a diverse universe as railroad freight traffic. The *international* rate data were, incidentally, developed from actual revenue statistics and are of higher quality. The second difficulty arises out of the Canadian waybill sample's treatment of railway subsidies. The effects of the Maritime Freight Rates Act subsidy and part of a general subsidy (paid to the railways until the end of 1966 to offset higher labour costs) are included; the effects of other subsidies are excluded. Adjustment is, unfortunately, impossible.

There is a fairly obvious difference in the average lengths of haul among international, U.S., and Canadian traffic. For Canadian exports (Table 84) the unweighted averages for the eight commodity groups are 1,452 miles for international, 760 miles for U.S., and 794 miles for Canadian. For Canadian imports (Table 86) the figures are 1,228 miles, 730 miles, and 599 miles.

[101]See note to Table 85 explaining the use of 1963 U.S. data.

Canadian and U.S. lengths of haul equal (or nearly equal) to the international haul could have been selected, but this would have meant using only a fraction of the traffic sampled in each commodity group. Such arbitrary selection was believed to be most undesirable, and in any case, the analytical procedures which have been developed circumvent the potential difficulty of varying lengths of haul.

The general level of international rates for export commodity groups is higher than the U.S. rate level for the same groups. Statistical analysis of the rate levels was carried out by means of the following regression equation:

$$Y = f(X_1, X_2, X_3, X_4)$$

where

Y = revenue per ton-mile in cents
X_1 = distance in miles
X_2 = dummy variable for international traffic
X_3 = dummy variable for U.S. traffic
X_4 = dummy variable for Canadian traffic.

In computation the dummy variable for Canada (X_4) was dropped.[102]

The choice of independent variables in this equation carries the implicit assumption that, within each commodity group, distance is the only real variable affecting the level of rates. Variations in rates within commodity groups that are not explained by variations in distance must therefore be due to the *type* of rate—international, U.S., or Canadian. Differences among international, U.S., and Canadian rate levels could be due to cost differences, differences in regulatory policy, or differences in railroad rate practices. For the time being, we will assume that rate differences are due to either or both of the last two of these influences. Consideration of possible cost differences will be left to later.

The data in Table 85 provided 21 observations. The three rate-distance combinations for agricultural machinery were eliminated from the analysis because of the magnitude of the rate (revenue per ton-mile) and the positive relationship between rate and distance. The following values for the equation were developed:

$$Y = 2.166 - .0005224X_1 + .3293X_2 - .05120X_3$$
$$(.0001242) \quad (.2117) \quad (.1722)$$

Standard errors for each regression coefficient are shown in brackets below each coefficient. The multiple coefficient of correlation was .7418.

The regression equation indicates that rates on international export traffic

[102]If one dummy variable is not dropped, all the dummy variables assume an insignificant relationship to the dependent variable—in this case, revenue per ton-mile.

are higher than rates on similar U.S. traffic, the effects of differences in length of haul having been accounted for. The percentage by which international rates on exports are higher than U.S. rates depends on the length of haul. For varying lengths of haul the following estimates may be made:

Length of haul (miles)	International rate (cents)	U.S. rate (cents)	International rate ÷ U.S. rate
300	2.339	1.958	119
500	2.234	1.854	120
1,000	1.973	1.592	124
1,500	1.712	1.331	129
2,000	1.451	1.070	136
2,500	1.189	0.809	147

We are less confident of these results than of the more general statement that international rates are higher than U.S. rates. This is because the regression coefficient for the U.S. dummy variable (X_3) is rather insig-

TABLE 86
FREIGHT RATES OF SELECTED CANADIAN IMPORTS, 1965
(cents per ton-mile)

Commodity	International		United States		Canada	
	Rate	Length of haul (miles)	Rate	Length of haul (miles)	Rate	Length of haul (miles)
Fresh and frozen fruits and vegetables[a]	1.72	2,616	1.60	1,669	1.66	730
Cotton	1.65	1,525	1.92	670	*	*
Chemicals	2.54	960	2.11	674	2.48	603
Primary and manufactured iron and steel	3.05	774	2.20	404	1.70	606
Agricultural machinery	3.91	1,099	3.63	770	4.17	1,206
Industrial machinery	3.70	1,155	3.43	920	3.93	647
Motor vehicle parts	5.32	467	3.48	736	4.17	402

Sources: International rates: Table 84; other rates from sources given for Table 85.
Note: U.S. data are for 1963. A major change in the freight commodity classification in the United States has made U.S. 1964 statistics non-comparable with the international statistics, which were collected for 1964. Differences between the two years on an aggregate basis are quite minor. Revenue per ton-mile declined by 2.1 percent, and average length of haul declined by 0.6 percent. It is believed that differences between the two years for the commodity groups shown in this table are similarly minor. An exception is chemicals, for which the average U.S. rate appears to have declined by about 15 percent between 1963 and 1964.
[a]See Table 66 for the composition of these commodity groups.
*Cotton traffic within Canada is too atypical for relevant rate comparisons.

nificant, since the standard error for this coefficient is over three times as large as the coefficient itself. Canadian rates would lie just above U.S. rates and could be estimated by putting X_2 and X_3 equal to zero.

Similar analysis was carried out with respect to the general level of railroad freight rates on Canadian imports from the United States. The general form of the regression equation was the same as for exports. Once again the Canadian dummy variable (X_4) was deleted for computation.

Table 86 provided 17 observations of rate-distance combinations for imports. Agricultural machinery was again eliminated from the regression analysis because of the distinctive positive relationship between distance and revenue per ton-mile. The following values for the equation were developed:

$$Y = 3.498 - .0008232X_1 + 1.005X_2 - .02842X_3$$
$$(.0004385) \quad (.6824) \quad (.6117)$$

Standard errors for each regression coefficient are shown in brackets below each coefficient. The multiple coefficient of correlation was .5870.

The regression equation indicates that rates on international import traffic are higher than rates on similar U.S. domestic traffic, the effects of differences in length of haul having been accounted for. The percentage by which international rates on Canadian imports are higher than U.S. rates depends on the length of haul. The following estimates may be made using varying lengths of haul:

Length of haul (miles)	International rate (cents)	U.S. rate (cents)	International rate ÷ U.S. rate
300	4.256	3.223	132
500	4.091	3.058	134
1,000	3.680	2.646	139
1,500	3.268	2.235	146
2,000	2.857	1.823	157
2,500	2.445	1.412	173

In evaluating these results we must keep in mind the low level of significance obtained for the regression coefficient of X_4 (the U.S. dummy variable). Canadian rate levels would, according to our import regression equation, be about equal to U.S. rate levels and, therefore, significantly lower than international rate levels.

From the foregoing discussion it is apparent that rates on Canadian exports to the United States are much lower (by about 50 percent) than rates on Canadian imports from the United States. Does this rate pattern represent a substantial divergence from costs and can it be said to reflect a policy of retarding imports and promoting exports? We would answer no. First, international lengths of haul are about 225 miles longer on exports than on imports. Second, and much more important, the export commodity groups are cheaper to transport. Their weight/volume ratio is higher, they are lower valued, they are easier to handle, and they move in larger volume between fewer origins and destinations.

D.   COMMODITY COMPARISONS OF INTERNATIONAL AND DOMESTIC RATES

More precise information analyzing the effects of international rate levels on trade can be developed from rates within commodity groups. In this way some conclusions may be drawn concerning the market-competitive impact of rate levels. For exports, nine possible types of rate-distance relationships exist as between international and U.S. traffic. These are as follows:

1. international rate (int R) higher than U.S. rate (USR) and international haul (int H) longer than U.S. haul (USH).
2. int R higher than USR and int H shorter than USH
3. int R higher than USR and int H equal to USH
4. int R less than USR and int H longer than USH
5. int R less than USR and int H shorter than USH
6. int R less than USR and int H equal to USH
7. int R equal to USR and int H longer than USH
8. int R equal to USR and int H shorter than USH
9. int R equal to USR and int H equal to USH.

Equality between rates or hauls is assumed to exist when international and U.S. values are within plus or minus 5 percent of each other.

If we accept the proposition that the normative relationship between rate and distance, within a given commodity group, is that a higher rate should be associated with a shorter length of haul (or that a lower rate should be associated with a longer length of haul), then we can develop guides to the impact of rate differences on trade. The nine types of rate-distance relationships may be distributed as follows:

exports (or imports) encouraged   5, 6, 8
exports (or imports) discouraged   1, 3, 7
indeterminate effect on exports (or imports)   2, 4
no effect on exports   9.

The encouragement or discouragement of exports from Canada to the United States exists, of course, relative to the situation as it would be if rate and length of haul were correctly related in terms of cost. Type 9 is an obvious example of such a correct relationship. Types 2 and 4 might also represent this optimum, but we cannot be sure without more precise analysis. We continue the underlying assumption that there are no significant cost differences between international and U.S. rail operations.

Examination of Table 85 shows that 5 of the 8 commodity groups fall into the "indeterminate" result. The breakdown of the comparison between international and U.S. rate levels is as follows:

indeterminate effect on exports: type 4 lumber and plywood
                                   aluminum and alloys
                                   nickel and alloys
                                   primary and manufactured
                                     iron and steel
                                   woodpulp
exports discouraged: type 1 newsprint
                       type 7 fertilizers
                       agricultural machinery.

A similar type of comparison can be made for Canadian imports from the United States. The basis for the comparison is the difference between international rates and Canadian rates. The nine rate-comparison types are modified appropriately—Canadian rates and hauls are substituted for U.S. rates and hauls. From Table 86 we can show that for 4 of the 6 commodity groups for which comparisons are possible (no relevant Canadian rate exists for cotton), the pattern of international and Canadian rates tends to discourage imports. The detailed results are as follows:

imports discouraged: type 7 fresh and frozen fruit and vegetables
                       chemicals
                       type 1 primary and manufactured iron and steel
                       motor vehicle parts
imports encouraged: type 5 agricultural machinery
indeterminate effect on imports: type 4 industrial machinery.

Analysis of the export and import rate relationships described above must be preceded by amendment of the export results. First, the fertilizers commodity group should be shifted from the "exports discouraged" category to the "indeterminate effect" category. This is in line with the 1964 increase in fertilizer freight rates mentioned in the note to Table 85. Second, a shift in the opposite direction should be made for lumber and plywood. This commodity group should be shifted from the "indeterminate effect" category to the "exports discouraged" category. The reason for this is the small amount (.07 cents) by which the international rate is lower than the U.S.

rate, considering that the international length of haul is almost 700 miles greater. A difference of such magnitude in distance shipped should be reflected in a more substantial decline in revenue per ton-mile.

The best general guide to the impact of these rate/distance anomalies on trade flows between the two countries is the freight factors—the importance of the freight rate in the total destination value of each commodity group. Freight factors for the three "discouraged" exports are estimated at 20 percent for lumber and plywood, 14 percent for newsprint, and 4 percent for agricultural machinery.[103] Given the relative approximate magnitudes of the rate/distance anomalies as shown in Table 85, we would conclude that newsprint exports are more constrained by high international freight rates than are exports of lumber and agricultural machinery. In considering newsprint exports, however, it must be remembered that market areas are traditionally allocated, within the newsprint industry, among different mills. Such cartel-like practices are likely to have a far greater impact on trade than is the difference between U.S. and international rate levels.

Freight factors for the four "discouraged" imports have been estimated as follows: fresh and frozen fruits and vegetables, 24 percent; primary and manufactured iron and steel, 12 percent; chemicals, 7 percent; and motor vehicle parts, 3 percent. The freight factor for the sole "encouraged" import, agricultural machinery, is estimated to be 5 percent.[104] Examination of Table 86 shows that the magnitude of the international/Canadian rate/distance anomaly is greatest for iron and steel, followed by motor vehicle parts, fruits and vegetables, agricultural machinery, and chemicals, in that order. We conclude that the level of international freight rates has its relatively greatest import-depressing effect in the case of iron and steel. Fruits and vegetables would come second, were it not for the monopoly, at most times of the year, represented by U.S. sources of supply for the products in this group. This, coupled with a rather inelastic demand for food products in general, impels us to modify the impact of the international rate level for this commodity group. For this reason, we would probably be correct in concluding that chemicals imports are more affected by high international rates (vis-à-vis Canadian rates). Conclusions regarding the last "discouraged" import group, motor vehicle parts, could at best be described as tenuous, given the low freight factor and the integrated structure of the automotive industry.

Agricultural machinery is an interesting case with respect to *both* imports

[103]Freight factors are crude estimates of the Canadian average for rail exports as developed from various sources.
[104]Freight factors are crude estimates of the Canadian average for rail imports as developed from various sources.

and exports. The rate structure discourages exports from Canada to the United States and encourages imports into Canada from the United States. The import rate is 6 percent below the Canadian rate on an average length of haul that is 9 percent shorter than the Canadian haul. The export rate is 4 percent above the U.S. rate on an average length of haul that is 24 percent longer than the U.S. haul. Freight factors are low, however—approximately 4 percent for exports and 5 percent for imports. Therefore, it is difficult to be very confident about any general conclusions that might be developed from these relationships.[105] The work of the Royal Commission on Farm Machinery, which is at present investigating the farm machinery industry, will presumably shed more light on this question.

E. FREIGHT-RATE IMPACT ON REGIONAL EXPORT ADVANTAGE

The question of the relative advantages enjoyed by different Canadian regions in exporting to the United States is of some interest. Relevant rate and distance information, by province, for the various export commodity groups was presented in Table 83.

An equation of the following form was used in analysis of this regional export data.

$$Y = f(X_1, X_2, X_3, X_4, X_5, X_6)$$

where

Y = revenue per ton-mile in cents
X_1 = distance in miles
X_2 = dummy variable for Atlantic
X_3 = dummy variable for Quebec
X_4 = dummy variable for Ontario
X_5 = dummy variable for Prairies
X_6 = dummy variable for B.C.

In computation, one dummy variable again had to be dropped; X_6, the B.C. variable, was chosen. The data in Table 83 provided 24 observations, with agricultural machinery again being excluded. The following values for the equation were developed:

$$Y = 1.984 - .0004367X_1 + .3472X_2 + .4248X_3 + .2135X_4 + .0947X_5$$
$$(.0001410)\quad (.2799)\quad (.2791)\quad (.2638)\quad (.2303)$$

[105]It has been suggested that the high Canadian rates on farm machinery (which account for the import "encouragement" and at least partly for the export "discouragement") may be related to the low rates Canadian railways are required to charge for transporting export grain. At best, this explanation could only be partial, considering the variety of agricultural machinery and agricultural products transported by the railways.

Standard errors for each regression coefficient are shown in brackets below each coefficient. The multiple coefficient of correlation was .7836.

According to the equation, railroad freight rates on exports are highest from Quebec origins, followed by origins in the Atlantic provinces. Ontario, the Prairies, and British Columbia follow, in that order. Satisfactory levels of statistical significance were, however, obtained only for the Quebec and Atlantic dummy variables. Rates for a haul of 1,000 miles for a commodity that was a composite of the 7 export groups could be estimated as follows:

	Rate (cents)	Ratio to B.C. rate
Atlantic	1.89	122
Quebec	1.97	127
Ontario	1.76	114
Prairies	1.64	106
B.C.	1.55	100

Having in mind the low levels of significance obtained for the coefficients of X_4 and X_5, we should probably not attach too great weight to these results, but they are certainly suggestive of differential railroad freight-rate treatment on exports as between different Canadian regions.

F.   RELATIVE COST LEVELS IN NORTH AMERICAN RAIL TRANSPORTATION

Barton's 1941 study of international freight rates concluded, tentatively, that Canadian railroad operating costs were higher (.802 cents per revenue freight ton-mile as against .703 cents) than U.S. railroad operating costs.[106] Since international traffic involves some Canadian and some U.S. operation, the implication of this relationship is that the level of international rates should be above the level of U.S. rates and below the level of Canadian rates.

Such an implication can only be tentative, however. There is no particular reason to assume that cost levels averaged over all Canadian railway operations are representative of cost levels on the Canadian portion of international railway operations. We might, in fact, suspect that they were *not* particularly representative, since much U.S.-destined Canadian rail traffic moves over intensively utilized rail lines. Offsetting this is the poorer utilization of freight cars in the United States[107] and, presumably, on international traffic. Canadian railways consider that freight-car cycles (a cycle runs from

[106]Barton, "Principal International and Interterritorial Class-Rate Structures," Table IX, p. 54.
[107]The ratio of freight car-miles to total number of freight cars is about 25 percent higher in Canada than in the United States (calculated from DBS and Association of American Railroads statistics and assuming relatively equal numbers of Canadian- and U.S.-owned freight cars operating in the other country).

origin to destination and back to origin) are about 50 percent longer in international movements than in all-Canadian movements. We would further argue that international rail movements have higher operating costs than comparable U.S. domestic movements, anticipating the conclusions of the later section of this chapter that deals with customs regulations and procedures in international railroad operations.

A further qualification is required. Cost *averages*, such as we are about to develop, can only be approximations of the actual costs associated with particular movements of a particular commodity between particular points. Cost averages are far less reliable than rate or revenue averages, since the latter generally vary little within a reasonably well-defined situation.

Official statistics provide little help in comparing rail cost levels in Canada and the United States. Operating costs per revenue freight ton-mile in 1964 were 1.17 cents in the United States and 1.46 cents in Canada.[108] The cost measure, however, includes all railway expenses, while the output measure is for freight only. A more inclusive output measure is gross ton-miles, the combined weight of cars, passengers, and freight multiplied by distance. Operating costs per gross ton-mile in 1964 were 0.506 cents in the United States and 0.621 cents in Canada.[109] Thus Canadian cost levels appear to be 25 percent higher than U.S. levels, using the revenue ton-mile measure, and 23 percent higher, using the preferred gross ton-mile measure, in both cases ignoring exchange rate differences.

These are, of course, average cost levels applying to freight and passenger service. For purposes of rate evaluation we would be more interested in the marginal costs of freight transportation. The best U.S. estimates are those developed by Meyer and his associates. For comparison with Canadian variable cost data, they must be converted from cents per gross ton-mile to cents per revenue ton-mile, but this is easily done. According to Meyer's 1952–55 results, the long-run marginal cost of freight transportation was .3271 cents per gross ton-mile[110] or, applying gross/revenue relationships, .6961 cents per revenue ton-mile. The ratio of the 1952–55 U.S. railway materials and wage cost index to the 1964 index is 80.3/113.1.[111] Therefore

[108]Calculated from Association of American Railroads (AAR), *Yearbook of Railroad Facts*, 1967, Washington, AAR, 1967, pp. 16 and 32, and DBS, *Railway Transport*, 1964, Part I, *Comparative Summary Statistics 1960–1964* (1966), Table 8, p. 10, and Table 9, p. 12.
[109]Canadian figure calculated from DBS, *Railway Transport*, 1964, Part I; U.S. figure calculated from AAR, *Yearbook of Railroad Facts*, 1967, and Interstate Commerce Commission, *Rail Carload Unit Costs by Territories for the Year 1964* (1966), p. 39. Canadian average passenger car weight was used in developing passenger portion of U.S. gross ton-mile estimate.
[110]Meyer, *et al.*, *The Economics of Competition in the Transportation Industries*, p. 62.
[111]AAR, *Yearbook of Railroad Facts*, p. 79.

the 1964 figure for Meyer's long-run marginal cost is .9801 cents per revenue ton-mile.

Canadian variable cost estimates were developed in the course of the grain cost investigations carried out during the most recent Royal Commission on Transportation. The following costs may be developed:[112]

	Canadian National	Canadian Pacific
1958 long-run freight variable cost	$421.0 million	$230.8 million
1958 revenue freight ton-miles	$35.08 billion	$26.87 billion
1958 freight variable cost per revenue freight ton-mile	1.200 cents	0.859 cents

The weighted average of these costs is 1.053 cents per revenue ton-mile. Using the U.S. railroad cost index (because a comparable Canadian index is not available), the 1964 cost would be 1.184 cents per revenue ton-mile. Considering the relative general price trends in Canada and the United States in this period, this gives a conservative upward adjustment in this cost estimate.

If we assume equivalence between long-run marginal cost and long-run variable cost and again ignore the lower value of the Canadian dollar, Canadian costs per revenue ton-mile are .2039 cents higher than U.S. costs. The difference is 20.8 percent.

The implication of this result, which is admittedly based on very crude cost estimates that are crude averages of diverse components, is that international railroad freight rates *should* be higher than U.S. domestic freight rates. This is true to the extent that international traffic involves transportation over Canadian rail lines whose costs are typical of the national Canadian pattern. If we use the 40 percent Canadian—60 percent U.S. division of international traffic referred to earlier in this chapter, then Canadian railway costs 20 percent higher than U.S. railway costs should be reflected in international rates that are 8 percent higher than U.S. rates and 10 percent lower than Canadian rates.

The earlier comparative analysis of international and U.S. rates indicated, however, that international export rates were between 19 percent and 47 percent higher than U.S. rates, depending on the length of haul. Import rates were between 32 percent and 73 percent higher for international hauls.

[112]Cost information from D. H. Hay, "The Problem of Grain Costing," Royal Commission on Transportation, *Report*, Vol. III, Ottawa, Queen's Printer, 1962, pp. 347 and 355; Canadian National traffic from Canada, DBS, *Canadian National Railways 1923–65*; Canadian Pacific traffic from Canada, DBS, *Canadian Pacific Railway Company 1923–65*.

Moreover, international rates were higher than Canadian rates, despite the international traffic cost advantage resulting from 60 percent of the haul occurring under lower U.S. costs. Such disparities are far greater than would be indicated by the cost differences between the two countries and, if not accountable by the special costs involved in transborder railway operations, can only be attributed to railway pricing policies.

Insight into the effect of too high international freight rates on Canada-U.S. trade must depend on freight factors for the commodities involved. Freight factors for 3 export groups and 5 import groups have already been estimated; these were the groups for which the rate/distance relationships were obviously discriminatory against (or, in one case, in favour of) international trade. For other imports and exports we can, limited by the information available, do no more than suggest that the general level of international rail freight rates generally discriminates against trade between Canada and the United States. We suspect that the impact of this discrimination is not overwhelming (because freight factors tend to be low on many trade items, particularly those comprising Canadian imports) but could not substantiate this suspicion without much more information on rates and costs and greatly extended and refined analysis.

Customs regulations and procedures and international railroad operations

It has been argued (in various interviews in connection with this study) that the delays and costs associated with operating freight trains across the border are no more onerous than those that occur when freight trains are interchanged between two railroads within the United States.[113] This view seems overly optimistic, for two reasons. First, it ignores the problems raised by customs clearance procedures for transborder trains. Second, and more important, such a view neglects the obstacles that Canadian and U.S. tariff regulations place before the free and efficient exchange and utilization of railroad freight-car equipment in international service.

A.   BORDER-CROSSING PROCEDURES

Traffic moving between Canada and the United States in both directions may clear customs either at the border or at destination. Border clearance is preferred by railways and shippers because it avoids the possibility of delays at destination when goods cannot clear customs because of weekend

[113]According to John Meyer and his associates such interchanges occur every 228.5 miles in the United States. Meyer, *et al.*, *The Economics of Competition in the Transportation Industries*, p. 193.

arrival. Customs requirements and operating and safety procedures do, however, force delays at border points. At the "best" border crossing point on one of the major Canadian railways, for instance, the time spent by through trains at the border averages six hours. In the United States, where interchange is frequent but customs procedures are absent, the *average* interchange time has been estimated at six hours.[114]

B. TARIFF REGULATIONS FOR RAILROAD FREIGHT EQUIPMENT

Tariff regulations of both Canada and the United States pose greater difficulties for transborder railroad operations. These difficulties arise out of restrictions on the duty-free use of locomotives and freight cars engaged in international railroad operations. On the U.S. side, Customs Regulation 5.12 allows free entry to locomotives and cars built in Canada and operating across the border. On the return trip, locomotives entered duty-free can only be used to power through trains which cross the international boundary back into Canada. This requirement, although it is somewhat restrictive, does not seem to create serious inefficiencies in international rail transportation, since transborder operation of locomotives is not necessarily required.

The restrictions imposed on freight-car use are more of a problem. On the return trip, a freight car can only be used, empty or loaded, in through trains returning to Canada and "for such local traffic as is reasonably incidental to its economical and prompt return"[115] to Canada. Use of Canadian-built freight-car equipment for U.S. domestic traffic that is *not* ancillary to the equipment's prompt return to Canada invokes payment of the 18 percent U.S. tariff on the equipment. Moreover, each use of a car for this type of traffic that is separated by a return trip to Canada counts as a new importation.[116]

Canadian railroad equipment tariff regulations are set out in Tariff Item 436. U.S.-owned locomotives and cars are admitted duty-free into Canada when used in transborder rail service, provided that reciprocal

[114]*Ibid.* This estimate, moreover, is for 1955. Improvements in railroad operating practices and facilities have presumably reduced interchange times. A two-hour reduction in this time, *if* it resulted in an additional two hours' freight-train movement, would, using 1966 U.S. average speeds and freight-train loads, result in an additional 68,640 net ton-miles. At the average 1966 U.S. rail freight revenue of 1.257 cents, this output would have a market value of about $860. (AAR, *Yearbook of Railroad Facts*, 1967.) The same value might be applied as an estimate of the cost of border interchange over non-border interchange, assuming the former had a time disadvantage of two hours.

[115]U.S. Customs Regulation 5.12.

[116]This makes it virtually impossible for Canadian-built freight cars to be used in car-leasing schemes that involve the use of equipment in Canada and the United States at different times of the year.

treatment is afforded Canadian-built equipment by the United States (as it is). U.S.-owned equipment may be used "temporarily in the transportation of goods from a place in Canada to another place in Canada . . . subject to a duty . . . ."[117] The duty is a special one charged on a per month basis against the number of U.S. cars of a particular type operating in Canada less the number of Canadian cars of the same type operating in the United States. For locomotives the duty is apparently levied against the gross number of U.S. locomotives temporarily in Canadian service. The monthly freight-car duty varies by type of car, ranging from $25 for some types of tank cars to $5 for box cars. Regulations made pursuant to Tariff Item 436 do not specify a duty rate for locomotives.

Two further differences between Canadian and U.S. regulations require explicit mention. Once a piece of railway equipment, to be used in Canadian domestic service for a period longer than one year, has paid the *regular* Canadian tariff applicable on imports of such equipment, future re-imports of this piece of equipment are duty-free. This is a provision somewhat more favourable to the efficient international use of freight equipment than the comparable U.S. regulation, as it was described above. A second difference between the two countries involves allowing a car to engage in domestic freight service that is "incidental" to the prompt return of the car to the other country. Such service is allowed without payment of any duty in the United States; in Canada, payment of the per month duty may be involved, depending on the balance between U.S. cars in Canada and Canadian cars in the United States. This duty is, of course, quite nominal in amount.

One unexpected advantage, to the Canadian railroads at least, comes from U.S. tariff regulations on freight cars. The threat of customs action gives Canadian railroads, who may have up to 25 percent of their freight-car fleets in the United States at any one time, another weapon in their efforts to maintain effective control over their freight equipment. Since a "national freight car shortage"[118] exists in the United States, such efforts are of considerable importance to the Canadian railroads. When freight cars are in short supply, their return to the owning railroad is apt to be very slow. Similar widespread shortages of freight cars have not recently been common in Canada.

To sum up the section, we must first note the objective of U.S. and Canada policy in this area. Simply stated, it is the protection of each nation's freight-equipment-manufacturing industry. But this objective impinges on the stated objectives of both countries in transportation. The provision of efficient

---

[117]Tariff Item 436. "Temporarily" is now interpreted to mean periods of not more than one year. For longer Canadian service, regular import duties must be paid.
[118]This is the title of one section in the ICC's 1966 annual report, pp. 91–4.

transportation service is hindered because the flexibility of freight-car distribution is restricted and the selection of optimal car-routing patterns is difficult. A freight car carrying Canadian pulp to Atlanta, for instance, could not
be routed to New Orleans to pick up traffic for St. Louis, where the car could
be loaded with traffic destined for Canada. Such a routing for a Canadian-
owned car would require full customs entry and tariff payment.

Since low utilization of freight-car equipment is recognized as one of the
railroads' major problems,[119] the existence of customs regulations that augment this problem for international traffic is unfortunate. The ideal solution
would seem to be that railroad freight equipment be treated as an instrument
of international trade and be allowed to move freely between both countries.

Conclusions

The importance of railway transport in North American trade was reiterated
at the beginning of this chapter. In the course of the chapter we discussed
four areas where government and industry policies create difficulties for the
free flow of trade between Canada and the United States.[120]

International railroad rate-making practices were one such difficulty. We
judged them to be excessively cumbersome and hypothesized their effect as
the perpetuation of existing commodity and geographic North American
trading patterns. Prejudice in favour of the *status quo* frustrates the swift
adjustment of international trade flows to new cost and market conditions.

Customs regulations involved in border-crossing and operation of foreign-
owned railway equipment interfere with efficient international railroad
operations. Such interference presumably has effects on rate levels and
service quality that can only tend to discourage trade, although the magnitude
of the discouragement may be minor.

Extensive analysis of the level of international railroad freight rates was
presented. The belief that international rates were 10 percent higher than
U.S. rates was shown to be incorrect, at least in the terms in which it is
usually expressed. Analysis of the general level of international rates on
commodities important in Canada–U.S. trade indicated that for exports
these rates were much more than 10 percent above U.S. rates. Import rates
were an even greater percentage higher than U.S. domestic rates. Furthermore, international rates on both imports and exports were higher than

[119]*Ibid.*

[120]Piggyback (or trailer-on-flat-car—TOFC) operations constitute another area where
government policy creates difficulties for the free flow of trade. Because most of these
difficulties are created in the course of highway transport regulation, consideration of
piggyback will be left to the next chapter.

Canadian rates. Analysis by commodity group indicated that three export groups (newsprint, lumber and plywood, and agricultural machinery) and four import groups (iron and steel, chemicals, fruits and vegetables, and motor vehicle parts) were discriminated against. Imports of agricultural machinery from the United States were encouraged. Among Canadian regions Quebec and the Atlantic provinces paid higher freight rates on exports to the United States.

Canadian railway costs were estimated to be approximately 20 percent higher than U.S. costs. Therefore the costs of transporting international traffic were said to be higher by a lesser percentage—perhaps 8 percent higher. International rates, when compared to U.S. rates, exceed this percentage difference, suggesting a general influence of discriminatory railway pricing.

The regulation of international railroad traffic was discussed at length. The greater reliance on railroad promotion in Canada than in the United States was noted, but it was concluded that this was unlikely to have any significant direct effect on trade between the two countries. Particular attention was paid to the dominance of U.S. regulation and U.S. regulatory norms over international traffic. It was suggested that the total Canadian abandonment of this regulatory field was ill-advised, especially in view of the new system and philosophy of transport regulation that have been instituted in Canada. Given the substantial lack of agreement between the new Canadian regulation and U.S. regulation, it seems desirable that steps be taken to improve (or, more correctly, to institute) coordination of the regulation of international rail traffic. The Canadian Transport Commission will, presumably, undertake actively to promote this coordination in light of the new expression of national transportation policy in Canada.[121]

---

[121]According to Section 1 of the National Transportation Act, it is desirable that "each mode of transport, so far as practicable, carries traffic to or from any point in Canada under tolls and conditions that do not constitute . . . an . . . unreasonable discouragement to . . . export trade in or from any region of Canada. . . ."

5. Highway Transportation and Canada-U.S. Trade

Introduction

Highway transport is the dominant mode of transportation for Canada's imports from the United States, measured in terms of value. It is second to rail transport in Canada's exports to the United States. In both directions highway transport's share of transborder trade value is growing rapidly, mainly because of the increased flows of trade in manufactured goods generated by the Automotive Free Trade Agreement of 1965.

According to statistics presented in chapter 2, 27 percent of Canada's 1965 exports to the United States, measured in value terms, moved by truck. Highway transport dominated 7 of the 24 export commodity groups—meat, fish, distilled alcoholic beverages, nickel ore and scrap, communications and laboratory equipment, motor vehicles and trailers, and motor vehicle parts. It was also estimated (in chapter 2) that 51 percent of Canada's imports from the United States in 1964 were transported by highway. This was the dominant mode of transport for 6 of the 18 import commodity groups for which modal share information could be constructed. These six were as follows: meat, cotton fabrics, plastics, aluminum and alloys, motor vehicles and trailers, and aircraft and parts. Trucking was estimated to account for over 50 percent of import values in the other 73 percent of imports where land modal shares could only be roughly estimated.

The statistical weaknesses that partially cripple any attempt to study the trucking industry were noted in chapter 2. Despite these weaknesses we were able to identify Ontario as the most important province of origin and destination for truck-borne trade with the United States. Quebec ranked second. The importance of Ontario is of significance in this chapter, in which we examine the impact of highway transport policy on trade flows between Canada and the United States. Important too is the rapid growth in trucking's share of North American trade.

Canadian highway transport policy

A. THE CANADIAN TRUCKING INDUSTRY

There are two segments of the highway transport industry in both Canada and the United States—for-hire trucking and private trucking. For-hire trucking involves the transportation of freight owned by someone other than the owner of the vehicle. Private trucking, on the other hand, occurs when a firm uses its own trucks to transport its own freight. The direct impact of regulatory policy is greater on for-hire trucking than on private trucking, although the ultimate repercussions of regulatory policy affect the entire highway transport industry. Government highway transport policies of a promotional type tend, on the other hand, to affect both segments of the industry directly.

The Canadian for-hire trucking industry included 4,333 firms in 1965. Operating revenues for intercity freight transportation totaled $640 million. Just over 45,000 people were employed in the for-hire trucking industry.[1] Despite the large number of firms engaged in for-hire trucking, a relative handful dominated the industry. One hundred and seventy-one carriers (about 4 percent of the total number of firms) accounted for 64 percent of intercity freight revenues and 61 percent of employment.[2]

There is some ownership of Canadian trucking companies by U.S. interests. Several of the larger Canadian truckers are U.S.-owned, and the frequency of acquisitions seems to be increasing. Within the last three years three large Canadian trucking companies, operating a total of 1,138 trailers (the total for-hire carriers is 27,474), have been acquired by U.S. firms.[3] In most provinces such acquisitions require regulatory approval. This has so far been granted but would likely become more difficult to obtain if a sizable proportion of any province's trucking industry were becoming owned in the United States. The reason for U.S. interest in purchasing Canadian trucking companies will become clear when we discuss restrictions on the licensing of truckers to operate across the international boundary.

B. FEDERAL REGULATION OF HIGHWAY TRANSPORTATION

Under the British North America Act, the government of Canada has jurisdiction over extra-provincial trucking. This jurisdiction was confirmed by

[1]Canada, Dominion Bureau of Statistics, *Motor Carriers—Freight (Common and Contract)*, 1965, Part II, *Classes 3 and 4* (Ottawa: Queen's Printer, 1967), Table 1, p. 9. The statistics include all trucking companies—Classes 1, 2, 3, and 4.
[2]*Ibid.*, Part I, *Classes 1 and 2, 1965*, Table 1, p. 11.
[3]John Schreiner, "Trucking Takeover Extends U.S. Links," *Financial Post*, June 3, 1967, p. 4. Total number of trailers from DBS, *Motor Carriers—Freight*, 1965, Part II, Table 1, p. 9.

the Judicial Committee of the British Privy Council in one of the last occasions on which that body was called upon to act as final arbiter in a matter involving the Canadian constitution. The case decided has become known as the Winner Case.[4] It involved a bus company operating from the United States through New Brunswick to Nova Scotia and the scope of the regulatory authority of the New Brunswick Motor Carrier Board. According to the Privy Council, the province had no authority to regulate extra-provincial traffic and, moreover, the extra-provincial operations of an extra-provincial trucking firm could not be separated for the purpose of committing them to provincial regulation.

This decision left much of the for-hire trucking industry in Canada free of any regulation. To fill this gap, Parliament passed the Motor Vehicle Transport Act.[5] This Act, assented to only four months after the Privy Council's decision in the Winner case, in effect delegated the federal government's powers over extra-provincial motor carriers to the provincial governments. Provincial regulatory agencies were authorized to exercise the federal government's power in regulating extra-provincial trucking. Section 3 of the Act states as follows:

Where in any province a licence is by the law of the province required for the operation of a local undertaking, no person shall operate an extra-provincial undertaking in that province unless he holds a licence issued under the authority of this Act.

The provincial transport board in each province may in its discretion issue a licence to a person to operate an extra-provincial undertaking into or through the province upon the like terms and conditions and in the like manner as if the extra-provincial undertaking operated in the province were a local undertaking.

The Motor Vehicle Transport Act has not proved an effective solution to the problem of motor-carrier regulation. This is because it fails to deal with two realities of Canadian trucking regulation. These are the differing regulatory philosophies, standards, and procedures among the provinces and the lack of coordination among the agencies of different provinces that are necessarily involved in regulating extra-provincial truck transportation.[6]

The above discussion has primarily dealt with operating licence regulation. One other aspect of trucking regulation—rates—is also dealt with in the

---

[4][1950] 3 Dominion Law Reports, 207; [1954] 4 DLR, 529; and [1954] 4 DLR, 657.
[5]2–3 Eliz. II, c. 59.
[6]For a recent example of lack of regulatory coordination, see *Kleysen's Cartage Co. Ltd. v. The Motor Carrier Board of Manitoba*, 49 WWR 577 (1964). The case involved the transportation of building materials from Manitoba to Saskatchewan. Kleysen held an appropriate operating licence issued by the Saskatchewan Highway Traffic Board, but his Manitoba Motor Carrier Board Licence was not valid for the transportation being undertaken. The decision of the Court of Queen's Bench Chambers of Manitoba was that Kleysen could not engage in the transportation at issue.

Motor Vehicle Transport Act. Provincial regulatory boards are given power to control the rates charged by extra-provincial carriers if the rates of local carriers are regulated. The experience with the rate-regulation provisions of the Act has been unfavourable; some provinces have failed to maintain the equality of treatment between extra- and intra-provincial carriers called for in the Act.

The prospect of significant improvement in the present situation is contained in the recent National Transportation Act. Part III of the Act, which has yet to be proclaimed, gives the Canadian Transport Commission regulatory authority over "transport for hire or reward by a motor vehicle undertaking connecting a province with any other or others of the provinces or extending beyond the limits of a province."[7] The Commission's powers are specified in three areas: the issuing of operating licences, the filing of tariffs, and the disallowance of rates, either because they are so low as to be non-compensatory or because they are so high as to take advantage of a monopoly situation. In addition, the Commission is given power to make regulations respecting safety, service, accounting, finance, insurance, and documentation.

Desirable though the implementation of this system of regulation might be, it carries with it very substantial political difficulties. The provinces have grown, not unnaturally, to consider their exercise of federal power under the Motor Vehicle Transport Act as something done in their own right. There is clear indication that at least one of them, Quebec, is opposed to the institution of direct federal control over extra-provincial trucking.[8] In addition, a lack of enthusiasm on the part of several other provinces has been rumoured. The solution of the political aspects of this particular problem in

[7]National Transportation Act, sec. 4(e).
[8]The following quotations from a letter from Premier Johnson to Prime Minister Pearson, dated October 13, 1966, illustrate this opposition. "I shall not try to hide from you that, whatever may be the promises of future consultation, the government of Quebec looks most unfavourably upon the fact that the federal government wishes to acquire the right to exempt an undertaking from the jurisdiction of the provincial boards so as to place it under the authority of the future Canadian Transport Commission. Already, in 1954, Quebec had objected to the discretionary powers the federal government reserved itself under section 5 of the Motor Vehicle Transport Act; in our opinion, this was holding back with one hand what one was giving with the other. It seems now that our opinion was well founded. Indeed, the whole arrangement of 1954 is presently being questioned again. In fact, I was very surprised by the haste in which this measure concerning motor vehicle transport was submitted to parliament. Your letter dated August 4th, 1966 emphasizes the necessity of holding federal-provincial discussions so as to determine how we can best settle the problems that face us in this field. I wonder how such discussions could possibly be useful now that the federal government has already decided before-hand what would be their conclusions. If your government sincerely favours provincial consultation, it should necessarily proceed to such consultation before making its decisions, not after. The presentation of such a measure as the one provided for in Part III of Bill C-231 might eventually be the result of our discussions but

federal-provincial relations will have to be found before the benefits of an effective system of regulating extra-provincial trucking can be realized.[9]

C. PROVINCIAL REGULATION OF HIGHWAY TRANSPORTATION

All Canadian provinces except Newfoundland regulate for-hire trucking. In the remaining nine provinces motor carriers are required to hold or obtain certificates of public convenience and necessity before commencing operations. In Alberta this requirement is imposed only on extra-provincial operators, in apparent contravention of Section 3 of the Motor Vehicle Transport Act. All provinces except Alberta require motor carriers to file rates,[10] and five of the nine regulate rates as well. Regulation of rates here connotes the power to modify rates included in filed tariffs. Only two provinces, Prince Edward Island and Quebec, prescribe uniform methods of accounting for trucking companies under their jurisdiction,[11] although several provincial regulatory bodies make use of the reports which carriers file with the Dominion Bureau of Statistics.

Precise objective evaluation of the quality of provincial trucking regulation is difficult. However, the support given to Part III of the National Transportation Act by Canadian Trucking Associations, Inc.,[12] the national voice of the trucking industry, implies dissatisfaction with the present system.[13] This attitude can hardly stem from a feeling that the industry is overregulated,

---

it could certainly never be the preliminaries to them. For this is putting the cart before the horse." Canada, House of Commons, *Debates*, 111, p. 12347.

[9]The need for implementation of Part III of the National Transportation Act would, of course, become critical if anything should happen to the present arrangements under the Motor Vehicle Transport Act. One current threat is a case being heard by the Supreme Court of Canada that attacks the constitutionality of the Act. Although the Act was upheld by the High Court of Justice of Ontario (Regina v. Ontario Highway Transport Board, Ex parte Coughlin, [1966] 1 O.L.R., 183), the same decision by the Supreme Court is, of course, not guaranteed. A more durable, though less compelling, threat is the attitude of provincial regulatory boards and their willingness to continue to act under the Motor Vehicle Transport Act.

[10]The introduction of rate-filing in Ontario did not occur until May 1, 1963, and was preceded by intense debate. Two years later the debate was still continuing, with trucking companies generally in favour of filing and shippers generally opposed. The shippers argued that filing had encouraged price-fixing by truckers, while they replied that it had brought stability to an often turbulent industry. See "Ontario Rate Filing . . . after Two Years," *Canadian Transportation*, June 1965, pp. 28 ff.

[11]DBS, *The Motor Vehicle*, 1966, Part I, *Rates and Regulations* (1967), Table 4, pp. 18–19.

[12]See House of Commons, Standing Committee on Transport and Communications, *Minutes of Proceedings and Evidence*, Nov. 3, 1966, Ottawa, Queen's Printer, 1966, pp. 2357–63. This position represented a reversal of the CTA's long-standing opposition to direct federal regulation of extra-provincial trucking.

[13]The criticism of the Atlantic provinces' trucking regulations by the Atlantic Provinces Transportation Study might also be noted. See Economist Intelligence Unit, *Atlantic Provinces Transportation Study*, vol. V, *Legislation and Public Policy*, Ottawa, Queen's Printer, 1967, p. 146.

since it is widely believed in the trucking industry that both regulatory statutes and regulators are too weak.[14] It is typical, for example, for members of provincial bodies regulating trucking to be appointed without fixed term. This practice ensures continuing personal dependence on the provincial government and is generally regarded as poor administrative strategy.

The evidence suggests that provincial regulation of trucking has not been a success, particularly in the realm of extra-provincial trucking, where, at least, an alternative is available. In the view of one of the studies prepared for the 1961 Royal Commission on Transportation: "In the long run, it seems no more likely that the provinces can carry the full responsibilities of developing and regulating large-scale interprovincial trucking operations effectively than it was possible for them to carry the burden of railway building and regulation they attempted 50 to 70 years ago."[15] We would concur with this assessment. Significant improvement in the key regulatory areas of rates and operating licences is needed. Federal regulation would offer the possibility of improvement and would confer additional benefits by enhancing regulatory coordination of extra-provincial trucking.

D. PROMOTION OF HIGHWAY TRANSPORT

From regulatory policy we move to promotional policy. Three aspects of promotional policy may be identified: highway expenditure and the provision of highway facilities, highway taxation, and size and weight regulations for highway vehicles.

Highway expenditure data from 1960 through 1965 are shown in Table 87, divided between expenditures on highways and rural roads and expenditures on urban streets. Over this five-year period, total highway and street expenditures in Canada increased by $560 million, almost 60 percent. $432 million of the increase occurred in Ontario and Quebec. Between 1960 and 1965 Canadian paved highway mileage increased from 50,617 to 71,792. Total mileage of paved urban streets rose from 19,843 to 27,905.[16] Rural freeway mileage in 1965 was 1,646 miles, or about 2 percent of total paved rural mileage. Over 1,200 miles of this total was located in Ontario and Quebec.[17] Of the $1.6 billion spent on highways in 1965 by all levels of

[14]More concrete evidence is provided by a recent press report concerning illegal for-hire trucking in Ontario. A rough estimate in the report placed the annual revenue of these operations at $16 million. John Hunt, "A $16 Million Annual Haul," *Toronto Telegram*, July 22, 1967. Yet Ontario regulators have probably the largest enforcement staff in any province to ensure conformity to laws and regulations.
[15]D. W. Carr and Associates, "Truck-Rail Competition in Canada," Royal Commission on Transportation, *Report*, Vol. III (1962), p. 90.
[16]DBS, *Road and Street Mileage and Expenditure*, 1960 and 1965 (1961 and 1966).
[17]Canadian Good Roads Association, *Highway Finance*, 1965, Ottawa, Canadian Good Roads Association [1966], Table 11, p. 14.

TABLE 87

RURAL HIGHWAY AND URBAN STREET EXPENDITURES IN CANADA BY PROVINCE, 1960–65
(million dollars)

	1960			1961			1962		
	Rural[a]	Urban[b]	Total	Rural	Urban	Total	Rural	Urban	Total
Newfoundland	23.8	1.5	25.3	17.0	1.9	18.9	20.9	1.7	22.7
Prince Edward Island	7.1	0.3	7.4	8.0	0.4	8.5	9.0	0.2	9.2
Nova Scotia	36.3	3.9	40.2	32.1	3.7	35.8	29.7	6.0	35.7
New Brunswick	38.6	3.1	41.7	35.8	3.7	39.5	32.7	4.1	36.7
Quebec	149.4	99.8	249.2	149.5	61.3	210.8	185.4	62.2	247.7
Ontario	241.8	58.6	300.4	237.9	105.8	343.7	240.7	116.5	357.1
Manitoba	42.0	11.7	53.7	34.4	10.5	44.9	34.8	11.9	46.7
Saskatchewan	49.8	11.5	61.3	44.5	10.8	55.4	45.0	10.5	55.4
Alberta	79.9	17.8	97.7	71.4	22.1	93.6	68.5	21.9	90.3
British Columbia	114.5	16.7	131.2	112.5	15.1	127.5	102.2	19.0	121.2
Canada[c]	783.4	225.0	1,008.4	743.2	235.3	978.5	768.9	253.9	1,022.8

	1963			1964			1965		
	Rural	Urban	Total	Rural	Urban	Total	Rural	Urban	Total
Newfoundland	35.5	2.7	38.2	55.2	3.8	59.0	56.5	4.1	60.7
Prince Edward Island	9.0	0.5	9.5	9.7	0.6	10.3	11.2	0.5	11.6
Nova Scotia	32.7	6.1	38.8	35.6	6.0	41.6	45.0	6.0	51.0
New Brunswick	35.1	3.8	38.9	42.2	4.2	46.4	46.6	4.7	51.3
Quebec	246.1	63.3	309.4	337.7	63.2	401.0	391.3	69.8	461.1
Ontario	286.1	147.3	433.4	330.4	134.9	465.3	360.3	160.8	521.1
Manitoba	35.8	14.3	50.1	42.3	14.6	56.9	49.6	20.2	69.8
Saskatchewan	47.8	13.6	61.4	54.1	13.5	67.6	68.7	18.5	87.2
Alberta	78.6	19.6	98.1	76.3	17.2	93.5	92.5	20.6	113.1
British Columbia	107.9	19.9	127.8	98.3	24.7	123.1	118.6	23.9	142.5
Canada	914.7	291.1	1,205.8	1,081.9	282.8	1,364.7	1,240.5	329.1	1,569.6

Source: DBS, *Road and Street Mileage and Expenditure*, various years.
[a] Includes some urban street expenditures by provincial governments in some provinces.
[b] Excludes some urban expenditures made by provincial governments and included under "rural."
[c] Excluding the Yukon and Northwest Territories.

government, $1.1 billion (70 percent) was provided by the ten provincial governments either directly or indirectly through municipal grants-in-aid. The federal government provided $161.1 million, and municipal governments, $323.1 million.[18]

The major responsibility for the provision of highway facilities rests with the provincial governments. Federal government participation is limited to the Trans-Canada Highway, roads in national parks and other federal areas, improvement of railway grade crossings, the Alaska highway and territorial roads, and developmental roads under the "roads-to-resources" program and the Atlantic regional development program.

Revenues collected from highway users amounted to $917.7 million in 1965.[19] The provincial breakdown is shown in Table 88. Table 88 includes only revenues from various highway– and street-connected licence fees and motive fuel taxes. It excludes some revenues that DBS includes in highway-use revenues, among them service station licences and fines for Motor Vehicle Act infractions.

TABLE 88
REVENUES FROM HIGHWAY USERS, BY
PROVINCE, 1965
(million dollars)

Newfoundland	15.3
Prince Edward Island	4.5
Nova Scotia	32.5
New Brunswick	26.5
Quebec	249.8
Ontario	345.3
Manitoba	52.8
Saskatchewan	39.5
Alberta	59.1
British Columbia	81.0
Canada[a]	906.3

Source: DBS, *The Motor Vehicle*, 1965, Part IV, *Revenues* (1966). The revenues are for fiscal years ending February 28 or March 31, 1966.
[a]Excluding the Yukon and Northwest Territories.

The above revenues are all provincially collected. Yet the federal government does receive some tax revenues that are sometimes attributed to highway use. Import duties on motor vehicles, parts, and accessories could be

[18]Calculated from DBS, *Road and Street Mileage and Expenditure*, 1965 (1966).
[19]DBS, *The Motor Vehicle*, 1965, Part IV: *Revenues* (1966). The revenues are for fiscal years ending February 28 or March 31, 1966. The total excludes the $30.5 million collected as road, bridge, tunnel, and ferry tolls. See DBS, *Road and Street Mileage and Expenditure*, 1965, Table 7, pp. 14–15.

included here. Also, the 11 percent federal sales tax brought in, from motor vehicles and motor vehicle parts and accessories, an estimated $300 million in 1964.[20] The propriety of describing this as highway-user revenue is, however, questionable, since this tax is levied on all goods produced in, or imported into, Canada. Also, consistency would require that provincial sales taxes on automotive products be included as highway-user revenues, a definition that is similarly unattractive. The same comments could be made about inclusion in highway-user revenues of proceeds from the corporate income tax on manufacturing and trade companies engaged in supplying and servicing vehicles. Such revenues would amount to perhaps several hundred million dollars annually.

TABLE 89

ESTIMATES OF HIGHWAY TAXES[a] PAID BY SELECTED MOTOR VEHICLES BY PROVINCE, 1966

	Medium passenger car[b]	Medium truck[c]	Tractor–semi-trailer[d]
Newfoundland	$94	$491	$2,108
Prince Edward Island	91	469	1,887
Nova Scotia	97	519	2,712
New Brunswick	98	479	2,443
Quebec	88	410	2,255
Ontario	84	481	2,364
Manitoba	85	492	2,352
Saskatchewan	75	472	2,199
Alberta	63	338	1,691
British Columbia	75	416	1,769

Source: DBS, *The Motor Vehicle*, 1966, Part I, *Rates and Regulations* (1967).
[a]Vehicle licence fees plus estimated fuel tax.
[b]115-inch wheelbase; 3,300 lb. tare weight.
[c]2 axles; 20,000 lb. gross vehicle weight.
[d]Diesel tractor 2-axle semi-trailer combination; 50,000 lb. gross vehicle weight.

The structure of highway taxes (limited, as explained above, to those collected by the provinces) differs among the provinces. Estimated taxes for selected motor vehicles are shown in Table 89. The varying incidence of provincial highway taxes on different types of vehicles shows quite clearly in the above table. Ontario, for example, imposes relatively low taxes on automobiles (fourth lowest), but relatively high taxes on tractor–semi-trailer

[20]Calculated from Motor Vehicle Manufacturers' Association, *Facts and Figures of the Automotive Industry*, 1966, Toronto, Motor Vehicle Manufacturers' Association, 1966.

combinations (third highest). Notable also is the rather uniformly high level, on all three classes of vehicles, of highway taxes in the Atlantic provinces. The question of what is a "fair" level of taxation for various classes of vehicles is not easily answered. The most recent (and, indeed, the *only*) comprehensive Canadian study of this question is twelve years out of date.[21] More timely and complete research has been carried out in the United States,[22] but it is not possible here to attempt to apply it to Canada. Neither is it possible to update the Canadian Tax Foundation's 1955 study.

TABLE 90

RELATIONSHIPS BETWEEN HIGHWAY EXPENDITURE AND
HIGHWAY USE, BY PROVINCE, 1965

	Estimated highway use (million vehicle-miles)	Expenditure per vehicle-mile (cents)	Highway-user revenue per vehicle-mile (cents)	Subsidy per vehicle-mile (cents)
Newfoundland	686	8.85	2.23	6.62
Prince Edward Island	274	4.23	1.64	2.59
Nova Scotia	1,742	2.93	1.87	1.06
New Brunswick	1,482	3.46	1.79	1.67
Quebec	15,408	2.99	1.62	1.37
Ontario	22,624	2.30	1.53	0.77
Manitoba	2,771	2.52	1.91	0.61
Saskatchewan	2,964	2.94	1.33	1.61
Alberta	4,939	2.29	1.20	1.09
British Columbia	5,776	2.47	1.40	1.07
Canada[a]	58,666	2.68	1.54	1.14

Sources: Highway use: Canadian Good Roads Association, *Highway Finance*, 1965, Ottawa, Canadian Good Roads Association, 1966, Table 8, p. 9 (based on fuel consumption); expenditure calculated from above Table 87; revenue calculated from Table 88; subsidy calculated by subtracting revenue per vehicle-mile from expenditure per vehicle-mile.
[a]Excluding Yukon and Northwest Territories.

We can, however, attempt some rough judgments concerning the relationship between highway and street expenditures and the revenues contributed by highway and street users. In Table 90 statistics are presented, by province, to show highway expenditures, user-generated revenues, estimated highway use, and subsidization of highway use from general government revenues. Two comments should precede discussion of Table 90. First, we must acknowledge that statistics of expenditure/revenue relationships for high-

[21]Canadian Tax Foundation, *Taxes and Traffic*, Toronto, Canadian Tax Foundation, 1955.
[22]Culminating in U.S., Congress, House, *Supplementary Report of the Highway Cost Allocation Study*, H. Doc. 124, 89th Congr., 1st sess., 1965.

ways for any one year could be suspect, given the potential interyear variation in each. However, examination of similar data for other years reveals little variation from the general pattern shown in Table 90. Second, the designation of the difference between highway expenditures and highway-user revenues as user "subsidy" necessarily involves the judgment that non-users should, as a group, have no responsibility for highway costs. Support for this judgment comes from the monumental highway cost allocation study in the United States.[23] While conditions in Canada are not identical,[24] they seem in the main similar enough to permit us to assert that all highway expenses *should* be met by highway users.

The far-right-hand column of Table 90 indicates the extent to which this standard is not being met in each of the provinces. Newfoundland, Prince Edward Island, New Brunswick, Saskatchewan, and Quebec are, in that order, above the national average of 1.14 cents per vehicle-mile. The other five provinces are below. The patterns shown in this table will have implications for trade between Canada and the United States after comparison with similar U.S. data.

E. HIGHWAY-TAX RECIPROCITY IN CANADA

We continue by evaluating the extent of highway-tax reciprocity in Canada. Reciprocity refers to agreements between two (or more) provinces under which vehicles registered in one province need pay only partial licence fees for using the highways of the other province. Reciprocity applies to licence fees only, but for tractor–semi-trailer combinations these are of significant magnitude. For the combination included in Table 89, annual licence fees alone would range from $409 in Quebec to $770 in Saskatchewan. The absence of reciprocity agreements thus imposes extra costs on inter-provincial highway transport and may in fact hinder the growth of these operations.

Eighteen combinations of provinces seem important at the present stage of development of Canadian trucking.[25] For only two of these (B.C.-Alberta and Ontario-Quebec) is there no significant reciprocity agreement. The lack

[23]See U.S., Congress, House, *Supplementary Report of the Highway Cost Allocation Study*, H. Doc. 124, 89th Congr., 1st sess., 1965, pp. 28–9. The study does not reach a final conclusion, but subsequent U.S. federal highway-taxation policy has implied the absence of a non-user share.

[24]Specifically, the secondary benefits from highway expenditure—for example, stimulation of economic development—may, for *some* roads, be greater. A case may be made, under these circumstances, for a non-user contribution to highway costs.

[25]B.C.–Alberta, B.C.–Saskatchewan, B.C.–Manitoba, Alberta–Saskatchewan, Alberta–Manitoba, Alberta–Ontario, Alberta–Quebec, Saskatchewan–Manitoba, Saskatchewan–Ontario, Manitoba–Ontario, Manitoba–Quebec, Ontario–Quebec, Quebec–New Brunswick, Quebec–Nova Scotia, Quebec–Prince Edward Island, New Brunswick–Nova Scotia, New Brunswick–Prince Edward Island, and Nova Scotia–Prince Edward Island.

of any agreement between Ontario and Quebec is, however, a critical matter, considering the importance of highway transport between the two provinces. For five combinations, all at least partly in the Atlantic region, full reciprocity exists. The other eleven combinations have partial reciprocity agreements that generally allow full reciprocity for all vehicles under 6,000 pounds gross vehicle weight and for vehicles carrying household goods and, for some, agricultural and resource products. Other vehicles must pay a partial fee of $10 per ton gross vehicle weight.[26] The combination tractor–semi-trailer of Table 88 would pay a partial fee of $250, less than any regular fee. But this still represents something of a discouragement to inter-provincial truck operations. Assuming 50,000 vehicle-miles per year, this vehicle would pay ½ cent more per vehicle-mile in inter-provincial operations than in intra-provincial operations.

F. SIZE, WEIGHT, AND SAFETY REGULATIONS

We conclude this section by examining another example of limited inter-provincial uniformity. This occurs with respect to size, weight, and safety regulations for motor vehicles. Length, width, and height limits are fairly uniform among the provinces, although variation of five feet in maximum vehicle lengths is common.[27] In addition, most provinces permit maximum gross vehicle weights (GVW) of 74,000 pounds, with some restrictions. Ontario allows vehicles of up to 126,000 pounds GVW, however. None of the four Atlantic provinces, it might be noted, allow "double-bottoms"—a tractor or truck pulling two trailers or one semi-trailer and a trailer. Safety regulations, which involve vehicle lighting, warning devices, other safety equipment, brakes, driver hours, etc., are quite variable among the ten provinces. The economic impact of this variation is probably slight, however. In a later section of this chapter we present specific comparisons of Canadian and U.S. size and weight limits as they affect international trucking.

U.S. highway transport policy

A. THE U.S. TRUCKING INDUSTRY

In 1965 there were 15,565 interstate motor carriers of property subject to Interstate Commerce Commission regulation. Operating revenues of these firms totaled $8,105 million in 1965.[28] Continuing statistics are not available

[26]DBS, *The Motor Vehicle*, 1966, Part I, *Rates and Regulations* (1967), Table 3, pp. 16–17.
[27]All data from *ibid.*, Tables 1 and 2, pp. 6–15.
[28]American Trucking Associations, *American Trucking Trends*, 1966, Washington, ATA, 1967.

for trucking companies that are not subject to ICC jurisdiction. However, a special census survey for 1963 reported that there were 42,986 such companies and that their operating revenues were $2,229 million.[29] Like its Canadian counterpart, the U.S. trucking industry is rather concentrated. One hundred and twenty (2.08 percent) of the 5,763 ICC-regulated carriers of general commodities accounted for over 54 percent of the total revenues ($5,582 million) in this segment of the industry.[30]

Information is not available concerning the extent of Canadian ownership of U.S. trucking companies. Such ownership is quite rare, but a few Canadian carriers have acquired U.S. carriers in the interests of obtaining their operating licences and thus enabling the Canadian carrier to offer through service to and from U.S. points. These acquisitions require Interstate Commerce Commission approval, but this would seem to be relatively easy to obtain, unless the acquisition threatened a substantial diminution in competition.

B.   THE REGULATION OF INTERSTATE HIGHWAY TRANSPORTATION

The division of motor carrier regulatory authority between state and federal governments was decided in the United States in 1925. Two Supreme Court decisions in that year held that state economic regulation of interstate motor carriers was unconstitutional, despite the absence at that time of federal legislation on the matter. These decisions created a regulatory vacuum that existed until the passage of the federal Motor Carrier Act (Part II of the Interstate Commerce Act) in 1935. Pressure for federal economic regulation of interstate trucking grew out of two conditions: a growing instability within the trucking industry and an intensification of truck competition with the already regulated railroads.

The system of regulation that has grown out of the Interstate Commerce Commission's application of the Motor Carrier Act has been subjected to much criticism; but before evaluating the complaints, a brief survey of federal economic regulation of interstate trucking is necessary. There are numerous exemptions to the Act, but the most significant are those afforded to the transportation of agricultural commodities and transportation within a "commercial zone."[31]

Common carriers operating in interstate commerce must obtain certificates of public convenience and necessity from the Interstate Commerce Commission. The certificate specifies routes and type of service that the carrier may

[29]U.S. Department of Commerce, Bureau of the Census, 1963 Census of Transportation, Motor Carrier Survey (1966), Table 2, p. 6.
[30]Interstate Commerce Commission, Eightieth Annual Report, Fiscal Year Ended June 30, 1966, Washington, U.S. Government Printing Office, 1966, Table 33, p. 168.
[31]Sec. 203(b)(6) and (8). A commercial zone is roughly equivalent to a metropolitan area.

provide. Since 1962, motor carriers operating in interstate commerce within one state have been exempted from the certificate requirement, if they have obtained appropriate authority from the state regulatory commission.[32] Carriers are required to file tariffs of their rates and observe these tariffs. Rates must be just and reasonable and not involve preference, prejudice, or discrimination to any person or region. The Commission may disallow rates on its own initiative or upon complaint.[33] Extensive financial control is exercised by the Commission, including approval of issuance of securities,[34] the holding of adequate liability insurance,[35] the filing of reports and adherence to a uniform system of accounts,[36] and the approval of combinations and consolidations of motor carriers.[37] Safety regulation, previously an ICC responsibility, has been transferred to the new Department of Transportation.

Under Section 205 of the Interstate Commerce Act, the Commission is required to carry out its regulatory responsibilities through a joint board of state and ICC representatives when three or fewer states are involved in the matter in question.[38] Joint board decisions have the same status as other initial Commission decisions; that is, they are final unless appealed to the appelate division of the Commission or to the Commission as a whole.

Such detailed economic regulation of such a sprawling and dynamic industry generates a large regulatory workload. For example, in the fiscal year ending June 30, 1966, the Commission received 8,681 applications respecting motor carrier operating rights. As of June 30, 1966, a total of 18,512 motor carrier operating authorities were in force. Common and contract carriers of freight filed 137,600 tariffs with the ICC in the 1965/66 fiscal year—over 18,000 of these were criticized.

Most of the criticism of federal trucking regulation in the United States has centred on the control of entry—the issuance of certificates and permits of convenience and necessity. The application of what is essentially a railroad-type rate structure to an industry whose demand and cost characteristics are quite different has been condemned,[39] but there seems to be a *relatively* small volume of criticism of ICC motor carrier rate regulation generally. Few observers, however, seem to be favourably impressed with the procedures and impact of entry control. The comments of a 1960 study prepared for the Department of Commerce are representative:

Restrictive entry control, such as that applicable to interstate trucking, lessens competition and may even create route monopolies or small-firm oligopolies that result in monopolistic price and service policies. The market structure of regulated

---

[32]Secs. 206 and 208.   [33]Secs. 216 and 217.   [34]Sec. 214.
[35]Sec. 215.   [36]Sec. 220.   [37]Sec. 5.
[38]The Commission *may* use a joint board when more than three states are involved.
[39]See, for example, George W. Wilson, "Effects of Value-of-Service Pricing upon Motor Common Carriers," *Journal of Political Economy*, LXIII, Aug. 1955, pp. 337–44.

motor transport has been greatly influenced and made less competitive by denial of a large proportion of the proposed new entries into regulated trucking and of the extensions of established firms into new service fields. It has also been affected by the separation of markets for truck service into numerous noncompeting groups of cariers prevented by commodity, route, gateway, territorial and service restrictions from invading or interpenetrating one another's designated routes and markets.[40]

The most significant question is whether the net cost of transport service to the public at large has been reduced by entry controls lessening competition and increasing the size and market dominance of the firms, even creating monopoly or near monopoly conditions on certain routes. It is extremely doubtful that entry regulation has reduced transport costs to the public.[41]

Perhaps the most telling criticism of existing regulation of entry into for-hire trucking is the extent to which this regulation is avoided. An ICC study estimated that in 1959, 11.2 billion ton-miles of illegal for-hire trucking were performed. This estimate of these "gray-area" operations is limited to unauthorized interstate transportation of freight by truck.[42] The total revenue ton-miles performed by properly authorized truckers was 101.4 billion in 1959; the illegal portion represents about 11 percent of this. The advantage of being a "gray-area" operator is, of course, freedom from the necessity of obtaining an ICC operating licence and from ICC rate regulation. The existence of such a large and, presumably, flourishing "gray-area" trucking industry indicates that regulated for-hire carriers have their competitive potential restricted by ICC regulation.

In light of the comments made in a previous section about the desirability of federal trucking regulation in Canada and in view of the importance of the operating authority question for international trucking, an explanation is in order. Our complaint is not against the concept or principle of control of entry into for-hire trucking but only against the way this control has been developed and applied in the United States. Two influences seem primarily responsible for the undesirable effects of entry control. One is the statutory exemption from federal regulation of the truck transportation of agricultural products. This freedom encourages illegal for-hire truck operations on the backhauls of agricultural products carriers. The other destructive influence is "fragmented motor carrier certification."[43] Many ICC motor carrier

[40]Ernest W. Williams, Jr., and David W. Bluestone, *Rationale of Federal Transportation Policy: Appendix to Federal Transportation Policy and Program*, Washington, U.S. Government Printing Office, 1960, pp. 12–13.
[41]*Ibid.*, pp. 14–15.
[42]See Interstate Commerce Commission, *Gray Area of Transportation Operations* (1960), p. 13.
[43]For discussion see U.S., Senate, Committee on Interstate and Foreign Commerce, *National Transportation Policy* (the Doyle report), 87th Congr., 1st sess., 1961, pp. 547–52.

certificates (operating licences) are inflexible with respect to points to be served, route(s) to be followed, and commodities to be carried. A minor adjustment in traffic patterns will therefore require formal amendment of the certificate. Such unrealistically rigid regulations add to the costs of carriers that obey the law and encourage others to break it. They constitute an impediment to efficient interstate and international commerce. To quote the Doyle report again: "It is in the long range public interest that concepts developed in an earlier day be not perpetuated when they impose an avoidable continuing cost upon transportation as a whole. It is in the true interest of all regulated motor carriers that operating costs of their industry not be increased in comparison with unregulated carriers by the imposition of unnecessary circuity, directional, intermediate point and gateway restrictions, commodity restrictions and other manmade handicaps which stand in the way of maximizing the potential of their service."[44]

C. PROMOTION OF HIGHWAY TRANSPORT

The discussion of U.S. policies towards promotion of highway transportation will follow the same general outline used for Canada. We will discuss, in turn, highway expenditure and highway facilities, highway taxation, and vehicle size and weight regulations.

TABLE 91
HIGHWAY EXPENDITURE IN THE UNITED STATES, 1960–65
(million dollars)

	1960	1961	1962	1963	1964	1965
Rural[a]	7,580	8,074	8,717	9,315	9,719	9,948
Urban[b]	1,350	1,454	1,508	1,539	1,593	1,664
Administration	483	521	537	573	684	743
Total	9,413	10,049	10,762	11,427	11,996	12,355

Source: U.S., Department of Transportation, Bureau of Public Roads, *Table HF-2*, various years, Washington, Bureau of Public Roads, various years.
[a]Includes some expenditures in urban areas.
[b]Excludes expenditures on municipal extensions of state rural highway systems; these are included under "rural."

Highway expenditure data from 1960 through 1965 are presented in Table 91 for the United States as a whole. Between 1960 and 1965 U.S. highway and street expenditures rose by $2.9 billion, an increase of about 31 percent. Surfaced highway mileage increased by 137,000 miles to 2.3 million miles, and the completed mileage of the multi-lane Interstate Highway

[44]*Ibid.*, p. 548.

System doubled to over 19,000 miles.[45] In 1964, excluding expenditures from the proceeds of bonds, the state governments supplied 56 percent of highway expenditures. The federal share was 34 percent, and the local government share was 10 percent.[46]

Highway expenditures for 1964 (the most recent year available) are presented in Table 92 for 23 states selected on the basis of their importance in Canada-U.S. truck transportation. In addition to this $9.7 billion, another $4.3 billion of revenues for highways was provided from various non-user sources. Among these sources were road, bridge, and ferry tolls ($620 million), general fund appropriations ($1,019 million), and property taxes ($1,046 million).

Table 94 shows for 1964 the estimated taxes that would have been paid by three vehicle types in each of the 23 selected states. The estimates include federal Highway Trust Fund payments[47] and state taxes of these types: registration fees, "other" fees, fuel taxes, mileage or ton-mile taxes, and carrier fees. State property taxes are excluded, as are all municipal road-user taxes. The difference in the tax levied on the same type of vehicle in different states is quite large, ranging from $78 to $119 for the passenger car, from $339 to $604 for the truck, and from $1,759 to $3,322 for the tractor–semi-trailer combination.

Working from Tables 92 and 93, we will develop for the United States, as was done in the previous section of this chapter for Canada, estimates of the relationship between highway expenditures and highway-user revenues. The qualifications that followed Table 90 in this chapter (which presented the same type of statistics for Canada that Table 95 does for the United States) need to be repeated here. We assume that the excess of highway expenditures over highway-user payments for highways constitutes a subsidy to highway users. Also, we must be aware that one year need not be representative of long-term revenue/expenditure relationships. However, as in the case of Canada, examination of other years does not reveal any major divergence from the pattern shown in Table 95.

[45]Automobile Manufacturers Association, *1967 Automobile Facts and Figures*, Detroit, AMA, 1967, p. 55.
[46]Association of American Railroads, *Comparative Transportation Statistics*, Washington, AAR, 1966, p. 54.
[47]The Highway Trust Fund receives all U.S. federal government highway-user tax revenues *except* the excise tax on automobiles, which was 10 per cent of the wholesale price until May, 1965. In 1964 the automobile excise tax generated $1,821 million, and other federal highway taxes, $5,635 million. U.S., Department of Commerce, Bureau of Public Roads, *Highway Statistics*, 1964, Tables E-7 and E-8, pp. 54–5. The case for including the automobile excise tax as a road-user tax is much stronger in the United States than in Canada because there is no general federal sales tax in the United States.

TABLE 92
RURAL HIGHWAY AND URBAN STREET EXPENDITURES IN THE UNITED
STATES AND SELECTED STATES, 1964
(million dollars)

TABLE 93
REVENUES FROM
HIGHWAY USERS, FOR
SELECTED STATES AND
THE UNITED STATES
AS A WHOLE, 1964
(million dollars)

	Rural*a*	Urban*b*	Administration	Total	
Connecticut	158.2	32.9	13.7	204.8	141.3
Delaware	53.8	1.4	4.8	60.0	27.1
Florida	280.7	36.8	28.4	345.9	242.1
Georgia	181.4	20.7	10.8	212.9	181.0
Illinois	473.2	95.7	35.7	604.6	545.6
Indiana	232.9	21.4	24.6	278.9	247.6
Maine	60.6	9.7	3.5	73.8	56.7
Maryland	152.6	20.6	10.5	183.7	166.8
Massachusetts	251.1	72.3	21.3	344.7	183.7
Michigan	284.1	71.5	33.9	389.5	390.2
Minnesota	230.3	38.8	8.9	278.0	222.2
New Hampshire	43.3	8.6	3.6	55.5	45.1
New Jersey	192.1	75.3	19.5	286.9	151.7
New York	673.1	146.6	42.6	862.3	518.5
North Carolina	161.5	25.0	14.0	200.5	214.3
North Dakota	68.9	7.1	2.7	78.7	59.1
Ohio	450.9	91.9	29.8	572.6	523.8
Pennsylvania	494.9	74.2	41.2	610.3	492.3
South Carolina	87.6	3.4	5.0	96.0	101.2
Vermont	42.8	2.7	1.9	47.4	40.5
Virginia	271.7	23.3	16.9	311.9	305.3
Washington	192.8	31.4	12.5	236.7	182.3
Wisconsin	176.3	45.2	12.9	234.4	179.9
Total 23 states	5,214.8	956.5	398.7	6,570.0	5,218.3
Total U.S.	9,719.4	1,592.6	683.0	11,995.0	9,712.7

Source: U.S., Department of Transportation, *Highway Statistics,*
1965, Washington, U.S. Government Printing Office, 1967, Table
F-2, p. 121.
*a*Includes some expenditures in urban areas.
*b*Excludes expenditures on municipal extensions of state rural highway systems; these are included under "rural."

Source: U.S.,
Department of
Transportation,
Bureau of Public
Roads, *Highway
Statistics,* 1965,
Table F-1, p. 120.

In four of the states shown separately in Table 95, highway expenditures
are effectively equal to highway-user revenues. These states are Michigan,
North Carolina, South Carolina, and Virginia. In all the others highway
users are subsidized from general government revenues, with the amount of
the subsidy ranging up to 1.29 cents in Delaware. The average subsidy for the
23 states was 0.28 cents per vehicle-mile, close to the U.S. average of 0.27
cents per vehicle-mile.

TABLE 94

ESTIMATES OF HIGHWAY TAXES PAID BY SELECTED MOTOR VEHICLES IN
SELECTED STATES, 1964

	Medium passenger car[a]			Medium truck[b]			Tractor-semi-trailer[c]		
	State	Federal	Total	State	Federal	Total	State	Federal	Total
Connecticut	$58	$30	$88	$286	$104	$390	$1,022	$967	$1,989
Delaware	48	30	78	282	104	386	897	967	1,864
Florida	65	30	95	452	104	556	1,403	967	2,370
Georgia	48	30	78	272	104	376	1,294	967	2,261
Illinois	49	30	79	330	104	434	1,464	967	2,431
Indiana	51	30	81	262	104	366	980	967	1,947
Maine	61	30	91	391	104	495	1,223	967	2,190
Maryland	48	30	78	235	104	339	886	967	1,853
Massachusetts	53	30	83	252	104	356	792	967	1,759
Michigan	50	30	80	365	104	469	1,340	967	2,307
Minnesota	67	30	97	296	104	400	1,387	967	2,354
New Hampshire	85	30	115	390	104	494	1,267	967	2,234
New Jersey	53	30	83	291	104	395	961	967	1,928
New York	55	30	85	295	104	399	2,355	967	3,322
North Carolina	55	30	85	500	104	604	1,538	967	2,505
North Dakota	74	30	104	355	104	459	1,395	967	2,362
Ohio	55	30	85	392	104	496	2,131	967	3,098
Pennsylvania	54	30	84	323	104	427	1,009	967	1,976
South Carolina	49	30	79	400	104	504	1,277	967	2,244
Vermont	73	30	103	439	104	543	1,257	967	2,224
Virginia	54	30	84	307	104	411	1,580	967	2,547
Washington	89	30	119	426	104	530	1,704	967	2,671
Wisconsin	54	30	84	425	104	529	1,370	967	2,337

Sources: State taxes: U.S., Department of Commerce, Bureau of Public Roads, *Road-User and Property Taxes on Selected Motor Vehicles*, 1964 (1964); Federal taxes: U.S., House, *Supplementary Report of the Highway Cost Allocation Study*, H. Doc. No. 124, 89th Congr., 1st sess., 1965, Table 3, pp. 10–14.
[a]119-inch wheelbase; 3,480 lb. tare weight.
[b]2 axles; 19,000 lb. gross vehicle weight.
[c]Diesel tractor; 2-axle semi-trailer; combination, 55,000 lb. gross vehicle weight.

D.   HIGHWAY TAX RECIPROCITY IN THE UNITED STATES

Highway tax reciprocity has received considerable attention in the United States. Two regional groupings of states extend reciprocal privileges among their members. One is located in the western United States and includes 16 states, while the other group has 15 states as members and is centred in the southeast states. Besides these instances of regional reciprocity, some states have established bilateral reciprocity with other states. Reciprocity is, however, by no means universal, particularly in the northeastern United States.

TABLE 95

RELATIONSHIPS BETWEEN HIGHWAY EXPENDITURE AND HIGHWAY USE,
FOR SELECTED STATES, 1964

	Estimated highway use (million vehicle-miles)	Expenditure per vehicle-mile (cents)	Highway-user revenue per vehicle-mile (cents)	Subsidy per vehicle-mile (cents)
Connecticut	11,878	1.72	1.19	0.53
Delaware	2,553	2.35	1.06	1.29
Florida	26,941	1.28	0.90	0.38
Georgia	20,198	1.05	0.90	0.15
Illinois	43,585	1.39	1.25	0.14
Indiana	24,384	1.14	1.02	0.12
Maine	4,652	1.59	1.22	0.37
Maryland	14,119	1.30	1.18	0.12
Massachusetts	20,730	1.66	0.89	0.77
Michigan	38,145	1.02	1.02	—
Minnesota	16,422	1.69	1.35	0.34
New Hampshire	2,895	1.92	1.56	0.36
New Jersey	28,764	1.00	0.53	0.47
New York	54,709	1.58	0.95	0.63
North Carolina	22,061	0.91	0.97	(0.06)*
North Dakota	3,011	2.61	1.96	0.65
Ohio	44,652	1.28	1.17	0.11
Pennsylvania	44,008	1.39	1.12	0.27
South Carolina	10,736	0.89	0.94	(0.05)*
Vermont	1,846	2.57	2.19	0.38
Virginia	18,741	1.67	1.63	0.04
Washington	13,593	1.74	1.34	0.40
Wisconsin	17,613	1.33	1.02	0.31
23 states (weighted average)	486,236	1.35	1.07	0.28
U.S.	841,909	1.42	1.15	0.27

Sources: Highway use: calculated from fuel consumption statistics in U.S., Department of Commerce, Bureau of Public Roads, *Highway Statistics*, 1964, Table G-23, p. 5, using 12.47 vehicle-miles per gallon of fuel consumed (from *Highway Statistics*, 1965, Table VM-1, p. 54); expenditure calculated from Table 92; revenue calculated from Table 93; subsidy calculated by subtracting revenue per vehicle-mile from expenditure per vehicle-mile.
*Highway-user revenue greater than highway expenditure.

E. SIZE, WEIGHT, AND SAFETY REGULATIONS

As in Canada, maximum allowable vehicle sizes and weights vary among different U.S. jurisdictions. Maximum permissible vehicle lengths for tractor–semi-trailers vary between 55 feet and 60 feet in most states; but three states allow this combination to be only 50 feet in length, while five others permit tractor–semi-trailer lengths of 65 feet.[48] The maximum weight permitted for

[48]All figures in this paragraph are from "State Size & Weight Limits for Truck-Trailer Combinations," *Transportation and Distribution Management*, Oct. 1966, p. 26.

a 4-axle tractor–semi-trailer is 58,420 pounds in Texas, while in Wisconsin this vehicle is permitted to weigh 67,500 pounds. All states specify tandem axle-load limits. Over one-half put the maximum at 32,000 pounds, but one state, Georgia, allows tandem axle loads of 40,680 pounds, and, at the other extreme, Ohio allows only 24,000 pounds.[49] Some evidence is available concerning the impact of differing state taxes and regulations on interstate commerce. A 1961 U.S. Department of Agriculture study[50] found that most interstate truckers of agricultural products claimed that state taxes and regulations "unduly" interfered with their operations. "Unduly" was construed to involve "serious inconvenience in terms of cost or time"; 81 percent of ICC-regulated, and 93 percent of non-regulated, carriers alleged such interference.[51] The most frequent complaints were against fuel-use taxes, difficulty of obtaining operating authority from state regulatory commissions, ton-mile and axle-mile taxes, and length-of-vehicle limitations.

Canadian and U.S. highway transport policies compared

The discussion in the preceding two sections shows clearly that there are significant differences between Canada and the United States with respect to several key aspects of highway transport policy. In this section we enumerate and evaluate these anomalies.

The U.S. for-hire trucking industry is larger, in terms of operating revenues, than its Canadian counterpart. All forms of highway transport, private and for-hire, are similarly more important in the United States than in Canada. In 1965 U.S. highway transport accounted for 371 billion revenue ton-miles of freight transportation, or 22.5 percent of the total. Canadian highway transport had only a 9.3 percent share of total transport output, with production of some 19 billion ton-miles.

In Canada the provinces exercise virtually all regulatory and promotional responsibilities with respect to trucking. Federal regulatory authority over extra-provincial trucking has been, in effect, delegated to the provinces. Also, the federal government in Canada has not been a continuing and active promoter of highway transport through assistance to highway construction.

[49]A recent study of the desirability of increasing maximum vehicle weights compared vehicle operating-cost savings and additional highway costs and concluded that these limits should be substantially raised for the Interstate Highway System. See U.S., House, *Maximum Desirable Dimensions and Weights of Vehicles Operated on the Federal-Aid Systems*, H. Doc. no. 354, 88th Congr., 2nd sess., 1964.
[50]*Effects of State and Local Regulations on Interstate Movement of Agricultural Products by Highway* (1961).
[51]*Ibid.*, p. v.

.

This situation may be about to change, but it has not yet done so. The U.S. federal government, on the other hand, administers wide-ranging and detailed regulation over most for-hire interstate trucking. In addition, the federal government in the United States has since 1916 participated in an extensive program of aid in highway construction. 1965 expenditures of all federal government agencies for highways amounted to $4,165 million;[52] the comparable Canadian figure, as mentioned above, was $161 million.

The quality of regulation imposed on for-hire trucking in Canada is variable, but over-all it cannot be given high marks for consistency, comprehensiveness, or effectiveness. More disturbing is the lack of coordination among different provincial regulatory bodies, even when they are regulating extra-provincial transport under federal law. Different complaints are typically directed against U.S. trucking regulation by the Interstate Commerce Commission. The ICC is said to be trying to overregulate the industry and is accused of creating unnecessary barriers to the efficient adjustment of for-hire trucking to changing competitive conditions. Between these extremes must lie a more nearly optimal system and philosophy of regulation—we suspect that it lies closer to the ICC model than to the present Canadian model.

Canada spends more on highways, in relation to the size of her economy, than does the United States. Moreover, Canadian highway expenditures have increased much more rapidly in recent years. Highway taxes tend to be slightly lower in Canada than in the United States on similar types of vehicles (as a comparison of Tables 89 and 94 shows), but the differences are in most cases not substantial. Canadian highway users receive a much higher subsidy from non-users than do U.S. highway users. For Canada the average subsidy in 1965 was 1.14 cents per vehicle-mile, while in the United States the 1964 subsidy averaged 0.27 cents per vehicle-mile. Public policy in Canada is therefore more expansionary towards highway travel of all types than is public policy in the United States.

Concerning highway tax reciprocity, comparison of provincial and state regulations indicates that Canadian trucking may be in a less favourable position than its U.S. counterpart. But while there are fewer complete reciprocity agreements in Canada, Canadian jurisdictions are much larger, and the Canadian highway tax structure is not complicated by fuel-use taxes and weight-distance taxes. Restrictions on vehicle sizes and weights are generally both more uniform and more liberal in Canada than in the United States.

Highway transport is, we might conclude, at an advantage in Canada relative to the United States insofar as promotion and size and weight restrictions influence the course of the industry, and at a disadvantage insofar as

[52]*Highway Statistics*, 1965, Table FA-5, p. 174.

economic regulation is important to the industry. But given the denser population of the United States, the greater abundance of traffic well suited to
truck transport, and the higher quality of the highway system[53] (which
reflects the longer sustained improvement effort in the United States), we
must conclude that highway transport is better suited to the U.S. situation,
that it is better developed, and that public policy is at least partly responsible
for this last result.

But the higher level of subsidy to Canadian trucking deserves further
attention. Canadian vehicle operators are subsidized by 0.87 cents per
vehicle-mile more than are U.S. vehicle operators (1.14 cents in Canada;
0.27 cents in the United States). A tractor–semi-trailer combination of
50,000 pounds gross vehicle weight (the type used as an example in Tables
89 and 94) would carry approximately 15 tons of freight. Thus a subsidy of
0.87 cents per vehicle-mile may be converted to a subsidy of 0.058 cents (or
0.58 mills) per revenue ton-mile. A one-way haul of 300 miles would
develop 4,500 revenue ton-miles and benefit from a highway subsidy of
$2.61. A truck of this type might travel 50,000 miles per year, in which case
its Canadian "advantage" would be $435 per year. If this typical vehicle
traveled fully loaded throughout its 50,000 annual mileage, gross line-haul
costs would be on the order of $16,250 per year.[54] The annual Canadian
cost advantage is therefore about 2.7 percent of line-haul operating costs.

We might conclude that, on balance, highway transport policy in Canada
is more expansionary than in the United States. But what is the direction of
the impact of this policy difference on Canada-U.S. trade? In general terms
the question is simple. East-west truck transport within Canada is encouraged
relative to north-south truck transport between the two countries; therefore
trade is discouraged. But the significance of this influence is open to question.
To develop more meaningful conclusions as to the impact of highway transport policy on trade between Canada and the United States, we need more
specific analysis of the influence of regulation and promotion on transborder
truck transport. This will be attempted in the next two sections.

The promotion of highway transportation and transborder trucking

Highways have no direct effect on international trade unless they are built in
places where they can serve such trade. The highway systems of the United

[53]In the U.S. 27,000 miles of rural freeway (*Highway Statistics*, 1965, Table SM-11,
p. 134); in Canada, 1,646 miles of rural freeway (see above).
[54]Assuming a cost of 1.3¢ per gross ton-mile. See Highway Research Board, Bulletin
301, *Line-Haul Trucking Costs in Relation to Vehicle Gross Weights*, Washington,
National Academy of Sciences-National Research Council, 1961, Table 31, p. 86.

States and Canada have more of an east-west orientation than a north-south orientation. This is, of course, especially true in Canada, where the major single highway project of the last decade has been the Trans-Canada Highway. But the U.S. highway system is similarly east-west in location. There are, for example, only 12 places on the Canada-U.S. boundary that are reached by segments of the Interstate Highway System. The state of Illinois, to take a typical eastern example, is served at its borders by 13 interstate highways.

The subjective impression that highway expenditures have, to some degree, been directed towards projects that do not serve Canada-U.S. trade routes can be reinforced by examining the average subsidy levels for the provinces and states that are especially important in transborder truck traffic. Two provinces (Ontario and Quebec) and six states (Michigan, New York, Ohio, Indiana, Illinois, and Pennsylvania) are included in this group. Ontario's subsidy per vehicle-mile is 0.37 cents below the Canadian average, while Quebec's, at 1.37 cents, is 0.23 cents above it. Moreover, all the states, with the exception of New York, have vehicle-mile subsidies that are equal to, or, for four of the six, less than, the national average of 0.27 cents. A truck operating between Toronto and Flint, Michigan, for example, a distance of 250 miles (175 miles in Ontario and 75 miles in Michigan), would enjoy an average subsidy per vehicle-mile of 0.54 cents or, at 50,000 miles per year, $270 per year. Between Toronto and Chicago the annual subsidy would be only $190 per year.

The degree of stimulation of highway transport is therefore considerably less on international routes than on all-Canadian routes. There, using the national average, the subsidy would be $570 per year for 50,000 miles per year. The all-U.S. subsidy for the same vehicle, again using the national average, would be $135 per year. Assuming perfect *pro rata* reciprocity[55] among participating jurisdictions, we would expect some slight stimulus to transborder truck transport relative to other transborder modes of transport and relative to U.S. domestic trucking, and some retardation relative to Canadian domestic trucking.

The regulation of international truck operations

The regulatory policies towards trucking of the U.S. federal government and the Canadian provincial governments constitute probably the most significant transportation deterrent to the free flow of North American trade. We

[55]*Pro rata* reciprocity involves the split payment of all highway taxes according to the proportion of total mileage traveled in various jurisdictions.

will be able in this section to be considerably more explicit concerning the details and incidence of these policies than we were able to be in the case of promotional policies.

A.   CONTROL OF ENTRY UNDER U.S. AND CANADIAN LAW

The most important regulatory difficulties involving transborder truck transportation occur in the control of entry into this type of service. This control is exercised in the United States by the Interstate Commerce Commission under Sections 202(a) and 203(a)(11) of the Interstate Commerce Act and in Canada by the various provincial regulatory commissions under federal authority conferred under Section 3 of the Motor Vehicle Transport Act.

The relevant section of the Interstate Commerce Act is Section 206, which reads, in part, as follows: "Except as otherwise provided in this section and in section 210a, no common carrier by motor vehicle subject to the provisions of this part shall engage in any interstate or foreign operation on any public highway, or within any reservation under the exclusive jurisdiction of the United States, unless there is in force with respect to such carrier a certificate of public convenience and necessity issued by the Commission authorizing such operations." Comparable Canadian provisions vary among provinces, but the general requirement is proof of public convenience and necessity. In fulfilment of this requirement the following criteria are typically applied in deciding on an application for operating authority:

1. The fitness of the applicant (his financial resources and responsibility and his business ability and trucking experience).
2. Evidence of the *need* of shippers for the proposed service.
3. The effect of the proposed service on carriers already licensed to provide this service.

Not surprisingly, the application of these standards is as subjective as the ICC's application of its legislative mandate.

B.   THE APPLICATION OF ENTRY CONTROL BY THE
     INTERSTATE COMMERCE COMMISSION

Four formal cases involving the issuance of transborder operating rights will illustrate the practical impact of entry control on international highway transportation. Two of the cases were decided by the Interstate Commerce Commission and two by the Ontario Highway Transport Board (OHTB). We will first examine the ICC cases. The first of these was decided in 1956 and involved the application of a Canadian trucker to haul petroleum and petroleum products from points in Minnesota to the international boundary en route to points in northwestern Ontario.[56] The applicant presented evidence of need for his proposed service by several petroleum-products users in northwestern Ontario. The application for grant of operating authority was opposed by two motor carriers already offering a partial substitute for the proposed service. The Commission refused the application, on the grounds that the applicant had not established that the public convenience and necessity required his proposed service. On the question of its ability to evaluate the needs of Canadian consignees for additional petroleum-products transport service, the ICC had this to say: "We do not have, of course, any jurisdiction over the operation conducted by applicant or opposing carriers in Canada, or the need for any additional service between points in Canada; but in deciding whether applicant has shown a need for the authority here sought between points in Minnesota we must necessarily give consideration to evidence submitted with respect to service needs involving points within Canada."[57]

This interpretation by the ICC of their international responsibilities might be considered disturbing as an intrusion into Canadian affairs, but a more recent Commission decision that takes an opposite point of view seems to offer far greater scope for interference with trade flows. This second case involved an application of a Canadian trucker to carry clay products from points in Ohio, West Virginia, Pennsylvania, and Maryland to the international boundary at the Niagara, Detroit, and St. Clair Rivers en route to Ontario destinations.[58]

The applicant presented quite specific information concerning the need for the service he was proposing to offer with specialized equipment. The grant of authority was opposed by three U.S. railroads and by several U.S. and Canadian trucking firms. These motor carriers were jointly engaged in offering interchange service, apparently with conventional equipment. The ICC decided against the application, on the grounds that existing service from the U.S. origins to the international boundary was adequate. The needs of Canadian users of brick and clay products were specifically excluded from consideration, a complete reversal from the 1956 Clarke Robertson's decision. The Commission's reason for this change read as follows:

We are not persuaded that there is any material inadequacy in the service presently authorized from the involved origins to the port of entry at Buffalo. Further, we do not believe that the asserted inadequacy of transportation service and facilities

[56]"Clarke Robertson's Transportation Limited Extension—Petroleum Products," 68 MCC 611 (1956).
[57]Ibid., p. 614.
[58]"Joseph Balazs, Sr., Common Carrier Application," 95 MCC 63 (1964).

within Canada is a relevant consideration in disposing of the instant applications. This is a matter for the Canadian authorities. For example, questions were raised at the continued hearing respecting the scope of the one protestant's authorized operations within Canada. It would be manifestly improper for us to presume to determine the scope of such operations and it would be equally inappropriate to presume to determine the adequacy of existing service within Canada, or the needs of Canadian shippers for additional service within Canada. We are not unmindful that consideration has sometimes been afforded service needs in Canada and the adequacy of existing service within Canada. However, in view of the issues raised on exceptions by the Canadian protestants, we believe that this is the appropriate time to reappraise the situation. In summary, we believe that sound regulatory policy dictates that our responsibility is to determine the public convenience and necessity insofar as operations within the United States are concerned while, at the same time, respecting fully the authority of foreign countries over foreign operations.[59]

The danger in this interpretation is that it would seem to exclude, as a general rule, new grants of operating authority for any single-carrier service operating across the international boundary. Additional discussion of the effects of interchange service on U.S.-Canadian trade will be presented later in this chapter.

C. THE APPLICATION OF ENTRY CONTROL IN ONTARIO

The first Ontario case was decided in 1965 and involved the application of a U.S. carrier of general freight, Transamerican Freight Lines Inc. Their application requested: "the right to carry International freight as a common carrier from the points it is licensed to serve in the United States directly to certain points in Southern Ontario and return via the Detroit and Niagara River Gateways."[60] The case is of interest because of what it reveals concerning the impact of current regulatory practices on operating efficiency in international trucking and also because of the insights it affords into the attitudes towards transborder trucking of part of the Canadian trucking industry and one provincial government.

Hearings in the Transamerican case began in October, 1962, and a final decision was not handed down by the OHTB until August, 1965. Ninety witnesses appeared to support the application and 76 U.S. and Canadian trucking companies opposed it. The Ontario Board approved the application, with modifications.[61] The OHTB based its decision entirely on the excessive delays entailed by the existing system. That system involved the interchange of freight between U.S. and Ontario carriers at the international border. In

[59]*Ibid.*, p. 636.
[60]Ontario Highway Transport Board, "Decision: Transamerican Freight Lines Inc.," Aug. 24, 1965 (mimeo.), pp. 3–4.
[61]These restricted the Ontario points served to Windsor, London, Hamilton, and Toronto and specified use of the Detroit gateway only.

some cases the connection involved simple interchange of trailers, while in many others trailers were actually loaded and unloaded at the border. Noting the reported delays of two to three days, the OHTB concluded that these border transfers were "seriously hampering industry in this Province"[62] and that the "broad public interest" required approval of Transamerican's application, despite the expected "dislocation of certain private interests."[63]

The Ontario Cabinet did not agree. The Ontario truckers who had acted as respondents in the Transamerican case appealed the OHTB's decision to the Cabinet.[64] Their decision on the appeal remains to be handed down. In effect, of course, this amounts to a denial of Transamerican's application. Protection of the existing inefficient arrangements for handling transborder truck traffic is apparently considered more important than the promotion of Canada's (and Ontario's) trade with the United States.

In the second Ontario case the government's general attitude in the Transamerican case was reflected in the Ontario Highway Transport Board's decision. The case involved the application of four automobile haulaway carriers for operating authority to carry vehicles from points in the United States through to various points in southern Ontario and, for one of the applicants, to points in northern Ontario.[65]

Three of the four applicants already held operating authority to carry vehicles just across the international boundary, presumably there to transfer them to Canadian truckers for delivery to dealers. The application was vigorously supported by Ford Motor Company and Ford Motor Company of Canada Limited. Ford's argument was based, essentially, on the need for efficient transportation to serve the new northbound movement of vehicles made possible by the Automotive Free Trade Agreement. The applicant carriers already provided service from U.S. assembly plants to U.S. destinations for Ford, and the company wished to obtain the same single-carrier service to Ontario destinations. The existing system of transfer, vehicle by vehicle, was alleged to be inefficient and expensive, and interchange of loaded trailers was judged to be impossible because of divergent traffic patterns.

The respondents, four Ontario truckers and a union, based their opposition

[62]Ibid., p. 7.
[63]Ibid., p. 10.
[64]The Cabinet's action does not represent quite as much interference with an independent commission as might appear. Under Ontario law it is actually the Minister of Transport who issues the operating licence to carriers, after the Ontario Highway Transport Board has established public convenience and necessity. But the Minister's action is usually a mere formality.
[65]Ontario Highway Transport Board, "In the Matter of the Application of Automobile Transport, Inc., E. and L. Transport Company, Nu-Car Carriers, Inc., and K. W. McKee Incorporated," Jan. 23, 1967 (mimeo.).

to the application on three contentions. First, neither General Motors or Chrysler had attempted to obtain changes in the existing transborder operating arrangements. This was offered as proof that Ford's attempt was unnecessary. Second, it was asserted the transfer operation was not inefficient because current licensing practices required it. To be at all logical, this contention necessarily involves redefinition of "inefficient." Third, the four respondents were willing and able to offer service from international border points and from Ford's Detroit assembly plants. This was true, but single-carrier service from other Ford assembly plants could not be offered.

The OHTB denied the applications. While agreeing that the transfer operation was less efficient than a single-line operation, the Board found more weighty conclusions on the other side of the question. The existing carriers could, in the Board's opinion, be used to greater advantage than had been the case in the past. Also, Canadian truck drivers "may be in jeopardy with loss of employment."[66] These two factors were, however, of minor weight compared to the apparently major importance placed on obtaining reciprocal treatment for Ontario vehicle haulers from the Interstate Commerce Commission. Since the southbound flow of vehicles moved via highway transport will in the near future be very much larger than the northbound flow, the OHTB was apparently concerned that Canadian motor carriers be given full opportunity to participate in this traffic. Thus, one of the matters considered by the Board was described in these terms: "Would the Canadian carriers in fact be able to obtain Interstate Commerce Commission authority to operate in the United States, and if so, would the various State requirements make it impossible for them to operate within the United States without a large financial outlay?"[67] Its answer to this question may be seen quite clearly in the following conclusion: "The Board further finds that whereas damages and delays inevitably occur in any motor vehicle transportation system that on the evidence before it, under the present system, the damage and delays are not of such a proportion as to warrant the change of the present policy of having American carriers operate in the United States of America, and Canadian carriers operate in the Province of Ontario. This policy would appear to be in line with that of the Interstate Commerce Commission policy, whereby very few Canadian carriers can penetrate beyond the municipalities located at the international boundary."[68]

D. PROCEDURES IN TRANSBORDER TRUCK OPERATIONS

It is apparent from the discussion of these four cases that obtaining through international operating authority is not an easy task, at least between the United States and Ontario. There is reason to believe that a similar condition

[66]Ibid., p. 5.　　　[67]Ibid., p. 4.　　　[68]Ibid., p. 5.

exists between the United States and most other provinces. The costs of this difficulty will be left for later; we now want to explore the extent of the barriers to free international trucking.

Very few motor carriers offer general freight service between inland (non-border) Canadian points and inland U.S. points in the eastern half of the continent. From such important Ontario centres as Hamilton and Toronto, for example, only two carriers offer through single-line general freight service to New York City.

In the absence of a single-line transborder operating authority, two alternatives exist. The trailer may be interchanged (attached to a tractor operated by a properly licensed carrier) or it may be unloaded and its cargo transferred to a trailer operated by a properly licensed carrier. Trailer interchange, however, involves the motor carriers in the payment of additional licence fees, unless suitable reciprocity agreements are in force. General reciprocity does not exist between eastern provinces and eastern states; this situation will be discussed later.

The existence in Ontario of one type of reciprocity scheme makes it possible to estimate the proportions of U.S. to Canadian truck traffic handled via interchange and via other means for that province. The scheme referred to is the system of transferable plates; these plates are issued to Ontario truckers to enable them to haul U.S.-owned trailers without payment of additional licence or carrier fees. In 1964, 255 transferable plates were issued and 22,734 individual trips made using these plates.[69] Assuming that on each trip 15 tons of freight were carried (a generous estimate), about 340,000 tons of freight entered Ontario under this arrangement in 1964. Total truck-carried imports into Ontario in 1964 were on the order of 800,000 tons, based on conservative estimating procedures.[70]

The remaining 460,000 tons entered under one of five methods. Some freight was transported by private trucks operated by the owner of the goods, some was transported via trailer interchange in trailers on which full Ontario licence and carrier fees had been paid,[71] some was transported by the few carriers authorized to provide through transborder service, and some was

[69]Annual Report of the Ontario Highway Transport Board for Year Ending December 31, 1965 (mimeo.), Exhibit E, and information supplied by the Automotive Transport Association of Ontario.
[70]The source of this estimate is the DBS publication, Travel between Canada and the United States, and its basis is as outlined in the chap. 2 estimates of transborder truck traffic. In 1964 there were 527,917 commercial vehicle entries into Ontario from the U.S. Assuming that 60 percent of these vehicles were loaded and that the average load was 2.5 tons, we arrive at our 800,000 ton estimate.
[71]Little of this traffic would be likely to fall into this category. The DBS motor transport traffic survey sampled 2,290 Ontario-registered trucks in 1964. Only 80 of these were also registered in the U.S., as would be required for this category.

consigned to border points in Ontario included in the operating authorities of U.S. carriers. Most of this freight, however, was unloaded at the border— on either the U.S. or Canadian side—and reloaded into a Canadian trailer.

E.   THE COSTS OF RESTRICTIVE LICENSING PRACTICES

Some estimates can be made of the costs of these policy-enforced practices. The Transamerican and automobile haulaway cases discussed above suggest that even trailer interchange may impose unnecessary delays in freight service. Meyer and his associates, using 1955 figures, used an estimate of 3 hours for an interchange.[72] There do not appear to have been since then any significant technological advances that would impel us to reduce this estimate. Exhibits presented by the Ford Motor Company during the OHTB hearings in the automobile case indicate that international rates involving interchange are higher than the rates would be for single-line service. On vehicles transported from Oakville, Ontario, to Youngstown, Ohio, the existing truck-freight rate was $58.30 per vehicle; using all-Canadian mileage-rate scales the rate would have been $44.70 per vehicle. In the other direction, vehicles transported from Mahwah, New Jersey, to Hamilton, Ontario, paid a truck-freight rate of $91.25 per vehicle; using a combination of U.S. and Canadian mileage-scale rates, the charge for this transportation would have been $82.70 per vehicle. There are, of course, differences between Canadian and U.S. motor carrier costs, and Canadian rates are *generally* lower than U.S. rates.[73] This might suggest that the Oakville-Youngstown hypothetical rate is too low, since most of the haul would be in the United States—but this rate would not be so high as to bring it to the level of the published rate. The Mahwah-Hamilton hypothetical rate is based on both U.S. and Canadian rate scales and so is not affected by these qualifications.

More solid evidence of the costs of interference with transborder truck operations is provided by Interstate Commerce Commission cost studies. The ICC's 1964 cost study for the Eastern-Central Territory, which covers motor common carriers operating in the states immediately south of eastern Canada, contains estimates of the costs of interchanging equipment and cargoes. These are shown in Table 96. These costs constitute an unnecessary impediment to the free flow of trade within North America. Yet they are probably not as significant as the time costs of delays at the border, as incurred by carriers, shippers, and consignees. The Transamerican case's reports of two—

[72]John R. Meyer, *et al., The Economics of Competition in the Transportation Industries,* Cambride, Mass., Harvard University Press, 1959, p. 193.
[73]Average for-hire motor carrier revenue in Canada in 1964 was 5.4 cents per revenue ton-mile (7.2 cents in Ontario). For the United States the 1964 figure was 6.1 cents. Canadian statistics from DBS, *Motor Transport Traffic: Canada,* 1964 (1967), Table 4, p. 15; U.S. statistics from ICC, *Transport Economics,* Aug. 1967, p. 3.

TABLE 96

COSTS OF MOTOR CARRIER INTERCHANGE, TOTAL CARGO LOAD OF 30,000
POUNDS, U.S. EAST-CENTRAL TERRITORY, 1964

Weight of shipment (lbs.)	Cost of trailer interchange ($/trailer)	Cost of trailer interchange ($/100 lbs. cargo)	Cost of cargo interchange ($/100 lbs.)
1,742[a]	[b]	[b]	0.551
10,000	11.40	0.038	0.443
15,000	11.40	0.038	0.397
30,000	11.40	0.038	0.342

Source: ICC, *Cost of Transporting Freight by Class I and Class II Motor Common Carriers of General Commodities: Eastern-Central Territory,* 1964, Washington, ICC, 1966, Table 2, pp. 21–2.
[a]Average shipment size for the East-Central Territory.
[b]Not shown separately—presumably also $11.40 per trailer or $0.038 per 100 lbs. cargo.

and three-day delays denote substantial costs to all three parties—the carrier because he must store the goods in trailers or in terminals and the shipper and consignee because transit time is increased in length and uncertainty.

Concerning interchange involving cargo transfer, it is argued that this procedure would occur anyway at the border, since there exists there a natural break-bulk and assembly point.[74] In general this argument is not tenable. The inherent nature of international traffic flows does not require that they be broken and reloaded at the border—it is regulatory and licensing policy that impels this unnecessary and wasteful procedure.

F. THE SOURCES OF RESTRICTED INTERNATIONAL OPERATING RIGHTS

We have thus far concentrated on motor carrier operations from the United States into Canada because the specific information available on international highway transport has been concerned with south-north traffic. This might imply that the blame for the paucity of international operating licences (as particularly evident between Ontario and the United States) rests with Canadian authorities. This does not seem to be the case; if we were assigning proportionate blame, we would have to lay the greater proportion on the U.S. Interstate Commerce Commission and its regulation of entry into trucking operations.

Canadian licensing authorities have tended to be rather reluctant to give their approval to the issuing of through international operating licences, but there is evidence that this attitude is a result of Canadian carriers' inability

[74]It is also argued that the break-bulk operation is required because of the variety of customs clearance instructions given by different importers. But this is not a convincing argument—the instructions could surely be standardized if more efficient transborder operations were implemented.

to obtain reciprocal treatment from the ICC.[75] This inability, we should emphasize, does not flow from an explicit ICC policy of discriminating against Canadian motor carriers in operating authority proceedings. Rather, it is naturally derived from the Commission's generally restrictive policies regarding the entry of new trucking firms. The following excerpt from a speech of a former ICC chairman sets this forth:

[Canadian] carriers . . . who actually render service in the United States, must . . . meet the safety and insurance requirements and must . . . obtain operating authority from the Interstate Commerce Commission. Again, however, this is not different, either in philosophy or procedure, from requirements imposed on our domestic carriers. The Commission issues certificates of public convenience and necessity to common carriers who prove a need for the proposed service which is unavailable from existing carriers. Only by requiring proof of public convenience and necessity can we avoid division of traffic among too many carriers resulting in destructive competition and deterioration in service.[76]

The effect of this policy may be described as follows. A U.S. common carrier trucking firm seeking, for example, authority to transport general commodities from Buffalo to Boston, New York, Philadelphia, and Baltimore or from Seattle to all points in California would be as unsuccessful as a Canadian carrier in obtaining this authority. In the Commission's view on these routes (selected as examples only), the public convenience and necessity would not require the licensing of additional carriers. For the purpose of issuing operating authorities, international traffic is considered to originate and terminate at the international boundary. This interpretation is in line with the Commission's recent Balazs decision (discussed above) but is completely at variance with its treatment of international railroad traffic in the course of rate regulation.

Until the Commission's approach is modified, Canadian regulators, under pressure from Canadian trucking interests, will find it very difficult to approve important grants of operating authority for U.S. carriers. The Canadian economy generally would benefit from even a one-sided liberal licensing policy in international trucking. But in practical terms such an enlightened and benevolent change of attitude is extremely unlikely. Improvement in the present restriction policies towards licensing international carriers can probably only be achieved on a *quid pro quo* basis. The need for an international negotiating mechanism in highway transport will become even more pressing as truck traffic between Canada and the United States multiplies.

[75]As, for example, in the automobile haulaway case in Ontario.
[76]Charles A. Webb, "International Transportation Relationship between Canada and the United States," remarks before the 20th Anniversary Convention of the National Tank Truck Carriers, Inc., Montreal, May 19, 1965, p. 3.

Freight rates in international trucking

Federal statutes in both Canada and the United States provide authority for regulating rates charged for international truck transportation. The U.S. Interstate Commerce Act gives this authority to the Interstate Commerce Commission,[77] while the Canadian Motor Vehicle Transport Act empowers provincial regulatory commissions to regulate rates charged by extra-provincial carriers if the rates of intra-provincial carriers are regulated.[78] Only five provinces qualify, however, and it appears that most of these have, for various reasons, decided not to try to influence extra-provincial rates, beyond requiring that tariffs be filed. The non-regulating provinces also require tariff-filing.

This leaves the Interstate Commerce Commission as the effective sole regulator of international highway transport rates. Yet the ICC has been very inactive in this area and has, as far as can be determined, never intervened actively in matters involving international trucking rates.

There is general agreement that international rates are higher than U.S. domestic or Canadian domestic rates—we saw evidence of this in the preceding section of this chapter. Other evidence might be presented. For example, motor carrier rates from Grand Rapids, Michigan, to Toronto (340 miles) are 16 to 28 percent higher than rates on similar commodities from Grand Rapids to Cincinnati (300 miles).[79] The longer haul to Toronto *should* have higher rates, but the difference should be on the order of 5 to 8 percent.[80] The reason for these anomalies is alleged to be the costs of interchange of equipment and cargo and the costs of conforming to customs requirements. We are unable, unfortunately, because of the lack of suitable rate information, to explore the validity of this allegation or to analyze the impact of higher international rates on commodity trade between Canada and the United States.

A brief explanation of the procedures followed by motor carriers in setting through international rates will be helpful. International truck rates are made through tariff bureaus, as are international rail rates. Four U.S. rate bureaus are involved with international truck rates, but the bulk of international traffic moves under rates set by one of these bureaus. This is the Niagara Frontier Tariff Bureau, which publishes through rates between 6 Canadian provinces (from Manitoba through to Prince Edward Island) and 32 U.S. states and the District of Columbia.

[77]Sec. 216(b).   [78]Sec. 4.
[79]Cecil V. Hynes, *Michigan and Ontario Trade and Transport Reciprocity*, East Lansing, Mich., Michigan State University Graduate School of Business Administration, 1966, Table V-1, p. 96.
[80]ICC, *Cost of Transporting Freight ... Eastern-Central Territory*, 1964, Table 11.

The procedure is similar to that previously described in connection with international railroad freight-rate bureaus. Any carrier or shipper may apply to the Bureau for a new rate or for a rate alteration. If the application is of minor interest, it is considered by a standing rate committee of Bureau staff that meets weekly; if the application is of major importance, it must be adjudicated by a general rate committee composed of Bureau members. This committee meets once a month. If the rate is approved, it is filed with the ICC and the appropriate provincial commission. If either committee rejects the rate application, the carriers involved may take independent action.

Other policies affecting international highway transport

A. VEHICLE-SIZE AND -WEIGHT REGULATIONS

We are concerned first with the impact of differences in maximum-vehicle-size and -weight regulations on international trucking. In order to keep the discussion short, we consider only the size and weight regulations for a combination of a 3-axle tractor and 2-axle semi-trailer. This is probably the most common type of vehicle used to transport general freight.

Of the eight Canadian provinces bordering on the United States, six permit this combination to be 60 feet in length.[81] Two, Nova Scotia and Manitoba, permit a length of 65 feet. Twenty of the 23 states included in Table 92 as being important in international highway transport limit the length of this combination to 55 feet. Of the remaining three, two, Washington and North Dakota, allow it to be 60 feet, while Minnesota permits a length of only 50 feet. The general pattern is, then, that this particular type of vehicle is allowed to be 5 feet longer in Canada than in the United States. Vehicles operated in international service must conform to the shortest length limit in force, and the 55-foot length in the United States may require use of a semi-trailer that is 5 feet shorter and has proportionately less cargo capacity. Some states, in fact, limit trailer lengths to 40 feet, 5 feet shorter than the typical Canadian maximum. Ton-mile operating costs will, therefore, be higher by an amount depending on cargo density.

All Canadian provinces allow a 3-axle tractor and 2-axle semi-trailer combination to be operated with a gross vehicle weight (GVW) of 74,000 pounds.[82] All but seven of the 23 important states allow a maximum GVW of between 73,000 and 73,500 pounds for this type of vehicle. Two more states

[81]Canadian regulations from DBS, *The Motor Vehicle*, 1966, Part I, *Rates and Regulations* (1967), Table 1, pp. 6–9; U.S. regulations from *Transportation & Distribution Management*, Oct. 1966, p. 26.
[82]In British Columbia the maximum ranges from 73,300 lbs. to 76,000 lbs., depending on the highway used.

impose a limit of 72,000 pounds, one state has a maximum of 71,000 pounds, and one more has a maximum of 70,000 pounds. Three states have maximum GVWs below 70,000 pounds: Washington at 68,000 pounds, Michigan at 67,000 pounds, and Vermont at 60,000 pounds. A vehicle operated from Quebec City to New York through Vermont (a total distance of about 500 miles) would incur an additional line-haul operating cost of about $52.80 because of the load restriction imposed by the Vermont regulation. This estimate assumes a one-way load of 24 tons and an empty backhaul.[83] For most transborder traffic, of course, no such cost penalty exists—maximum-vehicle-weight regulations are generally similar on both sides of the international boundary.

We would conclude, therefore, that the international anomalies in state and provincial vehicle-weight regulations do not in general create significant barriers to efficient international highway transport. Disparities in vehicle-size regulations present greater problems, however.

B.   HIGHWAY-TAX RECIPROCITY

Even more serious problems are caused by the lack of highway-tax reciprocity between provinces and states. Three western provinces (B.C., Alberta, and Manitoba) have reasonably extensive reciprocity agreements with U.S. states.[84] The remaining western province, Saskatchewan, has partial agreements with only three states, but only a limited volume of traffic is affected. Canada's Atlantic provinces offer reciprocity to U.S. states on a mutual agreement basis, but few agreements have been signed. Quebec has executed reciprocity agreements with the New England states, New York, Pennsylvania, and South Carolina.

Between Ontario and the United States reciprocity is much more limited. There are only two commercially significant aspects of Ontario-U.S. highway-tax reciprocity. One is the reciprocity for trailers operated near (within 10 or 20 miles) both sides of the international boundary. The other is the transferable plate scheme mentioned earlier in this section. Transferable plates are issued to Ontario motor carriers to allow them to haul trailers and semi-trailers registered in the United States without payment of individual vehicle registration fees. The plates are sold at the maximum vehicle licence fee ($372) and the maximum motor carrier fee ($157.50), giving a total cost of $529.50. They have the advantage of flexibility, and they certainly

[83]Revenue ton-miles would then total 12,000. The additional cost per revenue ton-mile of reducing payload weight from 73,000 lbs. to 60,000 lbs. is about 4.4 mills per revenue ton-mile. See Highway Research Board, Bulletin 301, Table 32, p. 87.
[84]Information from DBS, *The Motor Vehicle*, 1966, Part I, Table 3, pp. 16–17.

lower the costs of operating U.S. trailers in Ontario below what would be paid if each and every trailer brought into the province paid full licence and carrier fees. But the transferable plate system does not constitute a satisfactory substitute for reciprocity. At best it allows partial reciprocity for for-hire trucking, but none for private trucking. Moreover, not enough plates are issued to meet the demand—at least, this would seem to be indicated by the large volume of transborder traffic that does *not* move under transferable plates. The lack of full reciprocity combines with restrictive operating-authority policies to cause the inefficient cargo interchange at the border. A more pertinent criticism is that no U.S. jurisdiction has seen fit to offer Ontario trailers a comparable arrangement. Southbound traffic must therefore, if it is desired to avoid double licence and carrier fees, be carried in U.S. trailers or transshipped at the border.

C. MISCELLANEOUS TAX PROBLEMS

The short hauls typical of much transborder trucking create tax difficulties for Canadian carriers. In general, it is the Canadian carrier which operates into the United States (to Buffalo or Detroit, for instance) to effect trailer or cargo interchange. Although in the case of Ontario these international carriers travel only short distances in the United States and are free from state licence fees, they are liable for the U.S. federal highway-use tax. This tax requires the payment of an annual fee of $3.00 per 100 pounds for all vehicles of over 26,000 pounds GVW. Tractor–semi-trailer combinations could thus expect to pay between $150 and $200 annually for a very limited use of U.S. federal-aid highways. In addition, Canadian truck drivers and Canadian truckers who operate trucks across the border are liable for unemployment and social security taxes under the Federal Insurance Contributions Act. This liability exists despite the partial nature of the drivers' employment within the United States and despite the non-liability for U.S. income taxes. Until the present inefficiencies of transborder operations can be corrected, the application of highway-use and FICA taxes against Canadian motor carriers and their employees seems inequitable.

Customs and international highway transport

The discussion in this section parallels the discussion of this topic with respect to railway transport in chapter 4. We first examine the procedures for customs clearance of truck-carried freight and follow this with an examination of customs treatment of vehicles used in international service.

A.   CUSTOMS CLEARANCE PROCEDURES

Canadian customs clearance is carried out at border points or at inland sufferance warehouses. Border clearance is probably preferred by trucking companies, under ideal conditions. However, at the busiest border points conditions are rarely ideal; congestion and delays slow down traffic and increase costs for carrier, shipper, and consignee. For this reason many truck-carried imports are cleared at inland sufferance warehouses. These facilities, located at inland receiving points, are licensed by the Department of National Revenue and provide for more efficient fulfillment of Canadian customs requirements.

These requirements are more cumbersome than their U.S. counterparts. U.S. customs clearance may be carried out at the border, where it is reported to be much faster than in Canada, or, in some cases, at final destination points. The restrictions posed by customs clearance procedures to the free flow of transborder truck traffic thus seem to arise mainly on the Canadian side of the border. Their over-all significance, however, is difficult to assess.

B.   TARIFF REGULATIONS AND HIGHWAY VEHICLES

Problems with customs treatment of vehicles used in international highway transport also seem to be more serious in Canada. There are two systems by which the Department of National Revenue keeps track of Canadian use of foreign (i.e., U.S.) equipment. These are the permit system and the post audit customs control system. On traffic inbound from the United States, a vehicle on which duty has not been paid can leave freight at only one point in Canada, unless it is carrying "goods of a nature that, in the opinion of the Deputy Minister, cannot be readily transferred to other motor vehicles. . . ."[85] This requirement is presumably interpreted liberally. A vehicle operated by a motor carrier working under the permit system may not carry any domestic Canadian freight—only freight for export may be loaded in Canada. A vehicle operated by a post audit carrier may, however, carry domestic Canadian traffic that is incidental to the international movement of the vehicle. However, under this provision domestic goods may only be loaded once on the inbound journey and once on the outbound journey, and the vehicle on which no duty has been paid may not proceed beyond the last point of discharge of imported goods for the purpose of picking up "incidental" domestic traffic. Two other restrictions might also be mentioned. U.S. vehicles are not allowed the same freedom in "in-bond" transportation that is given to Canadian vehicles. Also, "a tractor which has not been duty and

[85]All details in this paragraph are from Canada, Department of National Revenue, "Commercial Motor Vehicle (Customs) Regulations," Memorandum D3, Dec. 17, 1965 (mimeo.).

tax paid cannot be used to haul a trailer which it did not pick up at the frontier examining warehouse or originally bring into Canada. . . ."[86]
U.S. customs regulations are much simpler. Canadian trucks may enter the United States duty-free and may carry on the *return* journey domestic U.S. freight whose carriage is "reasonably incidental to its [the truck's] economical and prompt return" to Canada. This is the same provision that applies to railroad freight cars.[87] On comparison the Canadian regulations seem more restrictive, but it should be remembered that their application is spelled out in more detail. The precise interpretation of "reasonably incidental" in the U.S. rules could make them more restrictive than the Canadian rules.

Problems in transborder piggyback transportation

Piggyback (or trailer-on-flat-car—TOFC) operations constitute one of the significant transportation innovations of the last 15 years. Although the first movements of highway trailers on railroad flat cars occurred several decades ago, it was not until the middle 1950s that TOFC service became of importance in Canada and the United States.

Since then, growth has been rapid. Piggyback carloadings in the United States have increased from 168,000 in 1955 to 554,000 in 1960 and to over 1 million in 1965.[88] This five-fold increase in traffic over ten years testifies to the advantages of this hybrid method of transportation. Piggyback carloadings in 1966 were 1.2 million, a continuation of this upward trend.[89] In 1965 total tonnage originated in piggyback service was 22.8 million,[90] about 1.5 percent of total railroad tonnage originated. A few states accounted for a large proportion of the originated tonnage; in 1963 about 55 percent of total tons originated came from Illinois, New Jersey, New York, California, and Pennsylvania.[91] Major commodity groups carried by piggyback included canned and packaged food, manufactured iron and steel, and fresh meat. These accounted for about 17 percent of 1963 traffic.[92]

Canadian piggyback traffic has also shown rapid growth. In 1958, the

[86]Another problem in Ontario is that transferable plates may not be used for domestic Canadian transportation—the goods carried must be of foreign origin or destined to foreign consignees. Thus provincial policy ensures that there is little incidental domestic traffic carried by U.S. vehicles within Ontario.
[87]U.S. Customs Regulations 5.12 and 10.41.
[88]ICC, *Piggyback Traffic Characteristics* (1967), Table 1, p. 6.
[89]Association of American Railroads, "Piggyback: Pace-Setter of New Railroad Services," Jan. 1967, p. 1.
[90]*Ibid.*, Table 5, p. 16.
[91]*Ibid.*, Table 27, p. 40.   [92]*Ibid.*, Table B-3, pp. 58–60.

first year for which statistics are available, piggyback carloadings were 77,100. By 1960 they had increased to 154,900.[93] Piggyback traffic reached a peak in 1965 with 232,200 carloadings—traffic declined to 187,600 carloadings in 1966, and 1967 piggyback traffic is running 10 percent below 1966 levels.[94] The 1966 drop may be attributed to labour disputes in the trucking industry; reasons for the continued decline in 1967 are less obvious.

Despite the falling off in Canadian traffic over the past two years, TOFC service has still exhibited remarkable growth in both Canada and the United States. This may be attributed to its economic advantages, which involve, essentially, combining the local flexibility of truck transportation with the line-haul economy of rail transportation. Piggyback thus represents an effective coordination of the most advantageous attributes of both modes of transport. It is not, of course, suited to all transportation of all commodities. But for the transportation of merchandise freight under suitable conditions of haul and regularity, piggyback offers better service than rail transport at lower rates than truck transport.

This method of transport would seem likely to play an important role in trade between Canada and the United States, particularly, given the commodity content, in Canadian imports from the United States. Although no statistics on transborder piggyback traffic are available, there is relatively little use of this service in international railway transport.[95] This is despite the area and commodity pattern of TOFC traffic which exists within the United States and which might have been expected to be found in international transport as well.

Railroad policy is not primarily responsible for this lack of development, although the cumbersome rate-making procedures may have some effect here. Instead the low level of development of international piggyback traffic is caused by highway transport policy. In particular, it is caused by highway-taxation and operating-authority policies. As far as highway-tax reciprocity is concerned, it is fair to state that its absence harms TOFC service far more than conventional truck service. This is because TOFC operations involve little use of highways. When, as is the case in Ontario, all U.S. trailers delivered by piggyback must pay full licence fees before completing the last few miles of their haul from railroad piggyback ramp to destination,[96] piggyback loses much of its advantage.

[93]D. W. Carr and Associates, "Piggyback Transportation in Canada," Royal Commission on Transportation, Report, Vol. III, Ottawa, Queen's Printer, 1962, p. 101.
[94]DBS, Carloadings (weekly), various dates.
[95]This conclusion is based on interviews in connection with this study, as well as on an examination and appraisal of available transborder rail traffic statistics, which lump piggyback into a miscellaneous group.
[96]Railroads cannot obtain Ontario transferable plates for their piggyback trailers.

A similar result follows from restrictions on the operating authority of railroads to deliver piggyback trailers. In the United States the commercial-zone exemption under Part II of the Interstate Commerce Act relieves much piggyback traffic from the necessity of obtaining ICC operating authority. No such exemption exists in any Canadian province, although most provinces have been generous in their granting of special arrangements for the highway movement of piggyback trailers.

Conclusions

At the end of such a detailed examination of the intricacies of transborder truck transportation, it may be appropriate to restate the purpose of this chapter. We have tried to illuminate those policy aspects of highway transport in Canada, in the United States, and between the two countries that have relevance for the flow of commodity trade within North America. What we wish to do in this section is to draw the discussion of the chapter together; this process will be continued for all the modes of transport together in the final chapter of the study.

Which highway transport policies create barriers to free trade flows between Canada and the United States? For a start, we might turn to the anomalies between domestic highway policy in the two countries. There is something of a paradox here—Canadian policy appears somewhat more expansionary than U.S. policy, yet highway transportation in the latter country has reached a higher level of development. We attribute this to the economic geography of the United States, in the broadest sense of the term. Further, we conclude that the *direct* effects on trade of relatively greater Canadian stimulation of highway transport are not significant. The indicated advantage of all-Canadian highway transport of $300 to $400 per year per vehicle is difficult to relate to actual traffic patterns. It may have a significance in intermodal competition within Canada, but that is not directly relevant here.

Furthermore, there are more important policy issues to discuss. Probably the *most* important is regulation of operating licences for international truckers providing for-hire service. For reasons of broad policy, U.S. licensing policies are restrictive. They do not specifically discriminate against Canadian motor carriers seeking transborder operating authority, but the effect of these policies is the same as if they did. Quite naturally, several Canadian provinces retaliate against what *they* regard as discrimination by the Interstate Commerce Commission by making it very difficult for U.S. motor carriers to obtain transborder operating authority. Where such retaliation occurs, highway freight moving in international trade between Canada and the United States must be handled using the wasteful practice of trailer interchange or, worse, of cargo interchange.

The lack of several strategically important highway-tax-reciprocity agreements also creates barriers to international trade. Double taxation on highway vehicles is an unnecessary levy whose major effect (apart from minor supplements to governments' revenues) is to reduce the flexibility of motor-carrier-equipment utilization and to increase the costs of highway transport. Private and for-hire truckers are both affected, the latter usually more heavily.

The initial cause of the absence of needed reciprocity arrangements may, unlike the operating-authority problems mentioned above, lie on the Canadian side of the border. The following quotation is of interest in this connection.

Michigan officials have stated that they would welcome an extension of transport reciprocity with Ontario leading towards full and complete reciprocity for motor carrier operations. However, they are reluctant to grant further concessions to Ontario carriers until such time as Ontario will extend similar concessions to Michigan carriers.

Ontario officials have stated that because of limited highways and moderate sources of revenue to build and maintain the highways, they are not willing to grant more than limited reciprocity to Michigan for motor carrier operations in Ontario.[97]

Regulations concerning maximum size and weight of vehicles may add unnecessarily to the costs of international highway transport. However, over most routes followed by goods moving in either direction, differences in maximum weight are not too important. But restrictions on vehicle length seem to be a greater problem. Although the margin of difference is only five feet, it encourages inefficient routing and utilization of equipment, increases operating costs, and may necessitate cargo interchange. There is no real excuse for lack of uniformity in vehicle-size regulations and little more for non-uniform vehicle-weight regulations.

Three other policy areas were given brief discussion in this chapter. The miscellaneous U.S. federal taxes imposed in full measure on Canadian truckers that barely penetrate the international border are another unfortunate result of restrictive transborder licensing policies. These levies would be much "fairer" if Canadian carriers were allowed farther into the United States. Customs procedures and treatment of vehicles cause some increase in transborder operating costs. Streamlining of the procedures and liberalization of the vehicle regulations would seem to be in order. As far as the former are

[97]Hynes, *Michigan and Ontario Trade and Transport Reciprocity*, p. 112 (emphasis in original).

concerned, it is in Canada that most improvement seems to be needed; concerning the latter, both countries could offer more opportunity for efficient use of vehicles. Conclusions respecting international piggyback problems are difficult because of the lack of statistical information. However, it appears that this method of transport may suffer more from restrictive highway transport policies than does highway transport itself.

What can we conclude concerning the over-all impact of these policy difficulties? Specific commodity-oriented conclusions seem best left until a later chapter. But we are able to make meaningful general statements. There is a great need for a better coordination of highway transport policy as it affects international operations. There is in many areas scarcely any coordination now—the policies that influence transborder truck transport are in many cases no more than spillovers of domestically conceived and implemented policies. International highway transport must be viewed as more than a variety of domestic highway transport and, indeed, as more than an end in itself. It has an increasingly important role to play in the facilitation of trade in both directions between Canada and the United States, and the present frustration of that role is to be deplored. It seems that improvement must involve the fulfillment of two prerequisites: a modification of Interstate Commerce Commission policies towards licensing through international service, and the institution of federal regulation of extra-provincial highway transport in Canada.

6. Water Transportation and Canada-U.S. Trade

Introduction

In 1964, water transport accounted for $854 million of Canadian exports to the United States and $360 million of imports from it. Only a few commodities moved in volume by water, and the number of origins and destinations was similarly restricted. This, coupled with the federal regulation of water transport in both countries and the relative wealth of statistical sources, will make the analysis of this chapter more successful than that attempted in the last chapter for trucking.

Canadian water transport policy

We first examine Canada's policy towards its domestic water-borne commerce. Shipbuilding-industry policies also require brief study because of the close operating and corporate relationships between shipping and shipbuilding. Consideration of the St. Lawrence Seaway will be left to a later section.

The major statute affecting water transportation in Canada is the Canada Shipping Act.[1] This is an extremely complex piece of legislation that runs, as consolidated in 1952, to 301 pages for the Act and 275 pages for appended schedules. Amendments to the Canada Shipping Act since 1952 comprise a further 69 pages. Fortunately, little of this mass of material affects economic policy towards shipping; most of it is concerned with technical and safety aspects of vessel operation.

The economic impact of the Canada Shipping Act on the coasting trade[2] may be summarized as follows:

1. Only British ships may engage in the coasting trade of Canada. A British ship is one registered in a Commonwealth country and owned by a British subject or a corporation established and doing business in a Commonwealth country.[3]

[1]RSC 1952, c. 29.
[2]The coasting trade of Canada comprises the carriage of goods or passengers by water between two Canadian ports or places.   [3]*Ibid.*, sec. 669 and sec. 6.

2. Since 1965 only Canadian ships may engage in the coasting trade on the Great Lakes, which are defined to include Seven Islands and all ports above on the St. Lawrence–Great Lakes system.[4] A Canadian ship is one registered in Canada and owned by residents of Canada or a Canadian corporation.[5]

3. ". . . A ship built outside of Canada shall not, without the consent of the Minister [of Transport], be registered in Canada."[6] The ease with which this consent has been obtainable tends to have varied with the strength of the federal government's commitment to protect the Canadian shipbuilding industry. Foreign-built ships entered under Section 22 of the Shipping Act must, however, pay duty—except ships built in Commonwealth countries.

Exemption from the first two conditions is provided for in Section 673 of the Canada Shipping Act. Suspension of the coasting laws was first authorized in 1923 as an anti-combines measure.[7] Approval of registration of ships built outside Canada has already been mentioned.

Regulation of water transportation is also provided under the Transport Act.[8] The carriage of general cargo, bulk cargo,[9] and passengers on the Mackenzie River and of general cargo and passengers on the Great Lakes (here defined as all ports from Quebec City west) is subject to regulation by the Canadian Transport Commission. All companies operating vessels in these trades must hold a certificate of public convenience and necessity from the Commission. Tariffs of rates must be filed and adhered to and are subject to the Commission's approval. It appears that, so far as the Great Lakes are concerned, these regulations have had minimal impact on the shipping industry. The Commission's predecessor, the Board of Transport Commissioners, had little impact as a regulator, perhaps because of the exclusion of the all-important bulk cargo traffic from its jurisdiction.[10]

[4]13–14 Eliz. II, c. 39, sec. 38.
[5]RSC 1952, c. 29, sec. 7(3).
[6]*Ibid.*, sec. 22.
[7]Royal Commission on the Coasting Trade, *Report*, Ottawa, Queen's Printer, 1958, p. 9. A 1922 royal commission had found that a combine existed among shipping companies operating on the Great Lakes. The report of the Royal Commission on the Coasting Trade constitutes by far the best source for much of this chapter, despite nine years having elapsed since its publication.
[8]RSC, c. 271.
[9]"Bulk cargo" is defined as grain and grain products, crude ores and minerals, pulpwood, logs, woodpulp, waste paper, iron and steel scrap, and pig iron. *Ibid.*, sec. 2(1) (d). This definition is slightly more inclusive than that laid down for U.S. water transportation in Part III of the Interstate Commerce Act (see below).
[10]Only 12 percent of the Lakes fleet is licensed under the Transport Act. Board of Transport Commissioners, *Annual Report*, 1965, Ottawa, Queen's Printer, 1966, p. 21.

The Canadian Transport Commission also has jurisdiction for goods shipped under through bills of lading involving both rail and water transportation. For example, joint lake-rail or rail-lake-rail rates would be regulated under the Railway Act.[11]

Great Lakes bulk cargo traffic is subject to partial regulation under the Inland Water Freight Rates Act.[12] All grain shipped from Fort William or Port Arthur by water to points in Canada or the United States comes under this Act, which is administered by the Board of Grain Commissioners. The Board is required to examine all charter parties respecting this grain transportation. The power to set maximum rates is given to the Board but has not been used since 1959.[13] The Board, however, still reports the average Lake freight rates on grain from the Lakehead, based on its scrutiny of vessel charter confirmations. A more significant government influence on Great Lakes grain transportation exists through the monopsonistic power of the Canadian Wheat Board. The Board, which ships most Lakes wheat, is regarded by shipping companies as a very demanding rate negotiator.

The picture that emerges from this discussion is of a coastwise shipping industry in large part protected from any competition from "cheap" foreign shipping. Any British ship may engage in the coasting trade outside the Great Lakes, though, and this undoubtedly has some effect in lowering transport costs on the Atlantic and Pacific coasts. In the Lakes coasting trade, closed to non-Canadian ships since 1965, the influence of competition is indirect. However, much bulk cargo on the Lakes is destined to overseas points, and for this there is a ceiling to Lake freight rates. This traffic is coastwise because it is transported by Lake ship to transshipment ports en route to overseas ports. The rate ceiling is provided by the higher costs of operating ocean ships in the Lakes. Such higher costs are a matter of vessel construction, operation, and carrying capacity (10 to 15 percent less than in lakers of maximum Seaway dimensions). As long as Lake freight rates remain generally below this level, direct export via ocean vessels is discouraged. But for other bulk cargo and all general cargo no protection of this type exists. The regulation of rates on general cargo by the Canadian Transport Commission may protect shippers from the monopoly granted to Canadian water transport firms (as does the existence of land transport

[11]RSC, c. 234, secs. 2(10), 341(3), and 363.
[12]RSC, 1952, c. 153. This Act was another result of the 1922 royal commission mentioned earlier in this section.
[13]The Board's Order no. 21 under the Inland Water Freight Rates Act (March 10, 1959) canceled the existing maximum rates because "the opening of the St. Lawrence Seaway will result in changes in grain carriage which cannot now be accurately determined."

alternatives), but there is little influence of ocean shipping (i.e., non-Canadian) here; rather, Canadian shipping costs and charges rule.

Another aspect of government policy towards shipping is the provision of navigation facilities. For Canada this mainly includes the St. Lawrence Seaway, which will be discussed later, and wharf installations at the various ports. These latter are provided by the National Harbours Board and, since the Board's annual loss has recently averaged only $2 million,[14] may be assumed to constitute little artificial encouragement, by way of subsidy, to Canadian water transport. Construction and administration expenditures on harbour and river works by the federal Department of Public Works totaled $41 million in the fiscal year 1966/67, and Department of Transport expenditures on marine services (aids to navigation, Coast Guard, etc.) were $100 million.[15] Most of these outlays, of course, benefit international shipping, fishing, and recreation as well as coastal shipping. There are few direct user charges imposed on coastal shipping.

Shipbuilding assistance must also be discussed. Between 1955 and 1965 shipbuilding subsidies under the Canadian Vessel Construction Assistance Act amounted to $326 million for new construction.[16] Another $36 million was made available for conversions and major alterations. The Act also allowed freedom from recapture of depreciation by the income tax authorities in cases where ships were sold and replacements built in Canadian shipyards. Over the 1955–65 period a further $119 million subsidy was made available in this way.[17] In 1965 the shipbuilding subsidy activities of the federal government were curtailed. The subsidy available as a proportion of vessel cost was cut from 40 percent to 25 percent and will decline in stages to 17 percent in 1972.

There have been two major direct beneficiaries of the shipbuilding subsidy program. One is the Canadian shipbuilding industry and the other is the Canadian shipping industry, primarily the Great Lakes part of the industry.[18] Over 80 percent of the gross tonnage of the Canadian merchant fleet is in the Great Lakes fleet.[19] Eighty-three of the 210 ships in this fleet were con-

---

[14]National Harbours Board, *Annual Report*, 1965, Ottawa, Queen's Printer, 1966.
[15]Canada, *Estimates for the Fiscal Year Ending March 31, 1968*, Ottawa, Queen's Printer, 1967, pp. 420 and 504.
[16]Canadian Maritime Commission, *Annual Report*, 1965, Ottawa, Queen's Printer, 1965, Table VIII, p. 31.
[17]*Ibid.*, p. 15.
[18]It might be noted that the largest shipbuilding company in Canada, Davie Shipbuilding Limited, is a wholly owned subsidiary of the country's largest shipping company, Canada Steamship Lines, Limited. Other shipping-shipbuilding corporate relationships also exist.
[19]Calculated from Canadian Maritime Commission, "Canadian Merchant Fleet" (mimeo.), p. 1.

structed or converted in Canada between 1955 and the present, and these ships constitute perhaps two-thirds of total Canadian Lakes tonnage.

Direct operating subsidies are also made available to some coastal shipping companies. Subsidies amounting to $8.7 million were paid by the Canadian Maritime Commission in the 1966/67 fiscal year. In the same year the federal government paid $16.4 million to Canadian National Railways to cover deficits on certain Atlantic coast shipping services performed by the company.[20] The subsidies on transportation of coal and feed grain mentioned in chapter 4 are also relevant here. In particular, several million dollars of coal subventions are paid to water carriers each year.

This concludes our survey of policy towards domestic shipping in Canada. The policy is clearly one designed to effect the preservation of the Canadian coasting trade for Canadian shipping. This effect is particularly desired, it appears, for Canadian Great Lakes shipping. Combined with this protection has been a policy of promotion through shipbuilding subsidies and, to an unknown and probably minor degree, the provision of non-Seaway marine facilities and services.

U.S. water transport policy

The policies followed by the U.S. government with respect to the country's domestic shipping industry differ markedly from those applied to the ocean, or foreign-trade, shipping industry. The familiar operating-differential subsidy, construction-differential subsidy, and government cargo preference policies are only marginally applicable to domestic shipping. Thus almost all of the heated controversy that has surrounded these expensive subsidy programs (annually amounting to $187 million, $126 million, and $80 million, respectively)[21] has only incidental applicability to domestic water transport.

There are four geographical segments of the domestic U.S. water transportation industry. These are divided as follows: (1) Great Lakes; (2) inland waterway; (3) coastwise; (4) non-contiguous coastwise. Government policy with respect to each segment shows some variation.

[20]Canada, *Estimates for the Fiscal Year March 31, 1968*, pp. 526–7 and 553–4.
[21]Figures are for the 1965/66 fiscal year. Direct subsidy figures from U.S. Department of Commerce, Maritime Administration, *Annual Report*, 1966, pp. 16 and 22. Cargo preference indirect subsidy estimate from David Novick, ed., *Program Budgeting: Program Analysis and the Federal Budget*, Washington, U.S. Government Printing Office, 1965, Table 5, p. 110. Other estimates of the cargo preference subsidy range up to $160 million annually. Samuel B. Lawrence, *United States Merchant Shipping Policies and Politics*, Washington, The Brookings Institution, 1966, p. 50.

For all, however, competition from foreign-built and foreign-operated ships is prohibited. Section 27 of the Merchant Marine Act of 1920 (popularly known as "the Jones Act") reads in part as follows: "no merchandise shall be transported by water, or by land and water, on penalty of forfeiture thereof, between points in the United States . . ., either directly or via a foreign port, or for any part of the transportation, in any other vessel than a vessel built in and documented under the laws of the United States and owned by persons who are citizens of the United States. . . ."[22] Later parts of the section provide for emergency exceptions and exceptions for transport via Canadian railroads and connecting Canadian water carriers. This second exception is designed to apply to traffic between the continental United States and Alaska.

Water transportation on the Great Lakes and inland waterways is subject to the jurisdiction of the Interstate Commerce Commission (under Part III of the Interstate Commerce Act). The exemptions to this jurisdiction are, however, extensive, and only 11 percent of the total tonnage shipped by water is subject to ICC regulation.[23] Three exemptions account for this situation: bulk commodities including liquids, contract carriers[24] performing service that is not competitive with rail or motor common carriers, and contract carriers owned by their customers.[25]

For the remnant of traffic not covered by the foregoing exceptions, the ICC's regulation includes control of entry through the requirement of certificates (or, for contract carriers, permits) of convenience and necessity.[26] Rates of common carriers are controlled through tariff filing and various standards of "just and reasonable" rates. Contract carriers must file copies of their contracts.[27]

Shipping along and between the various coasts of the United States is controlled by the Federal Maritime Commission, acting under the Intercoastal Shipping Act of 1933 and the Shipping Act of 1916. The Intercoastal Shipping Act requires shipping companies to file tariffs of all rates and charges with the Commission. The Commission may accept or reject tariffs,

[22]46 USC 883. Foreign-built ships may be registered under the U.S. flag for foreign service, but they are ineligible for cargo preferences for a three-year period. This, added to the high costs of operating a U.S.-flag ship, makes such imports unappealing. *Ibid.*, p. 50.
[23]U.S. Army, Corps of Engineers, *Waterborne Commerce of the United States—Water Carriage Ton-Miles, National Summaries 1963, Supplement 2 to Part 5*, Washington, Corps of Engineers, 1965, Table 3.
[24]A contract carrier provides service "under individual contracts or agreements" including ship-chartering (49 USC 902(e)).
[25]49 USC 903.
[26]49 USC 909.
[27]49 USC 905 and 906.

depending on their ability to meet the familiar criteria of being "just and reasonable."[28] No control of entry into coastal shipping is provided.

The Shipping Act of 1916 gives the Federal Maritime Commission authority over agreements entered into by coastal shipping companies to fix rates, control competition, and allocate traffic. These anti-competitive practices are a traditional feature of the shipping industry,[29] and the Commission is directed by the statute to approve agreements of this type unless they are discriminatory, harmful to U.S. commerce, or contrary to the public interest.[30] There is also a requirement that rates be "just and reasonable."[31]

U.S. firms operating ships in domestic service receive no shipbuilding subsidies. Despite attempts at amendment, the Merchant Marine Act of 1936, under which the construction-differential subsidies are paid, makes subsidies available only for ships to be used in foreign commerce. Both shipbuilding and Great Lakes' shipping interests have made attempts to obtain subsidies for new vessel construction, pointing out that there have been virtually no additions to the U.S. Great Lakes fleet since World War II. This is in marked contrast to the situation in the Canadian Lakes fleet discussed earlier, although the contrast is muted somewhat by extensive programs of modernization in the U.S. fleet.[32] The failure of U.S. Great Lakes operators to achieve treatment in shipbuilding subsidies comparable to that received by ocean-shipping interests can probably be laid in part to the nature of operations on the Great Lakes. The majority of the tonnage in the U.S. Lakes fleet is owned by "captive" companies—firms that primarily transport cargo, mainly iron ore, for their parent corporations. It may be speculated that the U.S. government is not interested in providing the steel industry with a new fleet, partly at government expense.

The lack of shipbuilding subsidy for the coastal operators may be explained by the decline of shipping service between ports of the contiguous United

[28]46 USC 844 and 845a.
[29]For extensive discussion and evaluation of the activities of shipping conferences see Daniel Marx, *International Shipping Cartels*, Princeton, N.J., Princeton University Press, 1953, and S. G. Sturmey, *British Shipping and World Competition*, London, The Athlone Press, 1962.
[30]46 USC 814.
[31]46 USC 815–817.
[32]Annual reports of the Lake Carriers' Association—the U.S. Great Lakes shipping association—have for several years carried statements like the following: "For the second successive year, no construction or reconstruction was completed in the U.S. bulk cargo fleet." Lake Carriers' Association, *Annual Report*, 1963, Cleveland, Lake Carriers' Association, 1965, p. 37. However, plans have recently been announced to build new bulk carriers for the U.S. Lakes fleet. These ships will be up to 1,000 feet in length, longer than the Seaway locks, and their initial use, at least, will be limited. "Lake Erie Shipyards to Build Bulk Carriers of Record Size," *Toronto Globe and Mail*, Oct. 3, 1967, p. B7.

States because of competition from land transport and the lack of incentive to build new ships for the totally insulated trades between the contiguous and non-continguous parts of the country.

Port facilities in the United States are provided by federal, state, local, and private sources. Estimates developed by the Association of American Railroads place expenditures for providing port and navigation facilities at $825 million in 1964. An additional $178 million was spent in constructing, maintaining, and operating the 29,000 miles of inland and intra-coastal waterways.[33] Another estimate of the extent of public aid has been developed by John Meyer. Using the budget of the U.S. *federal* government, he estimates the following expenditures on intercity domestic transportation by water.

TABLE 97

U.S. FEDERAL BUDGET FOR INTERCITY DOMESTIC
WATER TRANSPORTATION, 1965 FISCAL YEAR
(million dollars)

Corps of Engineers:	
operating expenses	93.0
capital outlays: navigation projects	198.7
capital outlays: multi-purpose projects	17.5
other capital outlays	9.4
estimated share of general expenses	9.0
Tennessee Valley Authority:	
net operating cost	4.6
	332.2

Source: Adapted from John R. Meyer, "Transportation in the Program Budget," *Program Budgeting: Program Analysis and the Federal Budget*, ed. David Novick, Washington, U.S. Government Printing Office, 1965, Table 1, p. 108.

This gives us a means of deflating the Association of American Railroads' estimate, which included expenditures on behalf of international ocean transportation (but which also included state and local government expenditures, in part). Very few user taxes are paid by water transportation companies, although President Johnson proposed in 1966 a fuel tax of 2 cents per gallon to yield $8 million annually.[34] This has not yet been approved by Congress.

[33]Association of American Railroads, *Comparative Transportation Statistics*, Washington, AAR, 1966, pp. 29, 30, and 32. Excludes the St. Lawrence Seaway and expenditures by the Tennessee Valley Authority.
[34]*Ibid.*, p. 23.

Canadian and U.S. water transport policies compared

The first point to make in this comparison is that the U.S. domestic shipping industry is almost nine times as large as its Canadian counterpart.[35] Since there seems to be a common level of promotional and regulatory activity in both countries, this difference must be ascribed to geographical circumstance and, of course, to the greater size of the U.S. economy.

Policy towards domestic water transport appears, over-all, to be equally expansionary in both countries. Canada and the United States both exclude foreign shipping, with Canadian law being slightly more lenient, but only towards Commonwealth shipping on the two coasts. Each country submits segments of the industry to economic regulation by commission, but only a relatively minor portion is affected. The widely publicized difficulties that the Intercoastal Shipping Act presents for lumber producers in the Pacific northwest states have been well studied.[36] These producers are forced to use U.S. vessels in competing in U.S. Atlantic coast lumber markets while B.C. sawmills can use less expensive foreign vessels. This has placed U.S. sawmills at a cost disadvantage of up to $12 per 100 board feet.[37] A conflict between the coasting laws of the two countries also exists. This involves their inter-pretations of particular voyages as "coasting," and hence subject to cabotage control, and "international," and hence subject to no control. Canadian law, for example, would define the water portion of a crude oil movement from Alberta to Superior, Wisconsin, to Ontario as coasting, and the water portion of fruit and vegetable traffic from California to Vancouver to Alaska as inter-national. U.S. law would give an opposite definition to each case.

Domestic shipbuilding is promoted in both countries by requiring ships used in coastal shipping to be of domestic origin. The U.S. regulations are totally exclusive; but while Canadian law is more liberal, Canadian ship-builders have been protected by generous subsidy arrangements. This has had, as we shall see in the next section, an important effect on the transport of goods by water between the two countries.

Canada and the United States both provide navigation facilities virtually free to domestic water transport firms. The impact of this promotion is greater in the United States, however, because a wider network of inland waterways has been developed. There seems to be little desire to emulate this development in Canada.[38]

[35]On a ton-mile basis; see DBS, *Daily Bulletin*, February 13, 1967, p. 4, and Interstate Commerce Commission, *Transport Economics*, Sept. 1967, p. 10.
[36]For a discussion, see U.S., Senate, Committee on Commerce, *Problems of the Soft-wood Lumber Industry*, 87th Cong., 2nd sess., 1962, and U.S., Tariff Commission, *Softwood Lumber*, Washington, Tariff Commission, 1963.
[37]*Ibid.*, Table 15, p. 91.
[38]A private member's bill to canalize the Red and Saskatchewan Rivers (via Lake Win-

International water transportation between Canada and the United States

The provision of water transportation service between Canada and the United States is free from any direct control of nationality of vessel.[39] Yet tradition, geography, and domestic policy have combined to develop the pattern shown, for 1957 (the last pre-Seaway year) and 1965, in Table 98 for Canada-U.S. trade and Table 99 for U.S.-Canada trade.

TABLE 98
VESSEL REGISTRY ON IMPORTANT ROUTES IN CANADA-U.S. TRADE, 1957 AND 1965
(percentages of total cargo tonnages)

	1957				1965			
	Canada	U.S.	U.K.	Other	Canada	U.S.	U.K.	Other
Atlantic-Atlantic and Gulf	3.4	18.2	12.8	65.6	1.1	1.1	21.6	76.2
Atlantic-Great Lakes	91.7	—	*	8.3	78.6	9.3	6.5	6.2
Great Lakes-Great Lakes	72.4	26.9	—	0.7	52.1	26.8	0.8	20.3
Pacific-Pacific	32.8	50.1	*	17.1	61.4	12.3	*	26.3
Pacific-Atlantic and Gulf	—	9.1	*	90.9	—	—	4.1	95.9
Total, all routes	34.8	22.6	6.4	36.2	39.2	9.4	10.6	40.8

Source: DBS, *Shipping Report*, 1957 and 1965, Part I.
*Less than 0.1 percent.
Note: The routes selected are those presented in Tables 68–73. For descriptions of the routes see those tables.

The noteworthy change in Table 98 over the 1957–65 period is the declining importance of U.S. shipping[40] in transporting Canada's exports to the United States. This has occurred on all routes. However, 1957 U.S. flag participation was unusually high on the three all-ocean routes. Ocean freight rates were abnormally high in that year because of the Suez crisis, and U.S. ships were able to obtain some cargoes that would have been denied them were it not for the temporary shortage of shipping.

Canadian shipping[41] has increased its total participation in Canada-U.S. trade. This has occurred despite a decline in three of the four routes served by Canadian ships and is due to the continuing dominant position of

nipeg) between Winnipeg and Edmonton was "talked out" in the House of Commons in June 1967. *House of Commons Debates*, 2nd sess., 27th Parl., June 28, 1967, pp. 2090–97.
[39] However, "vessels of third-party states have no legal right of navigation without the permission of the riparian states." Don C. Piper, *The International Law of the Great Lakes: A Study of Canadian-United States Cooperation*, Durham, N.C., Duke University Press, 1967, p. 60. An excellent survey of the law of Great Lakes navigation is presented in this book (pp. 46–70).
[40] Defined to include only vessels owned *and* registered in the United States.
[41] Defined to include only vessels owned *and* registered in Canada.

TABLE 99

VESSEL REGISTRY ON IMPORTANT ROUTES IN U.S.-CANADA TRADE, 1957 AND 1965
(percentages of total cargo tonnages)

	1957				1965			
	Canada	U.S.	U.K.	Other	Canada	U.S.	U.K.	Other
Great Lakes–Great Lakes	73.7	25.5	0.4	0.4	65.4	9.6	1.3	23.7
Great Lakes-Atlantic	99.8	—	*	0.2	64.9	10.8	10.7	13.6
Atlantic and Gulf-Atlantic	9.2	31.7	8.1	51.0	2.1	4.8	10.5	82.6
Pacific-Pacific	27.3	64.6	1.3	6.8	47.9	40.1	*	12.0
Total, all routes	69.1	26.7	0.9	3.3	60.8	11.9	3.0	24.3

Source: As for Table 98.
Note: The routes selected are those presented in Tables 74–79. For descriptions of the routes see those tables.
*Less than 0.1 percent.

Canadian shipping in transportation to U.S. Great Lakes ports from Canadian Great Lakes and Atlantic ports. Much of Canadian-registered ship traffic between Pacific ports of both countries consists of barge traffic.

U.K. and foreign shipping carries virtually all goods moving by water from Canada to U.S. Atlantic and Gulf ports. Were it not for the suitability of barge transportation, they would also dominate traffic along the Pacific coast. We discuss this further following an examination of Table 99.

For water transport northbound from the United States to Canada, the major change over the eight-year period shown in Table 99 has been the increase in volume of goods carried by U.K.- and "other-"registered ships. Because of the volume of traffic involved (over 22 million tons in 1965), this has been of particular significance in traffic moving northbound on the Great Lakes. U.S. shipping has been the main loser on this route.

The share of Canadian shipping in Canadian imports from the United States has also declined, but Canadian ships still carry over 60 percent of these imports. This is a marked contrast to the export situation as presented in Table 98 and reflects the characteristics of the important northbound routes. The Atlantic coast route, over which almost 16 million tons of Canadian exports to the United States were carried in 1965 and on which Canadian shipping is non-competitive, accounted for only 1.4 million tons of imports from the United States in that year.

Comparing Tables 98 and 99 further, we note that the patterns of national participation over the four routes common to both trade directions are quite similar. Differences do exist, primarily because of commodity variations, but these are relatively minor. We would expect this, of course; shipowners are naturally adverse to empty return voyages, and rate policies usually reflect this. Thus, examining the volumes shown in Tables 73 and 79 of chapter 2, we would expect export rates to be lower than import rates on the Great Lakes–Great Lakes route. For the other three routes (Great Lakes–Atlantic, Atlantic–Atlantic, and Pacific–Pacific), the reverse should be true. However, the stimulus to imports on the Atlantic and Pacific coast routes might well be minimal because of commodity differences impelling empty northbound voyages.

The competitive position of Canadian and U.S. shipping

U.S.- and Canadian-registered ships together account for 48.6 percent of southbound and 72.7 percent of northbound commodity movements between the two countries. But vessels of these registries carry almost none of Canada's overseas trade. Canada, of course, has an ocean-going fleet of only four vessels,[42] so its 1963 participation in Canada's overseas trade of 0.3 percent (of total dry-cargo imports and exports)[43] is not surprising. But the U.S. ocean-going fleet amounted in 1963 to some 600 ships,[44] and these carried only 0.8 percent of Canada's overseas dry-cargo trade in that year.[45] U.S.-flag ships did carry 8.5 percent of total U.S. ocean-borne foreign trade in 1963 and 11 percent of dry-cargo trade,[46] but this was only made possible by the provision of operating subsidies and preferential treatment in the allocation of U.S. government cargoes.

The foregoing provides obvious indirect evidence of the inability of Canadian and U.S. vessels to compete in international ocean shipping. Direct evidence is also available. There were 317 U.S. ships under operating subsidy contracts in 1964. The average subsidy for 1964 was $655,000 per ship and amounted to 27 percent of freight and passenger revenues.[47] Almost one-half the direct operating expenses of these ships were paid from the operating subsidy.[48] We may conclude that U.S.-flag ships cost twice as much to operate as the comparable foreign-flag ships with which they compete.

The competitive disadvantage of Canadian ships is less, but still

[42]Canadian Maritime Commission, "Canadian Merchant Fleet," Dec. 31, 1966. Additional vessels are owned by Canadian companies but registered under foreign flags, principally in Bermuda.
[43]Canadian Maritime Commission, *Annual Report*, June 16, 1965, Ottawa, Queen's Printer, 1965, Table IV, p. 23.
[44]Lawrence, *United States Merchant Shipping Policies and Politics*, Table A3, p. 357.
[45]Canadian Maritime Commission, *Annual Report*, June 16, 1965.
[46]U.S., Department of Commerce, Maritime Administration, *Changing Patterns in U.S. Trade and Shipping Capacity* (1964), Table 2, pp. 16–17.
[47]Lawrence, *United States Merchant Shipping Policies and Politics*, Table 2, p. 206.
[48]*Ibid.*, pp. 205–6.

substantial. Although Canadian shipping interests have estimated the operating-cost differential for a 30,000- to 50,000-ton bulk carrier or tanker to be between $100,000 and $125,000 per year,[49] this figure seems low, even for vessels of this type. For smaller general-cargo ships, carefully determined estimates of cost differentials are available in the report of the Royal Commission on Coasting Trade. These are now ten years out of date and so probably underestimate the present difference. For a tramp vessel, built in the United Kingdom and capable of carrying 12,600 long tons of cargo, Canadian registry was estimated to impose a variable-expense penalty of $95,450 per year as compared to U.K. registry. Fixed expenses added a further $72,859. In percentage terms, Canadian registry added 27 percent to variable costs and 24 percent to total costs.[50] But Canadian registry tends to be limited, as we have pointed out, to Canadian-built ships. This widens the cost difference. A comparison of the cost of a ship built and registered in the United Kingdom and of the same ship built and registered in Canada yields the following results. For the Canadian vessel, variable costs are higher by $121,977 per year, or 34 percent; and total costs by $342,914 per year, or 49 percent.[51] The Canadian variable-expense disadvantage of $121,977 is equal to 26 percent of estimated variable expenses under Canadian registry. For purposes of rough general comparison, this figure may be placed against the 50 percent relationship between operating subsidy and direct operating expense given above for U.S. ships.

If Canadian and U.S. ships are so expensive to operate, why are they used to such a degree in carrying goods moving between the two countries? Several answers may be suggested. First, it is only traffic moving through the St. Lawrence Seaway that is predominantly carried by Canadian and U.S. ships (excluding the specialized movement along the Pacific coast). Second, ocean-going vessels are inherently less efficient within the Great Lakes–St. Lawrence area than the specialized Lake vessels. The size limitations of the Seaway locks combine with the design requirements of ocean shipping to give the largest Lake vessels a 15 to 20 percent capacity advantage over maximum-size ocean vessels in these trades. So ocean vessels cannot, as a rule, use Great Lakes and St. Lawrence cargo to augment their overseas cargoes. Normal trading patterns tend to discourage this, anyway. From this we deduce that foreign-registered ocean vessels are unlikely to be *able*, on a cost basis, to compete with the U.S. and, particularly, the Canadian Lake fleets for traffic moving between the two countries.

[49]J. D. Leitch, president of Upper Lakes Shipping Ltd., as reported in "Why We Should Have a Deepsea Fleet," *Canadian Transportation*, Feb. 1965, p. 44.
[50]Royal Commission on the Coasting Trade, *Report*, 1958, Table I, p. 114.
[51]*Ibid.*, Table I, p. 162.

This suggests another question. Why, then, do foreign shipping companies not enter the international Great Lakes and St. Lawrence trade with Lake fleets of their own? Some have done so, but there are important considerations that have limited this development. First, both the United States and Canada (since 1965) limit their domestic trade to their own ships. Thus foreign operators could engage in only one of the three route combinations (Canada-Canada, U.S.-U.S., and international), while U.S. and Canadian operators have access to two. For example, a Greek ship could not carry wheat from Duluth to Baie Comeau and return with iron ore from Seven Islands to Hamilton. And a Norwegian vessel would not have the option of carrying coal from Toledo to Port Credit or coal from Toledo to Buffalo. Second, Canadian and U.S. unions would surely react violently to any attempt of foreign ship operators to introduce their lower wage and manning scales into the Great Lakes. The possibilities for disruptive labour disputes on the Lakes are well known. Yet without the benefit of cheaper labour, one of the major advantages of foreign-registered-ship operation vanishes. Lower overseas construction costs would still provide some competitive edge, but this is dulled by Canadian shipbuilding subsidies and the difficulties inherent in bringing Lake-type vessels over long ocean voyages from their places of construction. Finally, the experience and specialized knowledge of Canadian and U.S. Lake shipping companies might make it difficult for foreign firms to enter the Great Lakes–St. Lawrence shipping market.

We have, then, an industry that is effectively protected from competition, at least from other shipping countries. Proceeding further, we may ask whether the industry exhibits signs of inter-firm competition. Evidence on this question is hard to collect. In the all-important bulk trades there are only a very few large shippers, and rate contracts are negotiated individually. Only fragmentary rate information is available publicly.

The market interplay between a few large buyers and a few large sellers may be expected to result in some inflation of price above that which would prevail under perfectly competitive conditions. On this issue, because of the lack of information, we are unable to do more than supply conjecture.

First, it must be pointed out that regulation of international water traffic by both governments is virtually non-existent. The only regulatory mechanisms are the Inland Water Freight Rates Act in Canada, which affects only a tiny part of Canada-U.S. water-borne traffic, and the Shipping Act of 1916 in the United States, under which shipping conference rates and practices are controlled. Formal shipping conferences play no part in water transport between the two countries.

Despite the absence of regulation and of competition from the ships of other nations, shipping-industry spokesmen argue that the industry is competitive. Three factors lend weight to this assertion. These are: (1) the market power of the largest shippers; (2) the existence of alternative shipping routes; (3) the existence of alternative modes of transport. Thus, although only a relatively few firms carry iron ore from Seven Islands to Cleveland, for example, their rates are controlled by the concentration of market power in the seller (the iron ore companies), the existence of an alternative route (via ocean vessel to U.S. Atlantic ports and thence by rail to steelmill locations), and the threat of the shipper's providing his own vessels. Similar comments can be made about virtually all the important (from the point of view of value) international Lakes–St. Lawrence trades. For many routes and commodities, it is the threat of rail competition that acts as a curb on rates, and there is a long and continuing history of competition between the railroads and Lake shipping companies, especially in the United States.[52] This competition, however, only puts a ceiling on Lake freight rates —it does not ensure that they will reach a competitively determined floor. Moreover, this floor could be determined only by the existence of direct competition, on the Lakes and the St. Lawrence, from foreign-registered ships of comparable design.[53]

Two pieces of evidence tend to support the contention that there are real non-competitive aspects to the domestic shipping industries of Canada and the United States. The first is somewhat dated now and refers only to Canada. During the years 1946 through 1958 the Board of Grain Commissioners set maximum rates on wheat carried from the Lakehead direct to Montreal. In only two of those years, 1954 and 1955, did the average rate charged fall below this maximum by even a fraction of a cent per bushel.[54] Since the opening of the Seaway, the rate has remained low, having fallen from 13 cents per bushel in 1960 to 9 cents per bushel by the summer of 1967.[55] There are three possible interpretations of this evidence.

1. The charging of identical rates on grain was a mere coincidence.
2. Shipping companies used to collude[56] to set rates on all cargoes over all routes, but no longer do so.

[52]See, for example, U.S., Senate, Committee on Commerce Hearings, *Great Lakes-St. Lawrence Seaway Transportation Study*, 88th Congr., 1st sess., 1964.
[53]One estimate for a Lake-ocean bulk carrier places daily operating costs under U.S. registry at 154 percent of costs under U.K. registry. U.S., Department of Agriculture, *Impact of the St. Lawrence Seaway on the Location of Grain Export Facilities*, Marketing Research Report no. 442, quoted in *ibid.*, Part 2, p. 492.
[54]Royal Commission on Coasting Trade, 1958, Fig. 4, p. 131 and Board of Grain Commissioners, *Annual Report*, 1958, Ottawa, Queen's Printer, 1956, Table G-11, p. 48.
[55]1960 rate for Lakehead-Montreal (direct) wheat from Board of Grain Commissioners, *Annual Report*, 1960, Table C-11, p. 32; 1967 rate from John Schreiner, "Lakes Settlement Boots Old Bottoms," *Financial Post*, Sept. 30, 1967, p. 10.
[56]Collusion here would almost certainly be informal and unorganized—perhaps even

3. Shipping companies used to collude to set rates on wheat cargoes moving from the Lakehead to St. Lawrence River ports but stopped when competition appeared from ocean vessels able to carry grain directly from the Lakehead to overseas destinations.

The third interpretation seems most plausible and points to similar pricing behaviour in similar situations—i.e., situations where the Lake shipping companies have a high degree of monopoly power.

We should also draw attention to the age of the Lake fleet. The U.S. fleet's advanced age has already been noted. But the Canadian fleet has a fairly high proportion of over-age ships too; 58 of the 210 Lakes vessels were built before 1920 and have not been rebuilt since.[57]

A balanced assessment of this section would have to conclude that the policies of the U.S. and Canadian governments have encouraged the development of conditions favourable to monopolistic shipping operations in one area of water transport between the two countries—the Great Lakes–St. Lawrence area. The degree to which the shipping industry, mainly concentrated on the Canadian side, has taken advantage of these conditions cannot be assessed.

The St. Lawrence Seaway

The St. Lawrence Seaway has had a major impact on trade between Canada and the United States. Shipments of iron ore from Labrador to U.S. Great Lakes have particularly benefited, as have shipments of U.S. grain to Quebec ports for Canadian consumption and for transshipment to overseas destinations. Yet there is evidence that present Seaway policies are not working towards the optimal use of this facility.

In April, 1959, the Seaway was completed and opened for traffic, 250 years after the first proposal for navigational improvement of the St. Lawrence River.[58] The Seaway is a joint undertaking of the St. Lawrence Seaway Authority of Canada and the Saint Lawrence Seaway Development Corporation of the United States. The two bodies have joint authority over the

unconscious. Formally organized price-setting seems most unlikely, since relations among the larger Lake shipping companies are far from cordial, as the 1963 Royal Commission investigating Great Lakes shipping-labour unrest discovered.
[57]Canadian Maritime Commission, "Canadian Merchant Fleet," Dec. 31, 1966. The oldest vessels tend to be concentrated among a few firms; most were purchased from U.S. shipping companies at very low prices.
[58]William R. Willoughby, *The St. Lawrence Waterway: A Study in Politics and Diplomacy*, Madison, Wis., University of Wisconsin Press, 1961, p. 4. Willoughby's book is the best account of the history of the Seaway.

Montreal–Lake Ontario section and the Welland Canal connecting Lake Ontario and Lake Erie. A total of $130 million was spent by the U.S. government on the new Montreal–Lake Ontario section.[59] The Canadian government spent $320 million on this section and Canadian investment in the Welland Canal is $213 million.[60]

TABLE 100

ORIGINAL TOLL SCHEDULE FOR THE ST. LAWRENCE SEAWAY

	Montreal-Lake Ontario	Welland	Complete transit
Charge per gross registered ton of the vessel	$ .04	$ .02	$ .06
Charge per ton of cargo: bulk[a]	.40	.02	.42
general	.90	.05	.95
Charge per passenger	3.50	4.00	7.50

Source: "St. Lawrence Seaway Tariff of Tolls," as reproduced in R. R. Baxter, ed., *Documents on the St. Lawrence Seaway*, New York, Praeger, 1961, pp. 77–80.
[a]Bulk cargo includes grain, cement, coal and coke, liquids, ores and minerals, pig iron, scrap iron and steel, pulpwood and logs, raw sugar, woodpulp, and domestic package freight. Domestic package freight is any non-bulk cargo moving between two Canadian ports or two U.S. ports.

The original toll schedule for the Seaway reads, in part, as given in Table 100. The toll schedule went on to state minimum tolls and tolls for partial transit. Canada was to receive all of the Welland tolls and 71 percent of the Montreal–Lake Ontario tolls. The United States was to receive 29 percent of the Montreal–Lake Ontario tolls. Over the first six years of Seaway operation, these tolls proved inadequate to develop the revenues that had been forecasted before the Seaway opened. By the end of 1964 the accumulated shortfall had reached $41 million, and accumulated revenues were 33 percent below the six-year estimate of $124 million.[61] Two developments contributed to this: Traffic was 23 percent below the estimate for the Montreal–Lake Ontario section and 25 percent below the estimate for the Welland Canal section. Moreover, the Canadian government had decided to discontinue the Welland Canal tolls in July, 1962.[62]

Both the U.S. and Canadian sections of the Seaway have operated at a loss. The Saint Lawrence Seaway Development Corporation was budgeted

[59]Association of American Railroads, *Competitive Transportation Statistics*, p. 77.
[60]St. Lawrence Seaway Authority, *Annual Report*, 1966, Ottawa, Queen's Printer, 1967, pp. 34–5.
[61]Association of American Railroads, *Competitive Transportation Statistics*, p. 79.
[62]*Ibid.*

for a net loss of $3.3 million in the 1965 fiscal year.[63] The St. Lawrence Seaway Authority had a $12.3 million loss in 1965.[64] Furthermore, no depreciation was charged on the Welland Canal facilities.[65]

Revision of the toll schedule was made in 1967. Canadian authorities proposed a toll structure incorporating a flat fee per lockage. This was in line with a consultant's report that had argued that the existing toll structure, emphasizing as it did cargo and vessel tonnage, was encouraging the inefficient use of the Seaway facilities. Thus, the toll on gross registered tonnage was to be replaced by a lockage fee to encourage ship operators to phase smaller vessels out of Seaway use.[66]

The St. Lawrence Seaway Authority adopted this approach in part. It put forward a plan involving a 10 percent increase in vessel and cargo tolls on the Montreal–Lake Ontario section and a lockage fee on the Welland section. The lockage fee was to rise from $20 per lockage in 1967 to $100 in 1971.[67]

Reaction of Seaway users was predictable. Both shipping companies and shippers predicted ruination, despite evidence presented by the Authority to show that the proposed toll increases amounted to ⅓ cent per bushel of grain and 11 cents per ton of iron ore or coal.[68] U.S. groups involved with the Seaway were particularly opposed to the toll increases[69] and were successful in having the U.S. government reject the advice of the Saint Lawrence Seaway Development Corporation and take a position opposing any toll increases. After negotiations the Welland lockage fee was agreed on, but the toll increase on the Montreal–Lake Ontario section was replaced by an increase, of 2 percent, to 73 percent, in Canada's share of the existing tolls. Even this substantial retreat from the earlier proposal was attacked. Carrier and shipper interests referred to the toll changes as "gross discrimination" and a "disappointing turn of events" and predicted increases in the costs of raw materials.[70]

Contrary to these expressions of outrage, tolls on the St. Lawrence

[63]John R. Meyer, "Transportation in the Program Budget," Table 1, p. 108 (see my Table 97 above).
[64]St. Lawrence Seaway Authority, *Annual Report*, 1966, p. 31.
[65]*Ibid.*, p. 21.
[66]J. Kates and Associates, *St. Lawrence Seaway Traffic Studies: Seaway Tolls Analysis and Recommendations*, Toronto, J. Kates and Associates, 1965, p. 1.
[67]St. Lawrence Seaway Authority, "Summary of Future Traffic Estimates and Toll Requirements," April 1966, p. 1.
[68]*Ibid.*, p. 8. The total value at destination of goods shipped through the Montreal–Lake Ontario section of the Seaway in 1964 was estimated at $3.0 billion. The toll increase proposed for this section amounted to 0.07 percent of this value.
[69]For evidence of earlier concern see U.S., Senate, Committee on Commerce, *Hearings, Great Lakes-St. Lawrence Seaway Transportation Study*, 88th Congr., 2nd sess., 1964.
[70]Geoffrey Stevens, "New Seaway Split Gives Canada 2% More," Toronto *Globe and Mail*, March 14, 1967, p. B1.

Seaway are too low and are collected in a way that does not encourage the efficient use of the facility. This first conclusion is obvious after the most cursory glance at the Seaway's financial results. Subsidization of this transport facility gives carriers and shippers transportation service at a price below the cost of the Seaway to the North American economy as a whole. It does not, however, promote the flow of goods between the two countries. Seaway tolls are too unimportant to have much impact of this sort, and we are forced to conclude that the present toll situation represents an unjustified subsidy that is split between the shipping companies and their customers.

TABLE 101
IMPACT OF SHIFT TO STRAIGHT $400 LOCKAGE FEE ON
SEAWAY TRAFFIC, MONTREAL-LAKE ONTARIO UPBOUND, 1964

	Vessel size under 7,000 GRT	Vessel size 17,000 GRT and over
No. of transits	2,253	207
Percentage of transits	66	6
Cargo tonnage	5,196,000	5,120,000
Percentage of cargo tonnage	28	28
Toll paid	$3,098,000	$2,195,626
Toll per cargo ton	$.60	$.43
Lockage fee payable	$9,000,000	$830,000
Lockage fee per cargo ton	$1.73	$.16
Per cargo ton change with lockage fee	+$1.13	−$.27

The toll structure does, however, have a direct impact on trade between the two countries. Since the structure discriminates, in terms of Seaway capacity utilized, against large ships, goods shipped in such vessels pay more than they should whereas goods shipped in small vessels pay less than they should. Table 101 shows the impact of a shift to a straight $400 lockage fee on 1964 upbound Montreal–Lake Ontario traffic.[71] A change of this magnitude might be expected, for example, to encourage the shipment of Labrador iron ore to the United States via the Seaway and, perhaps, to discourage the use of the water transportation of newsprint to U.S. Great Lakes destinations. Other similar effects could be hypothesized; they would all involve benefit to goods shipped in large "Seaway-efficient" ships and adjustment for goods shipped in small "Seaway-inefficient" ships.

[71]$400 fee developed by dividing 1964 average toll revenue per transit ($2,815) by number of locks (7). St. Lawrence Seaway Authority, *Annual Report*, 1965, p. 2. Traffic and toll data from St. Lawrence Seaway Authority, *Traffic Report of the St. Lawrence Seaway*, 1964, p. 17.

Water transport policy and North American trade

Three conclusions important to this section have been developed in earlier parts of this chapter:

1. There are no significant anomalies between Canadian policy towards domestic water transport and U.S. policy towards domestic water transport. Although U.S. policy does not give its domestic shipping industry the benefit of shipbuilding subsidies and Canadian policy does bestow this advantage on Canadian shipping, this difference has little effect on international trade. Even with comparable subsidies U.S. ships would probably not be competitive with Canadian ships, and even if they were, it would make no difference to commodity trade between the two countries. For that matter, U.S. shipping companies can take advantage of Canadian shipbuilding subsidies by forming subsidiary companies in Canada. Many have done so, to the outrage of Canadian shipping interests.[72] But this has no meaning for our assessment of trade effects. Policy harmonization, then, is not an issue in water transportation.
2. Foreign shipping (i.e., non-U.S. and non-Canadian) tends to dominate water transport between Canada and the United States over ocean routes (the Pacific coast is a special case). But within the Great Lakes and St. Lawrence River, purely domestic regulation, tradition, and potential labour problems have combined to exclude most foreign shipping. More expensive North American ships, mainly Canadian, transport most traffic (in both volume and value terms) between the Great Lakes ports of both countries and between U.S. Great Lakes ports and Canadian Atlantic ports.
3. Tolls on the St. Lawrence Seaway are too low and discriminate against commodities carried in large vessels—i.e., against bulk commodities such as iron ore, grain, and coal. The low level of tolls works to the disadvantage of competing modes of transport but probably has little effect in stimulating additional flows of traffic through the Seaway. It has even less effect on the flow of goods between Canada and the United States. The inequities of the toll structure, however, are probably of greater significance.

From these three conclusions it is obvious that on only two water transport routes—Great Lakes–Great Lakes and Great Lakes–Atlantic—does transport policy have an impact on trade flows. The use of higher cost Canadian and U.S. ships should tend to discourage trade in both directions, while the impact of Seaway toll policy is less consistent. Three of the six export com-

---

[72]For a detailed account see "Does Canadian Lakes Fleet Face U.S. Takeover Peril?" *Financial Post*, Feb. 11, 1967, p. 23.

modity groups included in Tables 68–73 of chapter 2 are affected significantly. These are iron ore, newsprint, and iron and steel. The other three export groups (lumber, fish, and woodpulp) are mainly exported via ocean routes. Iron ore exports (which move in large ships) are discriminated against by the Seaway toll structure, while the structure discriminates in favour of newsprint and iron and steel exports (which move in small ships). The low level of tolls is of benefit to all three groups. Freight-factor information for the three affected commodity groups indicates that the impact of policy on trade flows is likely to be significant for iron ore exports, of lesser significance for newsprint exports, and probably insignificant for primary and manufactured iron and steel exports.[73]

Four of the five import commodity groups included in Tables 74–79 of chapter 2 are brought to Canada from U.S. Great Lakes ports. These are coal and coke, iron ore, soybeans, and unmilled cereals. All are bulk commodities, and so all are disadvantaged by the present Seaway toll structure. Most of the imports in these commodity groups, however, pass through only one of the Seaway sections, and so the subsidy afforded by the low Seaway tolls is less important. Freight-factor information indicates that iron ore and coal imports are most susceptible to influence by water transport policy, with imports of unmilled cereals and soybeans being rather less susceptible, in that order.[74]

[73]Freight factors for Great Lakes exports of these commodity groups are estimated as follows: iron ore, 45 percent total transportation, 19 percent Lakes transportation; newsprint, 15 percent Lakes transportation; iron and steel, 6 percent Lakes transportation. It was assumed that origins and destinations for the latter two export groups were located at waterside. These freight factors are crude estimates developed from various sources.

[74]Freight factors for Great Lakes imports of these commodity groups are estimated as follows: iron ore, 26 percent total transportation, 15 percent Lakes transportation; coal, 38 percent total transportation, 13 percent Lakes transportation; unmilled cereals, 18 percent total transportation, 8 percent Lakes transportation; soybeans, 7 percent total transportation, 4 percent Lakes transportation. These freight facors are crude estimates developed from various sources.

7. North American Free Trade and Canadian Transportation

Introduction

The Automotive Free Trade Agreement of 1965 provides a starting point for this chapter, which is concerned with the impact of freer trade between Canada and the United States on the Canadian transportation industries. We discussed the interrelation of Canadian transportation and Canadian commercial policy in chapter 3; it seems clear that significant reductions in tariffs and other trade barriers would have important repercussions on Canadian transportation.

To the extent that it may be a prototype for future trade agreements between Canada and the United States, the automotive agreement can provide a guide to the future of Canadian transportation industries. The key change, from the transportation point of view, would be the replacement, presumably partial, of an east-west flow of goods, particularly manufactured products, with a north-south flow of these products. The two major Canadian railroads, which now dominate long-haul transportation of manufactured products from central Canada to the Maritimes and western Canada, would appear to be the major losers.

Canadian railroads and the Automotive Free Trade Agreement of 1965

We will return later to consider the general potential for rail traffic loss if freer North American trade were to be instituted. In the meantime, we will examine the automotive agreement's impact on the traffic patterns of Canadian railroads.[1] Two difficulties limit the scope of our analysis. One is, unfortunately, familiar: the automotive agreement's impact on highway transport cannot be studied empirically because statistics are not available.

[1]Our neglect of the impact of the automotive agreement on U.S. transportation is based on two related considerations. First, the potential changes in traffic are of only marginal significance to the much larger U.S. transportation industries. Second, because of this, there will be less pressure on public policy generated during the adjustment of the transport system to the new traffic patterns.

Second, not all the production and distribution adjustments being carried out as a result of the agreement have made their full effects felt.

The automotive agreement provides U.S. and Canadian automotive manufacturers with free entry into both countries for vehicles and parts if the manufacturers meet certain commitments regarding the preservation and expansion of the Canadian automotive industry.[2] The purposes of the agreement are set forth in its Article I:

The Governments of the United States and Canada, pursuant to the above principles, shall seek the early achievement of the following objectives:
(a) The creation of a broader market for automotive products within which the full benefits of specialization and large-scale production can be achieved;
(b) The liberalization of United States and Canadian automotive trade in respect of tariff barriers and other factors tending to impede it, with a view to enabling the industries of both countries to participate on a fair and equitable basis in the expanding total market of the two countries;
(c) The development of conditions in which market forces may operate effectively to attain the most economic pattern of investment, production and trade. It shall be the policy of each Government to avoid actions which would frustrate the achievement of these objectives.

From this, the intent is clear: free trade in motor vehicles and parts is expected to benefit both the U.S. and Canadian economies by encouraging more efficient production and distribution of motor vehicles.

These efficiencies are to be achieved, in part, by introducing model specialization in Canadian assembly plants. These plants had previously produced practically all models and styles in each manufacturer's line, thus incurring a substantial cost penalty. Model specialization means, however, that the Canadian automobile and truck markets will no longer be supplied solely from Canadian assembly plants. Where appropriate, U.S.-built and -assembled vehicles will supply Canadian markets. Thus a predominantly east-west flow of finished vehicles will be replaced by a flow that will tend, increasingly, to be north-south in direction.

Table 102 presents statistics showing the geographical distribution of the Canadian automobile and truck markets, together with the railroads' role in distributing vehicles to these markets.

The railroads' share of the transportation market for new passenger cars ranges from 90 to 95 percent in western Canada and the Maritimes down to less than 50 percent in Ontario and Quebec (if we use a conversion factor of 1.8 tons per car). The railroads' market share in transportation of new trucks is more difficult to estimate because of the variety of vehicle weights

[2]The details of the agreement are neatly summarized in Paul Wonnacott and R. J. Wonnacott, "The Automotive Agreement of 1965," *Canadian Journal of Economics and Political Science*, XXXIII, May 1967, pp. 269–84.

TABLE 102

SALES OF TRUCKS AND NORTH AMERICAN PASSENGER CARS, WITH
RAILROAD TERMINATING TRAFFIC, BY PROVINCE, 1964 AND 1966

	1964		1966	
	Sales (units)	Railroad terminating traffic (tons)	Sales (units)	Railroad terminating traffic (tons)
		CARS		
Atlantic provinces	39,420	60,195[a]	48,780	98,041[a]
Quebec	143,687	113,745	161,827	106,406
Ontario	226,670	232,086	258,531	233,148
Western provinces	141,046	228,727	157,848	257,697
Total	550,823	635,473	626,986	695,292
		TRUCKS		
Atlantic provinces	10,000	18,059[b]	11,146	25,732[b]
Quebec	21,642	7,518	22,849	12,273
Ontario	35,637	1,570	42,799	25,387
Western provinces	41,703	55,403	55,519	95,366
Total	108,982	82,550	132,313	158,758

Sources: Sales: Motor Vehicle Manufacturers' Association, *Facts and Figures of the Automotive Industry*, 1967, Toronto, Motor Vehicle Manufacturers' Association, 1967, Table 24, p. 23; Traffic: DBS, *Railway Freight Traffic*, 1964 and 1966 (1965 and 1967).
[a]Includes FCC 613: "automobiles, passenger."
[b]Includes FCC 615: "automobiles, freight."

and the probability that these are not evenly distributed regionally. In 1964 the railroads received $21.3 million for carrying cars and trucks from Canadian origins to Canadian destinations; in 1965 revenues reached $26.5 million.[3] Of the 1965 revenues, $20.7 million were received for carriage of cars and $5.8 million for carriage of trucks. The new passenger-car revenues were the fifth highest among the several hundred groups in the freight commodity classification. For rail transport between Canadian points, only wheat, bituminous coal, lumber, and manufactured iron and steel generated higher revenues.

Table 103 shows the distribution of revenue received by the railroads for various interregional movements of cars and trucks. According to the figures shown in Table 103, 62 percent of 1965 railway freight revenue from cars and trucks was accounted for by movements from eastern to western Canada.

[3]Board of Transport Commissioners, *Waybill Analysis: Carload All-Rail Traffic*, 1964 and 1965, Ottawa, Queen's Printer, 1965 and 1966. The revenue estimates were developed from a one percent sample of waybills and are subject to unspecified sampling error.

TABLE 103
RAILROAD FREIGHT REVENUE FOR TRANSPORTATION OF
CARS AND TRUCKS, 1965
(thousand dollars)

	Movement	
Cars	Eastern-Western[a]	12,221
	Eastern-Maritime	3,501
	Eastern-Eastern	3,308
	Other	1,665
Trucks	Eastern-Western	4,159
	Eastern-Maritime	1,136
	Eastern-Eastern	364
	Other	117

Source: Board of Transport Commissioners, *Waybill Analysis: Carload All-Rail Traffic*, 1965, Ottawa, Queen's Printer, 1966.
[a]"Western" includes northwestern Ontario and the four western provinces; "Eastern" includes the remainder of Ontario and most of Quebec; "Maritime" includes eastern Quebec and the four Atlantic provinces.

Traffic from Ontario and Quebec to the Atlantic region accounted for a further 18 percent.

The effects of the automotive agreement on distribution patterns of cars and trucks and on railway freight traffic are outlined in Table 104. Three significant changes may be observed in this table. They are the increase in imports of cars and trucks into Ontario and Quebec and the increase of imports of cars into western Canada. In the two cases involving changes in the pattern of new car traffic, there has been a presumably related reduction in traffic received from Canadian origins.

In terms of significance for Canadian railroads, it is the replacement in western markets of cars from eastern Canada by cars from the United States that is of most concern. Between 1965 and 1966 an additional 26,000 tons of cars were imported into western Canada by railroad, and receipts from eastern Canada dropped by 37,000 tons. Sales remained approximately constant in the two years. At an average revenue of $65 per ton,[4] the 37,000-ton decline represented a revenue loss of $2.4 million, less, of course, revenue earned for the relatively short in-Canada haul of U.S.-produced cars.

It appears that the replacement of Canadian-produced cars by U.S.-produced cars in western Canada will increase considerably. Future production and distribution plans of two of the "Big Three" automobile manufacturers call for increasing north-south shipments of vehicles. Indeed, analysis of the

[4]Calculated from Board of Transport Commissioners, *Waybill Analysis: Carload All-Rail Traffic*, 1965.

latest available railway traffic figures does reveal a substantial intensification of north-south traffic dominance between the first quarter of 1966 and the first quarter of 1967. In the first three months of 1966, rail-borne imports of cars and trucks were 4,000 tons and 5,000 tons, respectively. By the first three months of 1967 this traffic had expanded to 52,000 tons of cars and 9,000 tons of trucks.[5] Canadian factory shipments of cars and trucks

TABLE 104
CHANGES IN THE PATTERNS OF RAILWAY FREIGHT TRAFFIC IN
CARS AND TRUCKS, 1964–66
(thousand tons)

Destination		Received from U.S.	Received from Ontario and Quebec	Received from local origins	Total
CARS[a]					
Western Canada:	1964	6	220	3	229
	1965	3	269	3	275
	1966	29	226	4	258
Atlantic provinces:	1964	—	49	12	61
	1965	—	62	28	91
	1966	—	68	30	98
Ontario and Quebec:	1964	2	—	126	128
	1965	9	—	141	150
	1966	44	—	108	162
TRUCKS[b]					
Western Canada:	1964	2	52	2	55
	1965	2	82	3	86
	1966	2	91	2	95
Atlantic provinces:	1964	—	17	1	18
	1965	—	21	5	25
	1966	—	20	5	26
Ontario and Quebec:	1964	2	—	8	10
	1965	5	—	14	19
	1966	22	—	15	37

Source: DBS, *Railway Freight Traffic*, 1964, 1965, and 1966 (1965, 1966, and 1967).
Note: It was assumed, in developing these statistics, that vehicles received from the U.S. in a region were terminated in that region.
[a]Includes FCC 613: "Automobiles, passenger."
[b]Includes FCC 615: "Automobiles, freight."

were lower by about 10 percent (24,000 units) in the first quarter of 1967 than in the corresponding period in 1966. Comparing these figures with Table 104, we see that in this one quarter of 1967, rail-borne imports of cars were 71 percent of the total for the whole of 1966. First-quarter truck imports were 40 percent of the 1966 total.

[5]DBS, *Railway Freight Traffic*, first quarter, 1966, and first quarter, 1967. A regional breakdown is not available.

Clearly, a continuation of present trends would result in the Canadian railways losing the bulk of their long-haul traffic in new motor vehicles to western Canada. The potential revenue loss would appear to amount to some $16 million at a maximum, using 1965 figures. But there are several new sources of traffic to set against this loss. These are as follows:

1. Canadian portion of imports of new motor vehicles into western Canada.
2. Canadian portion of imports of new motor vehicles into Ontario and Quebec.
3. Canadian portion of exports of new motor vehicles from Ontario and Quebec to the United States.
4. Increased railway traffic in automotive parts within Canada and between Canada and the United States.

Each will be discussed.

The replacement, in western Canada, of vehicles manufactured in eastern Canada by vehicles manufactured in the United States will still leave the Canadian railways with at least the same weight of traffic. But their Canadian hauls will be much shorter. The major distribution points in western Canada will be Winnipeg (65-mile Canadian haul), Regina (160-mile Canadian haul), and Vancouver (30-mile Canadian haul). Revenues for these hauls will be only a fraction of the revenues for the average 1,700-mile haul from eastern Canada.

Somewhat similar comments could be made concerning the replacement of Canadian vehicles by U.S. vehicles in Ontario and Quebec. There, however, the geographic patterns of Canadian producing points, border crossings, and Canadian markets should tend to bring about approximately the same level of average revenue received per vehicle transported by Canadian railroads, no matter whether the points of origin are in Canada or the United States. In fact, even the supplying of these markets from U.S. assembly plants should benefit Canadian railroads, since longer hauls from these plants should result in the railroads carrying an increased proportion of the vehicles destined for Ontario and Quebec dealers.

Exports of new cars and trucks to the United States represent a new source of revenue to Canadian railroads. Rail-borne exports of cars increased from 2,000 tons in 1964 to 61,000 tons in 1965. Export traffic declined to 51,000 tons in 1966, but rail-borne exports of new cars in the first quarter of 1967 were 67,000 tons, compared to 7,000 tons in the same period a year earlier. Truck exports have increased steadily—from a few hundred tons in 1964 to 21,000 tons in 1965 and to 43,000 tons in 1966. Traffic in the first quarter of 1967 was 33,000 tons, far ahead of the year-earlier figure of 1,000 tons. Although Canadian hauls for this traffic are short, the volumes

involved are large and should continue to show substantial growth. Furthermore, some of the transportation in the United States will be performed by
U.S. subsidiaries of the two major Canadian railroads, particularly by Canadian National subsidiaries.

Since the automotive agreement, traffic in motor vehicle parts has shown
a greater absolute increase than has traffic in motor vehicles. The changes
are shown in Table 105. Increases in parts traffic to and from the United
States have been striking. Projecting the first-quarter figures, 1967 rail-
carried parts imports should amount to some 750,000 tons,[6] while Canadian railways should originate almost 300,000 tons of motor vehicle parts
destined for the United States.

TABLE 105
RAILWAY TRAFFIC IN MOTOR VEHICLE PARTS,[a] 1964–67
(thousand tons)

				1st quarter	
	1964	1965	1966	1966	1967
Canada-Canada	221	215	288	132	54
Canada-U.S.	52	94	205	44	73
U.S.-Canada	343	497	628	140	192

Source: DBS Railway Freight Traffic, various issues.
[a]Includes FCC 623: "Vehicle parts, n.o.s."

The four "new" sources of traffic for Canadian railways that have been
generated by the automotive agreement will probably not be sufficient to
offset completely, in revenue terms, the loss of new vehicle traffic to western
Canada. But they should be able to make up most of the revenue loss. In
addition, the agreement may stimulate the development of related secondary
manufacturing in Canada and should, in general, promote the efficient
organization of the Canadian economy. Canadian railroads should have a
great interest in this outcome.

However, if the railroads were to bear important burdens in the adjustment
of the Canadian economy to North American free trade in automotive products, there would be a strong case for their receiving special adjustment
assistance from the federal government. The provision of this assistance
would seem to be in line with the emphasis of the philosophy of the Royal

[6]In 1964 Canadian and U.S. railways together earned revenues of $5.6 million from
transporting parts from the United States to Canada. The Canadian share of this
revenue would be about one-third. Therefore, 1967 revenues of Canadian railroads
from northbound parts traffic would be in the order of $4 million. Revenues of U.S.
railroads owned by Canadian railroads would be additional to this.

Commission on Transportation. However, assistance to railway companies and their employees would have to be clearly identified as temporary in duration. Once successful transition had occurred—once the railways had made appropriate adjustments to their plant, and once displaced railway workers had found new jobs—adjustment assistance should stop.[7]

One final aspect of the railroads' position under the automotive agreement must be raised. The agreement was entered into without any consultation between the federal government and the railroads. This lack of consultation may have been unavoidable, since trade negotiations usually require a high degree of secrecy for success. Given this requirement, it would seem essential that Canadian railroads (and other transportation enterprises) make it their business to anticipate major shifts in Canada's foreign trade policy. The availability of forecasts and contingency plans covering the possible changes in Canadian foreign trade policy and patterns would remove the necessity of the railroads' making immediate and perhaps ill-considered rate and operating adjustments to emerging trade phenomena. An improved anticipation of future trade events might also discourage unwise decisions to invest in roadway or equipment that was doomed to redundancy.[8]

Canadian railroads and general North American free trade

In the next few pages we attempt to outline the probable impact on Canadian railroads of complete free trade between Canada and the United States. Our evaluation of the changes in trade flows will of necessity be at the level of crude conjecture, but we should at least be able to estimate the maximum traffic and revenue loss to Canadian railroads that North American free trade might bring.

Table 106 shows the revenues earned by Canadian railroads in 1965 for carrying certain commodities on interregional east-west and west-east hauls. Twelve commodity groups were constructed from the freight commodity classification. They were selected for inclusion in this table on the basis of an arbitrary assessment of the likelihood that U.S. origins would replace

[7]For a discussion of the strategy of transitional policies, see a forthcoming book in this PPAC series, Roy A. Matthews, *Easing the Adjustment to Freer Trade: A Program of Transitional Policies for Canada*, Toronto, University of Toronto Press.

[8]For example, Canadian railways now have approximately 200 tri-level automobile freight cars that have been idled because of reduced all-Canadian-vehicle traffic and that cannot be used to carry the increased flow of vehicles to the United States because their physical clearances (with respect to bridges, overpasses, etc.) are too high for the routes over which this traffic moves. These cars cost between $20,000 and $25,000 each new.

TABLE 106

FREIGHT REVENUES RECEIVED BY CANADIAN RAILWAYS FOR TRANSPORTATION
OF SELECTED COMMODITIES, 1965
(million dollars)

Commodity group	FCC no.	Western-Eastern Eastern-Western Western-Maritime Maritime-Western	Eastern-Maritime Maritime-Eastern
Coal and coke	305, 307	0.4	5.7
Chemicals, paint, plastics	527, 547, 549	5.0	0.8
Drugs	553	1.0	—
Industrial machinery and parts	595, 597	3.4	1.2
Tires	627	1.4	0.2
Electrical equipment	685	2.0	0.2
Furnaces	687	1.0	0.2
Glass and products	693, 695, 697	0.7	0.3
Major household appliances	707, 709, 711	2.7	0.4
Floor covering and furniture	713, 715	1.6	0.4
Canned and packaged food	763	7.2	4.8
Soap	769	2.1	0.3
Total		28.5	14.5

Source: Developed from Board of Transport Commissioners, *Waybill Analysis: Carload All-Rail Traffic*, 1965.

eastern Canadian origins as sources of supply for western and Atlantic markets and western and Atlantic origins as supply sources for eastern markets. This assessment was based mainly on current levels of Canadian tariffs. To repeat, the commodities included in Table 106 seem particularly likely to have their distribution patterns altered in the event of broad free trade between Canada and the United States. In 1965 railway freight revenues for these 12 commodity groups totaled $28.5 million for movements to and from western Canada and $14.5 million for movements in both directions between Ontario and Quebec and the Maritimes. These amounts presumably represent the maximum revenue loss of Canadian railroads. They do not, of course, take any account of increased revenues from a greater flow of Canadian exports to the United States.

However, to these 12 commodity groups we must add at least part of the revenues received by the railroads for hauling commodities included in the "Manufactures and miscellaneous, n.o.s." group (FCC 799). This group contains shipments in mixed carload lots and shipments of goods not shown separately in the freight commodity classification. Both components would presumably be weighted heavily by manufactured products. Revenues from traffic in this group to and from western Canada amounted to $47.1 million in 1965, while traffic between Ontario and Quebec and the Maritimes generated revenues of $9.0 million.[9] In addition, although revenue estimates cannot be developed, we should point out that a considerable volume of the Canadian railroads' less-than-carload traffic could be imperiled by the introduction of broad free trade within North America.

Substantial dislocation of existing traffic patterns is also a possibility within two other commodity groups in addition to those listed in Table 106. Free trade between Canada and the United States could alter existing flows of livestock and meat from western Canada and of primary and manufactured iron and steel to western Canada from Ontario and Quebec and the Maritimes and between Ontario and Quebec and the Maritimes. The railroads received revenues of $17.0 million in 1965 from the livestock and meat traffic from western Canada.[10] Western Canada traffic in primary and manufactured iron and steel generated revenues in 1965 of $22.8 million, while Maritimes traffic added a further $6.8 million.[11] While it seems most unlikely that all this traffic would disappear under Canada-U.S. free trade, some of it could be vulnerable.

In summary, Canadian railroads received freight revenues of $145.7 million in 1965 from east-west (and west-east) transportation of the commodities identified in earlier paragraphs in this section. The loss of even less than half this traffic could be expected to cause serious financial and economic difficulties for the railways. The financial difficulties would arise because most of the vulnerable traffic moves at rates that are set well above costs. In other words, much of the revenue loss would be reflected, at least immediately, in a reduction in railway profits. This would be serious, for, as we saw in chapter 4, railway profits hardly represent an adequate return on invested capital even now. The economic difficulties would involve the adjustment, over the long run, of the railways' plant and equipment. The adjustment would be impelled by the lower levels of traffic that could be expected because of the transformation of east-west traffic to north-south traffic. The adjustment process could be expected to be painful and of long duration. This expectation is based on the railways' long-standing inability, for a variety of reasons, mostly external, to rationalize their branch-line structure. Partial rationalization (retrenchment) of main-line investment could be expected to take even longer.

All of the preceding ignores, of course, the potential benefits of Canada-U.S. free trade to Canadian railways. Some of these benefits are direct and involve the generation of additional export and import traffic. Although this new traffic would be very likely to move, on the average, over much shorter

[9]Board of Transport Commissioners, *Waybill Analysis: Carload All-Rail Traffic*, 1965.
[10]*Ibid.* Includes FCC 203, 211, 215, 217, and 219.
[11]*Ibid.* Includes FCC 573, 575, 577, 581, 583, 585, 587, 589, and 779.

hauls within Canada, it could well make up in volume what it lacks in haul. The remainder of the potential benefits of free trade to Canadian railways are indirect and stem from the presumably greater vitality that such an arrangement would impart to the whole Canadian economy. Higher output per capita in Canada and a faster rate of economic growth should be reflected in more or less proportionately higher traffic levels for Canadian railways.

Canadian water and highway transportation and North American free trade

The discussion in this chapter has been almost exclusively concerned with the effects of Canada-U.S. free trade on the Canadian railway industry. An explanation for the neglect of the impact of free trade on the other major transportation industries thus seems in order.

Canada-U.S. free trade would appear likely to be of benefit to the Canadian water transportation industry. Canadian water carriers would experience an increase in traffic between U.S. and Canadian ports if tariffs were eliminated. At the same time, their domestic Canadian traffic seems generally impervious to diversion because of increased competition from U.S. imports. Concerning the possibility, admittedly remote, that a Canada-U.S. free trade arrangement would allow free cabotage rights to the water carriers of the two countries, we need only point to the cost advantage of Canadian water carriers (discussed in chapter 6) to demonstrate that this could be of substantial benefit to the Canadian industry. Canadian water carriers would be able to extend their relative domination of international Canada-U.S. trades into U.S. domestic trades, should present U.S. restrictions be relaxed.

The Canadian highway transportation industry would probably benefit more than any other part of the Canadian transportation sector from Canada-U.S. free trade. The augmented flow of goods between the two countries would in many instances be uniquely suited to truck transport. In addition, the loss of east-west traffic because of competition from U.S. imports should be relatively minor, simply because there is not too much of this traffic to be lost. Relaxation of restrictions on the transborder operations of motor carriers to allow Canadian carriers to operate into the United States and U.S. carriers to operate into Canada would work to the long-run advantage of Canadian carriers, it would appear. The introduction of "free trade" in highway transport should enable Canadian truckers to make use of their apparent cost advantage over U.S. truckers. This cost advantage is seen in differences between average revenues per ton-mile (the U.S. figure is 13 percent higher than the Canadian figure)[12] and in differences in average

[12]Chap. 5 above.

wage levels in trucking (the Canadian average wage was $5,435 in 1965; the U.S. average wage was $8,030 in 1965).[13] Assuming that this advantage could be maintained and regulatory and tax difficulties resolved, the prevalent fear of Canadian truckers regarding direct competition with U.S. truckers seems unreasonable. The industry should be able to benefit from the freeing of highway transport competition within North America. Whether this refinement were achieved or not, Canadian highway transport would receive major direct benefits from freedom of Canada-U.S. commodity trade.

There would undoubtedly be dislocations in Canadian transportation industries upon the implementation of free trade with the United States. Most of these problems would be short-lived, although in some cases, those involving Canadian railways, the transition period would be longer and more painful. But even here adjustment could be achieved, and we must reject outright any contention that the lowering of trade barriers between Canada and the United States should be impeded because of its effects on Canadian transportation. Such arguments seem to imply a reversal of appropriate priorities in public policy. We would, however, strongly recommend that the transportation industries receive every assistance to encourage their easy adjustment to the new environment. This assistance would include the fullest possible consultation and, where appropriate, financial aid to offset the cost burdens of adjustment.

[13]U.S. figure, American Trucking Associations, *American Trucking Trends*, 1966, Washington, ATA, 1967, p. 24; Canadian figure, calculated from DBS *Motor Carriers—Freight (Common and Contract)*, 1965, Part I: *Classes 1 and 2*, (1967), Table 3, p. 14 and Table 11, p. 24.

8. Conclusions and Recommendations

The first chapter of this study presented and discussed certain influences that transportation exerts on the location of economic activity and on the flow of trade between countries. In this concluding chapter we examine the impact of Canadian and U.S. transportation policy on trade flows and, by inference, on location of economic activity. Elements of transportation policy *can* have immense influence in altering transportation costs and rates from those that would prevail under purely economic influences. Our task here is therefore three-fold: we must summarize the features of transport policy that were discussed in chapters 3 through 6; we must evaluate the influence of transport policy on transport costs and rates; and we must examine the impact of the altered cost and rate levels on trade flows between Canada and the United States.

Transportation, trade, and location

The influence of transportation on the exchange of goods is felt, in the main, through the price charged for transport services. (This statement retains the assumption of chapter 1 that no explicit evaluation of service differentials and company logistics costs was to be made.[1]) The influence of transportation rates on the quantities of goods supplied and demanded depends on the elasticities of supply and demand and on the freight factor—the ratio of the freight rate to delivered price. For given elasticities of supply and demand, it is the freight factor that determines whether changes in the existing level of rates will have significant effects on the flow of goods between seller and buyer.

A related statement may be made concerning the influence of transportation on the relatively more stable patterns of industrial location. For industries where transportation of raw materials and/or finished products involves, for the firm, costs that are large relative to total costs of production and

[1]Chap. 1, pp. 16–17.

distribution, the transportation factor will be an important consideration in location decisions. In these situations, changes in transport rates are capable of making established locations economically untenable and of evoking and shaping decisions in favour of new production locations. Such influences are far less likely to occur if transport rates represent a relatively small portion of production and distribution costs.

The two foregoing paragraphs, however, both leave begging the most interesting and important question: how high is "relatively" high and what proportion of price or cost do transport rates have to represent before they *do* have an important effect on trade and location? Our evasion here is unfortunately still necessary for the time being, but we attempt to remedy it later in this chapter.

Transport policy: a summary

To summarize the policy influences discussed in earlier chapters, we begin by re-emphasizing the major role of transportation in Canadian national policy—in the broad sense. Historically, the transportation sector in Canada has been called upon to play economic, social, and political roles that far exceeded those expected of its U.S. counterpart. More important, major vestiges of this function still exist in Canadian transportation policy.

This should not be taken to imply that Canadian transportation policy is less amenable to revision than U.S. transportation. In an apparent paradox, the opposite is, in fact, true. The reasons for the relatively greater rigidity of U.S. transportation policy are rooted deep in the governmental, legal, and historical environment of each country.

Five aspects of transport policy are of interest to us here. These are rate regulation, control over operating licences, promotional policy, customs procedures, and rate-making and operating procedures of the transportation industries. The last aspect is included since these procedures are, because of the extensive regulation of transportation, a more or less implicit facet of public policy towards the transportation industries.

A. THE REGULATION OF FREIGHT RATES

Railroad freight rates on international traffic between Canada and the United States are regulated, in effect, by the U.S. Interstate Commerce Commission. The origins of this rather informal exercise of authority over transportation that is partly outside U.S. jurisdiction were described in chapter 4. But the *de facto* regulation of international rail rates by the United States is of concern for three reasons.

1. The over-all level of international freight rates appears to be well above the level of domestic U.S. (and Canadian) freight rates, allowing for approximate cost differentials.
2. Changes in the level of international freight rates tend to be tied to changes in the level of domestic U.S. freight rates.
3. There has been, since Canadian policy embraced competitive rate freedom for the railroads in early 1967, a fundamental difference in the philosophy and application of railway freight-rate regulation between Canada and the United States.

The existence of these three policy anomalies suggests that a revision of the existing mechanism for regulating international rail freight rates is in order.

It also appears, though from less satisfactory evidence, that international trucking rates are higher than domestic rates in either Canada or the United States. Generalization is difficult, however, because each province in Canada enforces its own particular mix of regulation and laissez-faire with respect to international trucking rates. At any rate, we can safely point to the general lack of interest, on both sides of the border, in the rates charged by for-hire motor carriers offering international service. In the case of highway transportation, however, more important transport-policy anomalies occur in the granting of operating licences to international carriers.

Only fragmentary information is available concerning the rates charged for water transportation between Canada and the United States. There is no important government control over rate levels, and, in fact, Canadian and U.S. licensing policies encourage cartel-like organization in much of the water transportation industry serving trade between the two countries. However, it would appear that the influences of competition from other modes of transport and of market power of major shippers and consignees control the rate excesses that public policy would appear to permit in water transportation.

B.   REGULATION OF OPERATING LICENCES

Regulation of licences to operate a transportation undertaking is not really a policy issue in railroad transport between Canada and the United States. Interchange points at the international boundary or at inland centres have been established by railways of the two countries for decades. Although there are instances of transborder operation and ownership, these are limited in extent. There have been no recent attempts by Canadian or U.S. railroads to "invade" the other's national territory.

Licensing policy is, however, a major policy issue in international highway transport. The Interstate Commerce Commission has interpreted its legislative mandate so as to develop regulatory policies in this area that are intricate in detail and restrictive in effect. New interstate motor carrier operating licences are difficult to obtain in the United States unless both the area to be served and the commodities to be carried are very much circumscribed. These policies are applied, quite impartially, to Canadian truckers wishing to serve U.S. points in through international service. Quite naturally, these truckers feel they are the victims of discrimination, forgetting that the operating certificates which they seek would be as difficult to obtain if they were domiciled in the United States. In some provinces disgruntled Canadian truckers have persuaded the provincial regulatory authorities to impose similar "discrimination" on U.S. truckers seeking equivalent operating licences in Canada. The result is to erect an invisible barrier at the international border. Unnecessary interchange of trailers and, too often, the transferring of the contents of trailers add significantly to the costs of providing international highway transport and markedly lower the quality of this service.

Neither the Canadian nor the U.S. government has any policy concerning the licensing of vessels or water carriers to operate between the two countries. But the spillover from domestic policies in this area is of great consequence. Thus, although the vessels of any nation *can* participate in Canada-U.S. water transport, their participation is mainly limited to the ocean trades on both coasts. Between 75 and 87 percent of cargo tonnages transported on the important St. Lawrence-Great Lakes routes moves in Canadian and U.S. vessels. These vessels are operated by high-cost carriers; their domination of these trades is in large measure due to Canadian and U.S. policies excluding foreign-registered ships from the equivalent domestic trades. The penalties of inflexibility that these policies impose on the prospective foreign operator are potentially severe—particularly when added to the difficulties of labour relations and vessel design that are inherent in foreign operators' participation in these inland international trades. The ultimate loser from these penalties is North American commodity trade, which must pay for the higher-cost service provided by the protected North American shipping firms.

C. PROMOTIONAL POLICIES TOWARDS TRANSPORTATION

Only part of the extensive and continuing promotion of railway transportation by the Canadian government directly affects international transportation. The commodity and regional subsidies do not apply to international traffic. But an unknown portion of the National Transportation Act subsidy is on account of traffic moving to and from the United States. Furthermore, as in the United States, the railroad system of today reflects past promotion of this mode of transport. It is interesting to speculate as to whether the railway facilities now available to international traffic would have been as extensive in the absence of government promotion of railroads. Perhaps these facilities, being north-south, would have been more extensive. In any event, railroad promotion is now a peculiarly Canadian phenomenon in North America and only marginally affects international rail transport.

Rough statistics developed (in chapter 5) showed that in both Canada and the United States public policy is to subsidize the provision of highways. The excess of highway expenditures over highway-user revenues benefits users. The benefit is about four times as large, on a vehicle-mile basis, in Canada as in the United States. Attempts were made earlier to relate this subsidy to transborder truck transportation. Also important here is the nature of highway-tax-reciprocity arrangements existing between provinces and states. In some cases these arrangements are limited in scope, and unfortunately, these are the cases which are most important in highway transport between Canada and the United States. Lack of uniformity in vehicle-size and -weight restrictions also imposes cost penalties on international trucking.

Canadian promotion of water transportation within North America is essentially concentrated on shipbuilding subsidies and, with U.S. participation, the St. Lawrence Seaway. As was pointed out in chapter 6, both the Seaway deficit and the Seaway toll structure are likely to affect Canada-U.S. trade. The former gives a slight encouragement to this trade, while the latter has a probably more significant impact on its composition. Canadian shipbuilding subsidies have stimulated the construction of newer and more efficient Canadian vessels, especially on the Great Lakes, lowering costs of water transportation and reducing the market share of U.S. water carriers. Within the United States there is extensive promotion of water transportation, but apart from the St. Lawrence Seaway, very little of this has any effect on Canada-U.S. water transportation.

D. CUSTOMS AND TRANSPORTATION

Customs procedures for rail and highway transportation can be treated together. In the case of water transportation this does not appear to be an area of difficulty. Customs poses two problems for international transportation—clearance procedures and entry of transportation equipment. Clearance procedures are not always as efficient as they could be from the point of view of the transportation company. In many cases they represent an exercise in administrative superfluity, being far more detailed and searching than is necessary for tariff or statistical purposes. Intensive and cumbersome clearance procedures add to the cost of transborder transportation and introduce unnecessary delays, lowering the quality of service. Customs treatment

of vehicles (trucks, tractors, trailers, locomotives, freight cars) is unsatis-
factory in terms of its effects on efficient international transport operations.
For trucking it reinforces the barriers imposed by restrictive licensing policies.
Enforced segregation of transportation equipment according to its country
of origin introduces uneconomic constraints in the quest for optimum
utilization of this equipment. The refusal to view the domestic use of transportation equipment as incidental to international trade and to permit its
duty-free entry as a means to international trade is regrettable.

E.   TRANSPORTATION INDUSTRY PRACTICES

The transportation industries themselves do not always act to further the
free flow of trade between Canada and the United States. A case in point
is the procedure by which the railroads set rates on international traffic. This
rate-making procedure is cumbersome and prone to delay. Moreover, it seems
almost to encourage discrimination against the expansion of North American
trade, particularly Canadian exports to the United States. Less equivocal
conclusions on this point are, unfortunately, impossible.

Transport policy, transport costs, and freight rates

We now come to the task of identifying the impact of transport policy on
costs and rates. Almost without exception, the features of Canadian and U.S.
transport policy summarized in the preceding pages act to increase transportation costs and rates for international transport. In some cases this influence
is directly on rates, while in others the impact occurs indirectly through
increasing costs or impairing the quality of service. The magnitude of these
influences is debatable, but there can be no question of their over-all direction. It is to raise the rates charged for transporting goods between Canada
and the United States.

Freight rates and North American trade

As we discussed at the beginning of this chapter, the influence of higher
freight rates on trade flows depends on a number of factors. These include the
prevailing elasticities of supply and demand and the freight factors. Generalization with respect to magnitudes is difficult for all three variables. We
have made very little attempt to discuss the elasticities of supply and demand
for the goods traded between Canada and the United States. The degree of
commodity specification required for meaningful use of such information

prompted this course of action. We did, in chapters 4 and 6, make some attempts to calculate freight factors, but the general requirements of specifying origin and destination make a more accurate determination of freight factors too involved for the purposes of this study.

It will be useful to indicate the general effects of Canada-U.S. transport policy on specific trade commodities. There are probably fewer effects likely to result from water transport policies than from land transport policies. However, the effective partial exclusion of foreign vessels from Great Lakes–St. Lawrence routes does result in some increase in shipping costs. This could tend to decrease Canadian exports of iron ore and newsprint and to decrease Canadian imports of iron ore, coal, and, perhaps, unmilled cereals.

The major impact of transport policy on commodity trade is felt through rail and highway transportation. International railroad freight rates are higher than domestic rates. Certain commodities were identified in chapter 4 as being particularly affected by this influence. For these commodities transport policies reduce trade. Included in this group were Canadian exports of lumber and plywood, newsprint, and agricultural machinery and Canadian imports of fruit and vegetables, iron and steel, chemicals, and motor vehicle parts. Canadian imports of agricultural machinery from the United States were encouraged by the level of international freight rates. However, these conclusions require qualification. Lacking specific cost information, we cannot say whether these rate differences were justified by cost differences. If they were, then the constriction of trade caused by higher international freight rates would be quite acceptable, reflecting as it would some of the real opportunity costs of international trade between Canada and the United States. We might add, however, that this explanation seems most unlikely to justify the pattern of international rail freight rates on agricultural machinery.

It appears, also, that rates charged for international highway transportation are above domestic rates. Detailed information is not available, but, given the commodity patterns of use of highway transport, we can supply conjecture concerning the incidence of this anomaly. Exports and imports of meat, motor vehicles and trailers, and most types of machinery and manufactured products would be discouraged. In addition, Canadian exports of fish, distilled alcoholic beverages, and nickel ore would be discouraged, as would Canadian imports of cotton fabrics and plastics.

We cannot develop any conclusions concerning the over-all *magnitude* of the impact of Canadian and U.S. transport policies on trade between the two countries. We cannot say that these policies reduced Canadian exports to the United States by X million in 1964 and reduced Canadian imports from the United States by Y million in the same year. But we can specify the over-all *direction* of impact—namely, *to reduce trade between the two countries.*

This occurs in three ways: a restriction in the range of goods traded, a restriction in the numbers of origins and destinations in each country, and a reduction, within the first two constraints, in the volume of goods traded. Moreover, we are probably safe in asserting that the interference with optimal trade flows will increase more than proportionately as total trade volume between Canada and the United States expands. This is because of the increasingly important role being played by the mode of international transport, trucking, that is subjected to the greatest policy barriers.

Recommendations

Harmonization of transport policies has been a major issue within most free trade groupings. The potential for partially frustrating the realization of benefits from free trade arrangements has impelled this interest. But with or without freer trade, transport policy harmonization is desirable between any pair or group of countries that have an interest in increasing their mutual trade. This latter objective seems to be part of both Canadian and U.S. trade policy at the present time, while a full-fledged free trade arrangement does not. The suggestions to be made here have relevance for the present gradual evolution towards freer North American trade; their implementation would be accorded higher priority as other impediments to the free exchange of goods disappeared.

The following changes in Canadian and U.S. transport policies are recommended:

1. *The institution of effective cooperation between the Canadian Transport Commission and the Interstate Commerce Commission in the regulation of international railroad freight rates.* It is highly desirable that an appropriate melding of Canadian and U.S. freight-rate policy replace the present total reliance on U.S. policy. This cooperative regulation should have, as its first specific objective, the modification of the unwieldy and discriminatory procedures by which the railroads establish international rates.
2. *A relaxation in the application of Interstate Commerce Commission motor carrier licensing policies to Canadian truckers seeking to operate through international service.* The complementary Canadian action would be the placing of international highway transportation under federal regulation. This would be followed by an appropriate expansion in the number of licences granted to U.S. motor carriers to operate into Canada.
3. *A concerted effort by state and provincial governments to augment exist-*

ing highway-tax-reciprocity agreements and to standardize vehicle-size and -weight regulations.

4. *Revision of tariff regulations in both countries to permit the free and efficient international use of transportation equipment.* This would mean, of course, that customs rules would no longer serve to protect the transportation equipment industries of both countries at the expense of a higher total volume of international trade.

5. *Relaxation of the protective emphasis of Canadian and U.S. water transport policies.* This would allow water-borne trade between the two countries to benefit from the influence of lower international shipping and of more competitive rate-making policies.

RELATED PUBLICATIONS BY THE
PRIVATE PLANNING ASSOCIATION OF CANADA

CANADIAN TRADE COMMITTEE PUBLICATIONS

THE WORLD ECONOMY

The World Economy at the Crossroads: A Survey of Current Problems of Money, Trade and Economic Development, by Harry G. Johnson, 1965.
The International Monetary System: Conflict and Reform, by Robert A. Mundell, 1965.
International Commodity Agreements, by William E. Haviland, 1963.

CANADA'S TRADE RELATIONSHIPS

Canada's International Trade: An Analysis of Recent Trends and Patterns, by Bruce Wilkinson, 1968.
Canada's Trade with the Communist Countries of Eastern Europe, by Ian M. Drummond, 1966.
Canada's Role in Britain's Trade, by Edward M. Cape, 1965.
The Common Agricultural Policy of the E.E.C. and Its Implications for Canada's Exports, by Sol Sinclair, 1964.
Canada's Interest in the Trade Problems of Less-Developed Countries, by Grant L. Reuber, 1964.

CANADA'S COMMERCIAL POLICY AND COMPETITIVE POSITION

Prices, Productivity, and Canada's Competitive Position, by N. H. Lithwick, 1967.
Industrial Structure in Canada's International Competitive Position: A Study of the Factors Affecting Economies of Scale and Specialization in Canadian Manufacturing, by H. Edward English, 1964.
Canada's Approach to Trade Negotiations, by L. D. Wilgress, 1963.

CANADIAN-AMERICAN COMMITTEE PUBLICATIONS

CANADA-U.S. ECONOMIC RELATIONS

Constructive Alternatives to Proposals for U.S. Import Quotas (a Statement by the Committee), 1968.
U.S.-Canadian Free Trade: The Potential Impact on the Canadian Economy, by Paul Wonnacott and Ronald J. Wonnacott, 1968.
The Role of International Unionism in Canada, by John H. G. Crispo, 1967.
A New Trade Strategy for Canada and the United States (a Statement by the Committee), 1966.
Capital Flows between Canada and the United States, by Irving Brecher, 1965.
A Possible Plan for a Canada-U.S. Free Trade Area (a Staff Report), 1965.
Invisible Trade Barriers between Canada and the United States, by Francis Masson and H. Edward English, 1963.
Non-Merchandise Transactions between Canada and the United States, by John W. Popkin, 1963.
Policies and Practices of United States Subsidiaries in Canada, by John Lindeman and Donald Armstrong, 1961.